THE TEAM-BUILDING WORKSHOP

THE TEAM-BUILDING WORKSHOP

A Trainer's Guide

Vivette Payne

AMACOM
American Management Association
New York • Atlanta • Boston • Chicago • Kansas City • San Francisco • Washington, D. C.
Brussels • Mexico City • Tokyo • Toronto

Special discounts on bulk quantities of AMACOM books are available to corporations, professional associations, and other organizations. For details, contact Special Sales Department, AMACOM, a division of American Management Association, 1601 Broadway, New York, NY 10019.
Tel: 212-903-8316. Fax: 212-903-8083.
E-mail: specialsls@amanet.org
Website: www.amacombooks.org/go/specialsales
To view all AMACOM titles go to: www.amacombooks.org

This publication is designed to provide accurate and authoritative information in regard to the subject matter covered. It is sold with the understanding that the publisher is not engaged in rendering legal, accounting, or other professional service. If legal advice or other expert assistance is required, the services of a competent professional person should be sought.

Library of Congress Cataloging-in-Publication Data

Payne, Vivette.
  The team-building workshop : a trainer's guide / Vivette Payne.
      p. cm.
  Includes bibliographical references and index.
  ISBN-10: 0-8144-7079-3
  ISBN-13: 978-0-8144-7079-4
  1. Teams in the workplace.   I. Title.
HD66.P39m2001
658.4′02—dc21

                                                    00-062079

Printing number

10 9 8 7 6 5 4

TABLE OF CONTENTS

INTRODUCTION

This book is designed to provide operating managers and practitioners—that is, trainers and consultants—with the tools they need to design, lead, and implement effective team building.

The Team-Building Workshop is a how-to book. This means it offers not just concepts about team building but provides techniques, assessments, planning guides, and other materials that make it easy to implement the concepts taught. Similarly, the tools and techniques provided are practical and readily adaptable to a variety of team situations.

The Team-Building Workshop enables operating managers, in their role as team leaders, to lead a team-building session with confidence. The six-step team-building process teaches them how to use team building to improve productivity, quality, customer satisfaction, task execution, and other important goals. In addition, this book is designed so that managers can facilitate team building themselves—without prior instruction or training.

The Team-Building Workshop is also useful for practitioners who seek new strategies, techniques, and team-building aids. These ready-to-use materials will supplement their expertise and can be customized to meet specific needs.

The book is divided into fifteen chapters. Chapter 1 describes the potential of teams and defines the concept of team building. This introductory chapter explains the value of team building and the key factors that are important for its success.

Chapter 2 helps operating managers and practitioners recognize when team building is a viable option. This chapter addresses the issue of readiness and provides guidance on how to evaluate opportune times for team building. Alternatives to team building are also presented.

Chapters 3 to 8 present detailed descriptions of each step in the six-step team-building process. Chapter 3 describes how to establish a collaborative contract with the team leader and team. It explains the importance of gaining the team's commitment and clarifying mutual expectations, and it suggests ways to handle resistance to team building. Chapter 4 teaches operating managers and practitioners how to gather information prior to team building and how to assess the team's needs. It describes the strengths and limitations of various information-gathering techniques. Chapter 5 describes how to analyze the data gathered, pinpoint the major issues, and deliver the feedback. Various formats for presenting the data and options for delivering feedback are discussed. Chapter 6 offers a Leader's Guide for designing and leading a two-day team-building workshop. All the materials required are explained, and sample charts, overheads, and handouts are included. The detailed explanation provided in the Leader's Guide walks you through every aspect of the team-building session from start to finish. Chapter 7 describes how to implement the results of team building. This ensures that the time invested in team building yields measurable results. A sample team-building summary report illustrates a method for documenting key agreements and decisions in a way that facilitates tracking results. Chapter 8 offers techniques for evaluating the effectiveness of the team-building workshop. These techniques help make team building an ongoing process.

Chapters 9 to 12 present team-building processes designed to meet special challenges. Chapter 9 describes strategies that help cross-functional project teams get off to a fast start. Chapter 10 provides team-building methods for resolving dysfunctional conflict. Chapter 11 offers techniques for aligning team goals with strategic direction and priorities. Finally, Chapter 12 teaches operating managers and practitioners how to use team building to deal with breakdowns in interpersonal relationships and rebuild trust.

Chapter 13 provides techniques for situations in which the two-day format is not feasible. These short interventions enable teams to deal with such issues as formulating their purpose and mission, clarifying roles and responsibilities, improving decision making and consensus-building, strengthening interpersonal relations, and improving team meetings. Operating managers and practitioners learn how to address these needs in one- to six-hour sessions. Chapter 14 provides several experiential exercises. These can be conducted as part of the two-day team-building session or as stand-alone interventions. Chapter 15 provides guidance on what organizations and team leaders should do to support teams.

THE POTENTIAL OF TEAMS

The tension in the room was palpable. The organization needed to find an economic and safe way to clean up and develop a new industrial site. Both the local community and two large organizations were depending on the success of this effort. So important was this project that top performers were assigned to it. They faced many demands. They had to meet community expectations and comply with government regulations. The schedule was tight and there was a lot to do. Weather, delays in getting equipment, and the need for training all presented serious challenges. But the team was confident in their ability to deal with these issues successfully. As one team member said, "We're not worried about schedules, equipment, or meeting everyone's expectations; we're concerned about working together as a team. That's the real challenge."

This story is repeated thousands of times each day. Organizations faced with competitive demands, critical goals, and changing business conditions choose to empower teams to deal with these issues. Teamwork has become a business strategy and team building is a major way in which organizations foster teamwork.

What's behind the move to teams? There is overwhelming evidence that high-performance organizations are comprised of high-performance teams. Everywhere you look, there is confirmation that teams play a key role in enabling strong competitive performance. Organizations in both the private and public sector compete for contracts, customer loyalty, market share, scholastic recognition, and other things. There is a continuing demand to do things better, faster, and cheaper. Employees seek more control over their work lives and want to make meaningful contributions to the organization's success.

Look at what's required today for organizational effectiveness, and the need for strong team performance becomes clear. For example, organizations compete for customers in a way they never have before. Business strategies that focus on customer retention, customer loyalty, and customer partnerships are commonplace. Responsiveness, service, quality, and sensitivity to customers' needs have never been greater. To ensure that these needs are met, organizations use teams rather than dividing up the work between different functional units.

Second, every facet of organizational life depends upon increasingly sophisticated technology. The proliferation of information and information technologies has made it impossible for individuals to perform their jobs alone. Systems are too complex for any one person to have all the expertise required. Today multifunctional teams manage these systems.

Third, competitive advantage depends upon executing tasks with simplicity and speed. To survive and compete globally companies must develop new products or services faster. This requires responsiveness, efficiency, and flexibility. All of this must be done without sacrificing quality or, in some instances, by improving the quality of products or services. Teams that can effectively integrate engineering, manufacturing, marketing, and other functions do this best.

Finally, for most organizations the world has become their marketplace. Managing costs is a major factor in their ability to deliver products and services at competitive prices. But there is also a need for employees with multiple skills and competencies to do the jobs that need to be done. This has led organizations to restructure around teams rather than individual jobs.

The potential of teams is unlimited. The challenge is enabling teams to deliver their best. Team building is a major strategy for helping teams achieve this.

The Value of Team Building

Team building has been a vehicle for helping individuals work better together to accomplish important results for several years. It became popular in the 1960s and continues to be used with all sorts of teams. Teams as diverse as executives of an international business group, managers of an urban settlement house, and a cross-functional team chartered to find alternative sources of fuel use team building to help them achieve their goals.

Most people who have experienced team building talk about how it benefited their team. They recognize the value of team building. But often, demanding schedules, concern about achieving tangible results, and other factors make teams and their leaders reluctant to engage in team building. Today's competitive environment sensitizes managers to the need to engage in activities that will ensure a good return on the time invested.

There are four factors that are important to remember when considering whether or not to do team building. These help ensure that time invested in team building yields results.

1. **Team building does not have to consume a lot of time in order to be of value.** Team-building sessions of one to two days can have a major impact on a team's subsequent performance. Performance is the key deliverable for teams. This applies to teams who make things, teams who lead others, and teams who recommend things. Every team faces its own unique challenges. In spite of these differences, there are common performance essentials that effective teams share.

    Every team needs a clear sense of its mission or shared purpose. This describes the team's reason for existence and the interdependence that makes them not just a group but a team. Similarly, teams need specific goals. These goals are unique to the team; they are the deliverables to which every team member commits. Goals give each person a focus, and, combined with clearly defined roles, describe what each person contributes to the team. These three components—shared purpose, specific goals, and clear roles—form the foundation of the team.

In addition, teams must agree on how they will work together. Their agreement on a common and collaborative approach defines how they make decisions, solve problems, resolve differences, share information, and do other things that enable them to work together effectively. Teams also need certain skills. These skills, technical or functional as well as interpersonal and decision-making, ensure that the team has the competencies required to execute its purpose and goals, and that each individual is capable of fulfilling his or her role. Along with skills, teams must be learning entities that seek continuous improvement in their results, processes, and relationships. Teams must be accountable for their own performance. Each person's sense of individual responsibility for the team's success helps to create an environment of shared responsibility and mutual accountability. Finally, a passion to deliver their individual and collective best characterizes effective teams.

Both new teams and teams that have been in existence for a while can use a short, one- to two-day team-building process to put in place all of these essentials of team effectiveness. A one- to two-day investment in team building is fundamental to the success of a new team. New teams accelerate their progress and development by using team building to establish purpose, goals, roles, approach, and accountability agreements. Teams that are struggling often find that one of the essentials of team effectiveness needs to be addressed. Doing so through team building gets the team on track. The one- to two-day investment yields long-lasting performance dividends.

2. **Team building needs to focus on strengthening team performance rather than promoting a team environment.** Team building is much more likely to benefit a team when it is designed to achieve specific performance results that meet the needs of customers, employees, and other key stakeholders. Team building for the sake of "creating a team environment" or "promoting teamwork" without more specific goals generally falls short of the projected performance impact. Just as teams need a reason to be a team, so team building needs a purpose that is worth the time and investment. For example, a large organization combined three functional departments into one. The manager and his two supervisors decided team building would bring together the employees of the newly constituted department and help them feel like one unit. Their communicated purpose for team building, "helping us all feel like one team," was met with cynicism and resistance. After working with a trainer, the managers redirected the purpose of the team building. They let employees know the two-day session would clarify the new team's purpose, establish goals for the next six months, and clarify each person's role. Immediately, there was enthusiasm for the team-building session. The employees were actually anxious to get

together and discuss these issues. The team building had moved from a general, "feel good" purpose to a session designed to achieve tangible and important outcomes.

3. **Typically, team building is most effective when led by an external trainer rather than the team leader**. This book enables operating managers or team leaders to conduct an effective team-building session. Sometimes this is the best approach. However, in most instances, it is beneficial for the operating manager to work with a trainer, either from within or outside the organization to lead the team-building session. Chapter 3 provides guidelines that help managers determine when they need a trainer's assistance. In general, it is important for both the leader and team members to be fully engaged in the team-building process. Someone must also ensure that the session meets its goals, that discussions stay on track, and that everyone participates. It is difficult for the team leader to play both roles of participant and facilitator. Often, the manager tends to dominate the session and drive for quick resolution of issues. Conversely, there are times when the manager takes such a passive role that the team feels a lack of concern or real interest in resolving key issues. Both kinds of behavior seriously jeopardize the success of team building. Working with a trainer, managers can be active participants, using their energy to create a productive and worthwhile session for everyone on the team. The trainer takes responsibility for leading discussions, keeping the session on track, and engaging everyone's participation. Together the manager and trainer ensure team building is successful.

4. **There must be a commitment to team building.** Like everything else that is important to the team's success, the team leader and team members must commit to the team-building process. As the six-step process illustrates, team building is a series of events and commitments. Although the two-day session is the focal point, the team must be willing to do what is required to diagnose the issues, to work on resolving them, to implement the agreements made, and to seek to upgrade their performance continuously.

   Likewise, team building usually results in a change in the way team members work, both individually and together. It is important that everyone on the team understands this and commits to making the necessary behavioral changes. Sometimes, the changes are major. For example, a leadership team responsible for managing research and development activities used team building to set strategic priorities and realign the responsibilities of each manager's work unit. Prior to the team-building effort, there was considerable overlap and duplication of work. In fact, each manager was apt to work on strategic initiatives independently and competitively. The outcome of the team-building effort required a commitment to share responsibility for the initiatives. This meant the team as a whole needed to be successful in order for any one manager to be successful. The shift from competition to collaboration required a major change in the way the individuals worked together, shared information, and made decisions. It was not an easy change but the team believed the benefits were worth the effort. The commitment that resulted was dramatically improved execution and greater ability to influence subsequent R and D priorities.

WHAT IS TEAM BUILDING?

There is a clear need for teams in order to meet the challenges organizations face. But the challenge of team building consists in how to make teams work. Teams cannot just be created, they must be built. That's why team building is so important.

What is team building? The concept of teams and team building has been a foundation of management since the 1960s. Although the value of team building was identified more than half a century ago, it has changed throughout the years.

Originally, team building was designed to improve interpersonal relations and social interactions. Because the concept of team building was derived from group dynamics, social psychology, and T-groups (i.e., sensitivity training that helps individuals develop greater self-awareness and become more sensitive to others), there was a heavy emphasis on relationship building, harmony, and group cohesion. As team building gained greater popularity in business organizations, the focus expanded to include a concern for achieving results, meeting goals, and accomplishing tasks. Today, team building typically addresses both aspects of performance: how teams accomplish their work and how team members relate to one another.

In its broadest sense, then, team building is a vehicle for ensuring that individuals work together harmoniously, productively, and effectively to maximize task accomplishment and goal achievement. In pursuit of this, team building takes many forms. Cross-functional teams responsible for creating new products or improving work processes use team building to agree on their shared purpose, team roles, boundary-spanning communication techniques, and similar aspects of their work together. Management teams employ team building to formulate business strategies and set future direction. Intact work teams, or intrafunctional teams, use team building to clarify their shared values, resolve interpersonal differences, and improve task execution. Still other groups engage in mental and physical challenge activities to build trust and unity.

Team building also has value for the individual team member. It helps a group of individuals maximize their collective contribution to the organization and integrate their personal goals with the organization's goals.

Team building is always done within the context of a specific purpose and is designed to meet specific objectives. The more measurable the objectives the better, because this allows the team to evaluate the effectiveness of team building. Team building may be one event or a series of events that are conducted over time. In either case, team building needs to be treated as an ongoing process.

There are six steps in the team-building process (Figure 1.1).

FIGURE 1.1

THE SIX-STEP TEAM-BUILDING PROCESS

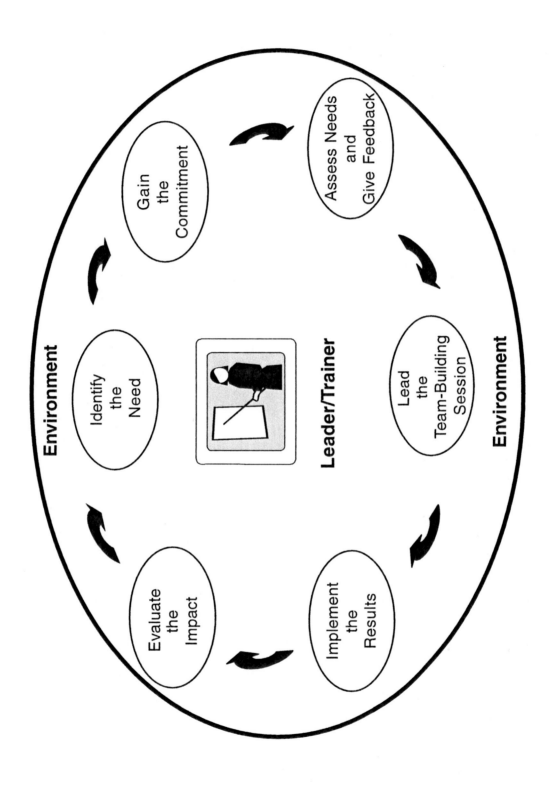

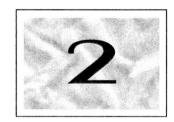

When to Do Team Building

Team building begins with a perceived need. The success of team building depends upon establishing that it is the best way to meet the identified need. Both operating managers and trainers may wonder, are there factors that indicate a need for team building? Obviously any type of breakdown in teamwork is an indicator. But team building can also enable vigorous performance in meeting strategic challenges.

TEAM-BUILDING INDICATORS

The following two assessments help identify the need to do team building. The Issue Identification Assessment (Figure 2.1) focuses on indicators of poor task execution and troubled interpersonal relationships. These are the traditional reasons teams engage in team building. For example, teams exhibiting poor communication, conflict, missed deadlines, low morale, or similar problems point to a need for team building. This assessment will help you pinpoint the specific issues that need to be addressed. The Strategic Impact Assessment (Figure 2.2) presents opportunities to do team building in response to strategic challenges or impending, or actual, change. Team members as well as the manager may complete the first assessment. The second assessment is designed for managers.

SIGNS OF TEAM DISTRESS

Signs of distress exhibited by team members also indicate a need for team building. The following represent various dysfunctional behaviors that divert individuals from doing the work of the team. The more widespread these

ISSUE IDENTIFICATION ASSESSMENT

Please indicate the extent to which the following problems are impacting team effectiveness.

	Not At All		Some Impact		High Impact
1. Low output and productivity.	1	2	3	4	5
2. Complaints within the team.	1	2	3	4	5
3. Confusion about roles.	1	2	3	4	5
4. Unclear assignments.	1	2	3	4	5
5. Lack of clear goals.	1	2	3	4	5
6. Low commitment to goals.	1	2	3	4	5
7. Lack of innovation.	1	2	3	4	5
8. Lack of initiative.	1	2	3	4	5
9. Problems working with the team leader.	1	2	3	4	5
10. People do not listen to each other.	1	2	3	4	5
11. People do not speak up and contribute ideas.	1	2	3	4	5
12. Lack of trust.	1	2	3	4	5
13. Decisions are made that people do not understand.	1	2	3	4	5
14. Decisions are made that people do not support.	1	2	3	4	5
15. People feel that good work is not recognized.	1	2	3	4	5
16. People feel that teamwork is not valued.	1	2	3	4	5
17. Different working approaches and styles inhibit collaboration.	1	2	3	4	5
18. People are not encouraged to work together.	1	2	3	4	5
19. There is favoritism with respect to assignments, how people are treated, etc.	1	2	3	4	5
20. People do not keep commitments.	1	2	3	4	5
21. Only a few people are involved in decisions.	1	2	3	4	5
22. Issues between team members remain unresolved.	1	2	3	4	5

	Not At All		Some Impact		High Impact
23. Meetings are ineffective.	1	2	3	4	5
24. There is a lack of information sharing among all team members.	1	2	3	4	5
25. The team does not have good working relationships with other teams.	1	2	3	4	5

Total: _____

Individual Scoring: Add up the scores for the twenty-five items. 100+ team building should be a top priority for your work unit. If you scored your team between 99–75, you should seriously consider a team-building session. If you scored your team between 74–50, there is some evidence that team building is warranted. This is particularly true if your score on seven to ten items is very high. If your score is between 49–25, there is little evidence your unit needs team building.

Group Scoring: If you administered this checklist to an entire group, calculate the group average and use the same scoring parameters as described above. In addition, identify those questions that have a broad distribution of responses from low to high. For example, three individuals responded 1, two individuals responded 3, and four individuals responded 5 in answering to a particular question. This indicates a need to address the issue, either through team building or some alternative.

STRATEGIC IMPACT ASSESSMENT

Please indicate the extent to which the following issues are impacting the team or are likely to impact the team over the next three to six months.

	Not At All	Some Impact	High Impact
1. The team must deal with a major new challenge.	Not At All	Some Impact	High Impact
2. A merger or acquisition has impacted roles, structure, lines of authority, values, etc.	Not At All	Some Impact	High Impact
3. The organization is undergoing a major change and the team is having problems dealing with it.	Not At All	Some Impact	High Impact
4. You, as the team leader, are new, or there are several new team members.	Not At All	Some Impact	High Impact
5. The team needs to better align its goals with the organization's strategy and goals.	Not At All	Some Impact	High Impact
6. The team is experiencing turnover and is losing high-quality individuals.	Not At All	Some Impact	High Impact
7. There is a need to strengthen quality, customer satisfaction, technology utilization, global execution, or other aspects of performance.	Not At All	Some Impact	High Impact
8. The team needs to agree on its strategic vision or clarify its shared values.	Not At All	Some Impact	High Impact
9. A large-scale transformation is planned or underway that will impact the team in significant ways.	Not At All	Some Impact	High Impact
10. The team is forming strategic alliances with other teams.	Not At All	Some Impact	High Impact
11. The team needs to work better with other teams in a boundaryless way.	Not At All	Some Impact	High Impact
12. There is a need to strengthen relationships with internal and/or external customers.	Not At All	Some Impact	High Impact

Scoring: If you identified any of the twelve items as High Impact, you should consider team building. Team building can help the group determine how to address the issue and ensure its ongoing effectiveness. In some instances, for example, numbers 10 and 11, it is important to do the team building with other teams. To address such issues as numbers 2, 3 or 9, the team leader will need to work with his or her manager and other key stakeholders to clarify the issues that need to be addressed in team building.

behaviors, the greater the urgency to do team building. These signs of distress are manifested by the following symptoms:

✓ Team Distress Checklist

- ❏ Irritability that diverts attention from work
- ❏ Decreased communication
- ❏ Reduced trust
- ❏ Decreased directness and openness
- ❏ Defensive behavior
- ❏ Protective behavior
- ❏ Blaming others
- ❏ Reduced risk taking
- ❏ Poor decision making
- ❏ Absenteeism
- ❏ Apathy or lack of interest
- ❏ Undermining others' efforts
- ❏ Complaints about lack of empowerment
- ❏ Increased conflict
- ❏ Complaints about other team members
- ❏ Avoidance of team interaction, that is, meetings

The manager must determine if these symptoms are widespread or only manifested in the behavior of one or two team members. When symptoms are widespread, team building can help uncover and address the underlying issues. Otherwise, the manager needs to address these symptoms on an individual basis. It is important to remember that deeper issues cause these symptoms. A thorough understanding of the deeper problems is important and guides the design of the team-building session.

READINESS TO DO TEAM BUILDING

In today's changing business environment, teams find themselves with a need to seize opportunities to strengthen performance or deal expeditiously with problems. The urgency of improving team performance is an important consideration about whether or not to engage in team building. Likewise, dealing with signs of distress motivates a desire to do team building. Operating managers must consider both the high price of unresolved problems and the high cost of missed opportunities. Teams can jeopardize their current performance or fail to turn around poor performance because they delay team building. The failure to prepare for change or to deal with it responsibly can, over time, become a major setback.

Timing then is an important issue in deciding when to do team building. When operating managers resolve to tackle problems or seize opportunities, this is the first step toward readiness. It means that the price of maintaining the status quo is greater than the cost of investing time, energy, and resources in team building. However, because team building generates changes in the way the team works, managers must genuinely desire these changes and, in fact, be prepared to accept them.

For example, the manager of a professional services team struggled with the need to do team building. She was comfortable involving herself in most of the team's decisions, sharing information selectively, and rarely exploring ways to improve services. But the pressure to provide faster service and stem growing customer dissatisfaction made action imperative. The manager recognized that reducing cycle time in responding to customers was crucial and that the team had to make this happen. She made the decision to engage in team building and, as a result, modify her leadership behavior.

The Manager's Team-Building Readiness Assessment (Figure 2.3) helps managers assess their readiness to do team building. Even if the prior assessments strongly indicate a need for team building, the leadership attitudes and behaviors described in this assessment are critical for success.

WHEN NOT TO DO TEAM BUILDING

Chapter 1 defined team building as a vehicle for helping individuals work together better and accomplish important results. This chapter has presented indicators of the need for team building and readiness assessments. But you also need to consider when it is not appropriate to do team building. There are times when readiness is high and indicators are strong, but team building is not the right solution. For example, a team of environmental compliance officers was experiencing several signs of distress. Apathy, low morale, and lack of commitment to team goals were all evident. There was also confusion about roles and little shared decision making. The trainer, working with the team leader, identified all of these issues and initiated a discussion about the need to do team building. However, the manager knew he was going to be reassigned within the next sixty days. He and the trainer decided not to engage in team building, feeling that it would be of more benefit to do it with the new manager in place. The delay meant team building could be used in conjunction with leadership change and give the team a new start. This was a wise decision. When the team building was done, it proved to be of enormous benefit. There *was* a sense of a new start, and team members willingly tackled the issues. Team performance, including morale and commitment, were turned around as a result.

As this example illustrates, there are times when, despite all the indicators and the leader's readiness, it is advisable to delay team building. There are other situations in which team building is not the appropriate way to meet the team's needs. The following guidelines will help you identify situations in which it is not appropriate to do team building (Figure 2.4). Alternative

MANAGER'S TEAM-BUILDING READINESS ASSESSMENT

As a manager or team leader, you believe there may be a need for team building. Consider the following statements. To what extent are you ready to engage in team building?

	Strongly Disagree	Disagree	Neutral	Agree	Strongly Agree	Not Applicable
1. You are comfortable sharing leadership and power with team members.	1	2	3	4	5	0
2. You want members of your team to be involved in making decisions.	1	2	3	4	5	0
3. You want to involve everyone on your team in helping to meet business and competitive challenges.	1	2	3	4	5	0
4. You want your team to help set goals and determine priorities.	1	2	3	4	5	0
5. You want a more collaborative environment.	1	2	3	4	5	0
6. You are interested in getting feedback about your effectiveness so that you can do a better job leading the team.	1	2	3	4	5	0
7. You want your team to be more involved in resolving day-to-day problems without your involvement.	1	2	3	4	5	0
8. You want everyone to know how their work supports your organization's strategic goals.	1	2	3	4	5	0
9. You want the team to help you deal with operating problems or improve processes.	1	2	3	4	5	0
10. You want to improve information sharing between yourself and team members, as well as between team members.	1	2	3	4	5	0
11. You feel it is important to uncover and deal with sensitive issues that exist in your team.	1	2	3	4	5	0
12. You want to resolve operating or interpersonal problems that exist on the team.	1	2	3	4	5	0
13. You want to give your team an opportunity to discuss what's working well on the team and what needs to be improved.	1	2	3	4	5	0

(continued)

	Strongly Disagree	Disagree	Neutral	Agree	Strongly Agree	Not Applicable
14. You plan to make major changes and want to get your team's buy-in and support.	1	2	3	4	5	0
15. You believe the team is working below its potential and you want to understand why and address it as a team.	1	2	3	4	5	0

Total: _____

Scoring: If your total score is between 53 and 75, you are probably ready to go ahead with a team building. If your score is between 38 and 52, talk the situation over with your team and others to see what needs to be done to get ready for team building. Examine closely the areas you rated below 3 and determine how to deal with this barrier to readiness. If your score is between 15 and 37, you are not prepared at the present time to engage in team building. Talk with an internal trainer, probably in human resources, who can help you identify what's hindering readiness.

ALTERNATIVES TO TEAM BUILDING

The following guidelines indicate situations in which team building is not the appropriate intervention. For each situation an alternative strategy is offered.

When Not To Do Team Building	Recommended Alternatives
Team members lack the skills required to do their job.	**Provide training for the team.** This is appropriate when teams are having problems making decisions or communicating. Indicators of poor decision making, communication, priority setting, etc., should be explored to determine if training is required rather than, or in conjunction with, team building.
The team does not have the resources it needs.	**This is an issue teams may not be able to solve.** You need to work with your boss to determine how to acquire the additional people, budget, equipment, or other resources the team needs to meet its goals.
Teamwork is not rewarded or reflected in the performance management system.	**This is an issue teams cannot resolve through team building.** Identify things within the team's authority that can be done to reward teamwork. However, compensation and performance management systems are bigger issues. Let human resources and others know the extent to which these issues are impeding team effectiveness.
Individual performance problems are impacting team effectiveness.	**Individual issues need to be addressed independently of team building.** Team building should not be done to handle performance issues. This can damage the morale of the entire team. Deal with these situations one-on-one.
The team is experiencing problems attracting or retaining individuals.	**This is not an issue that can be addressed through team building.** Work with human resources and others to evaluate recruiting strategies, reasons for turnover, assimilation techniques, and other factors, and take the appropriate action.

When Not To Do Team Building	Recommended Alternatives
Team members feel stuck and perceive there is a lack of opportunity for career **growth and development.**	**Organization-wide, companies need to put in place systems that allow individuals to develop their skills and talents.** You should do all you can to provide growth and learning opportunities for team members. This includes making sure individuals assigned to cross-functional project teams get the full benefit of this experience. For intact teams, you can use rotational assignments and special projects to increase personal satisfaction.
You lack the technical or functional expertise or interpersonal skills required.	**You need to have the expertise required to win the respect of team members and effectively lead the team.** Also, you need effective people management skills to facilitate group interaction. This can be addressed through training and coaching. Team building should not be conducted to help you acquire the skills required.
There is confusion about the team's authority.	**Although teams can clarify their shared purpose or mission, they may not be able to resolve problems related to their limits of authority.** This is particularly true for cross-functional project teams or problem-solving teams. When appropriate, the management sponsors and the team leader need to agree on scope of authority, boundaries, and limits.
It is not possible to get all the team members involved in team building.	**Sometimes there are geographical or logistical factors that impede a team's ability to come together for team building.** Alternatives include: 1. Convening a meeting of managers and supervisors and working with them to resolve issues. They can take the agreements back to their team. 2. If time is scarce, focus the team building on the key issues, so you can conduct team-building activities as part of regularly scheduled meetings.
The team has had a bad experience with team building.	**In these situations, it is important to delay team building.** Look for ways to set aside time in regular team meetings to help the team improve its effectiveness. As the team makes progress, it may become ready to engage in full-fledged team building.

strategies are recommended that will help the team get back on track or meet its needs.

This chapter described important prerequisites to engaging in team building. Although Chapter 4, Assess the Need, identifies how to target specific problems, the indicators discussed in this chapter are important warning signs. Sometimes they are so severe that the issues that need to be dealt with through team building are evident. But even in these circumstances, the team leader must be ready to engage in team building. Finally, it is important to use team building appropriately and find other ways to address issues team building cannot resolve.

Gain the Commitment

LEADING TEAM BUILDING

The decision to engage in team building begins with a contract, or agreement. It is important that managers, or team leaders, make explicit agreements about how they will work with a trainer. Sometimes managers may choose to lead team building. In these instances, managers contract with the team about mutual expectations. In either case, the first decision is, Who will lead the team building?

The team-building process, strategies, and techniques in this book are designed so team leaders can conduct team building without the help of an internal or external trainer. The fact that operating managers get their teams together for a sustained period of time to work on crucial issues is, in itself, a powerful intervention. When managers conduct the team building they gain a new appreciation of their leadership competence and strengthen or reaffirm their commitment to team effectiveness and efficiency. Team leaders who acquire team-building skills increase their confidence in themselves and are more comfortable dealing with issues that arise. In these situations, trainers coach managers on how to lead team building and maximize its effectiveness. Thus, there are some advantages to manager-led team building.

How then does the manager decide whether or not to lead the team-building session? The following assessment can help team leaders make this decision. (Figure 3.1)

Chapter 1 emphasized the importance of using a trainer to lead team building. However, if you answered Yes to most of the assessment questions, it is appropriate for you to lead team building. Otherwise, you will want to use an

19

LEADING TEAM-BUILDING SESSIONS

Team-building sessions can be led by the operating manager, or team leader, or a trainer from either inside or outside the organization. Check the appropriate response to each question. It will help you decide who should lead your team-building session.

	Yes	No	Not Sure
1. Do you want to *minimize* your participation in discussions and decision making?	❏	❏	❏
2. Will team members share information candidly if you lead the session?	❏	❏	❏
3. Does you team generally work together without a lot of conflict?	❏	❏	❏
4. Will team members see you as an equal participant rather than "the boss"?	❏	❏	❏
5. In meetings, do team members do most of the talking and generating of ideas?	❏	❏	❏
6. Do team members generally resolve interpersonal differences and other issues between themselves without your involvement?	❏	❏	❏
7. Do you feel you know enough about team building to design and lead a session without help?	❏	❏	❏
8. Will team members feel comfortable discussing issues that involve you if you lead the discussion?	❏	❏	❏
9. Do you feel the team is taking sufficient responsibility for its effectiveness?	❏	❏	❏
10. Is your team used to spending focused time away from day-to-day activities and working on issues of concern?	❏	❏	❏
11. Are you confident in your leadership style?	❏	❏	❏

	Yes	No	Not Sure
12. Are you confident that the team is not apprehensive about team building?	❏	❏	❏
13. Is it true that there are no long-standing issues that it will be difficult to change?	❏	❏	❏
14. Are you satisfied that you know how the group works together to solve problems and make decisions without your leading them?	❏	❏	❏

Total _____

Scoring: If you have checked eight or more Yes responses, you may not need a trainer to lead the team building. If you have four or more No responses, you probably need a trainer's help. If you have a mixture of Yes, No, and Not Sure responses, invite a trainer to talk over the situation and make a joint decision.

internal or external trainer. You and the team can benefit from a trainer's help in several ways:

- **The Leader's Participation**—Operating managers need to be fully engaged in the team building. It is important for them to contribute ideas, help make decisions and work to resolve issues. Trainer-led team building facilitates this involvement. Managers are relieved of the dual role of trying to lead the team-building process and can contribute to the discussion as a team-building participant. Using a trainer helps avoid a major pitfall of manager-led team building: the tendency of the manager to dominate the session. Trainers help balance the discussion and ensure everyone's ideas and concerns are heard.

- **Openness and Candor**—It is difficult for team members to be open and candid about problems when the manager is leading the team building. Individuals worry about the manager personalizing their concerns. Too often, a team downplays its issues for fear of offending its leader. Trainer-led team building allows team members to address their concerns to a neutral leader. The entire team benefits from a candid expression of what's working well and what's not working. For many teams, just the opportunity to talk directly about their concerns is a major step forward toward improved effectiveness.

- **Role Conflict**—When managers lead team building, participants tend to view them in their traditional role as "the boss." It is difficult for a team to divorce the manager from his or her day-to-day leadership authority and see the person as an equal participant. A team's struggle is usually evident when they defer to the manager to make decisions, break conflict deadlocks, or come up with the answer that resolves sensitive issues. Consequently, the team does not realize the full benefit of team building. Trainer-led team building makes it easier for team members to interact with the manager as an equal participant because the leadership role is elsewhere. In fact, this may be the first opportunity team members have to work with the manager in this way. It helps managers shift from their day-to-day role and work collegially with their team.

- **Sharing Leadership**—A major outcome of team building can be a realization that everyone on the team is accountable for the team's results. Trainer-led team building facilitates shared accountability for team performance. When operating managers lead team building, there is an implicit assumption that they are assuming ownership of the team's performance. Using a neutral trainer shifts this responsibility to the entire team and underscores the importance of each person's accountability to the team.

- **Facilitation Skills**—Team building is best led by individuals with strong facilitation and group process skills. Usually, these are trainers who bring their expertise to the team. Trainers are skilled in designing and leading team-building interventions that meet a variety of needs. Their ability to be flexible and creative ensures a team-building experience that is worthwhile.

CLARIFYING ROLES

Once the decision has been made to use a trainer, it is important to clarify his or her role. Together, the manager and trainer determine how this individual can best support the team-building process. The following roles are those most typically played by a trainer:

Advocate

The trainer seeks to influence the team leader to do certain things. This may include encouraging the manager to pursue specific team-building goals or identifying which issues have the greatest priority.

Specialist

Trainers can also offer specific expertise. This role is useful when team building is designed to accomplish tasks for which the trainer's special knowledge is helpful, such as strategy planning or process improvement.

Problem Solver

This is a traditional consulting role in which the trainer helps the team leader understand the deeper issues that need to be addressed, and how to structure the team building to meet these needs.

Data or Information Gatherer

In some instances the trainer's role is limited to gathering information from the team for the leader. The trainer works as an objective, unbiased data gatherer and provides the leader with an assessment of what's working well and what's not.

Facilitator

As a facilitator the trainer plays a neutral role in conducting the team building. This role uses the trainer's proven expertise to design and lead an effective team-building session. The ability to help the team deal with sensitive or controversial issues is a skill the trainer-facilitator brings to the leader.

Teacher

There may be times when the trainer instructs the manager how to conduct team building. Here, the individual's expertise is in teaching others how to execute the six-step process.

Coach

Trainers often play a coaching role in support of the team and team leader. As coaches they help leaders understand how they can maximize their participation in team building. Trainers coach leaders on such things as how to build trust and support for team building, how to maintain an open, nondefensive attitude, how to accept feedback from the team, and how to listen as an ally rather than an adversary.

Usually, the trainer will play several roles. For example, a CEO of a large organization wanted to use team building to increase interdepartmental cooperation and agree on strategic goals. The team building also provided a forum for presenting a plan to restructure the organization in a way that promoted greater synergy and global execution. The CEO decided to use an external trainer to help in designing and leading the team building. In addition to the role as facilitator, the trainer also provided strategic planning expertise and coached the CEO extensively. Finally, as an advocate, the trainer helped the CEO select the issues related to better cooperation and coordination that had to be addressed to ensure the success of the redesigned organization.

In another situation, the trainer was a member of the organization's internal training department. She worked with the leader of a cross-functional team chartered to upgrade the organization's information technology capability. The team was struggling and had made little progress in the three months it had been together. As a data gatherer, the internal trainer talked with each member of the team. She helped the team leader pinpoint the territorial and role-confusion issues that were hindering team cohesion and cooperation. Subsequently, the trainer facilitated a team building that successfully resolved these issues.

CONTRACTING WITH TRAINER

Operating managers need to make an explicit agreement with the trainer who will be designing, leading, and helping implement the results of team building. This agreement clearly describes what the manager and trainer expect of each other and how they plan to work together. This agreement needs to be revisited after Step 3 (Assess the Needs). After collecting data, the scope, expectations, roles, and other aspects of the agreement may change. Nevertheless, this initial contract establishes a framework for the manager and trainer to work together. At the minimum, the following elements need to be part of the contract:

1. **An understanding of the manager's perspective.** The manager needs to provide the trainer with the reasons why he or she believes team building is needed. This is the first agreement. Although many other things will be discussed, there must be up-front concurrence between the manager and trainer that team building is the right thing to do.

2. **The scope of the trainer's work.** The manager and trainer need to agree on the scope of the trainer's activity. For example, will the trainer explore all facets of the team's work or are there only certain issues he or she will pursue? Often, the scope changes after the formal assessment is conducted in Step 3. Nevertheless, there must be a tentative agreement on the breadth and depth of the trainer's work with the team.

3. **The role the trainer will play.** As mentioned above, there are several ways to use a trainer. The manager and trainer need to determine how to best use the individual's skills and expertise.

4. **The manager's expectations of team building.** It is important to clarify what benefits the manager expects from team building. These need to be expressed as tangible outcomes so the trainer can determine if they are realistic and attainable. Understanding the manager's expectations is another way to confirm that team building is the appropriate solution.

5. **Assessment and information-gathering process.** The trainer needs to describe the planned information gathering, or assessment, process. Together, the manager and trainer determine the most appropriate method. The size of the team, morale, comfort with team building, interpersonal dynamics, and other factors will influence the assessment method selected.

6. **Team-building deliverables.** The trainer must be clear about the products he or she is expected to provide at the conclusion of the team building. This agreement clarifies whether or not the manager is expecting a report or meeting summary that documents agreements, decisions, role descriptions, and similar outcomes.

7. **The manager's support and role.** The trainer and manager need to agree on how the manager will support the team-building process. This includes getting agreement on the manager's role. For example, the manager may want to provide assistance in setting up interviews, kick off the team-building session, or help present the feedback to the team.

8. **Clarifying the time schedule.** Clarifying dates, how long the team-building session will be, and the schedule for gathering information need to be discussed. This ensures the trainer understands things such as the team's time constraints or a manager's sense of urgency.

9. **Confidentiality.** Confidentiality is an important consideration for managers and team members. The manager needs to know that information gathered will not be discussed with his or her manager or peers. The trainer must also be able to assure team members that data collected will be summarized showing trends and themes without identifying individual responses.

10. **Follow-up.** The initial contract should describe how the trainer will work with the manager to follow up on the team-building session.

The following exhibit provides a list of contracting questions (Figure 3.2). Using these, a good contract can be established.

Contracting is best done face-to-face with the manager whose team will be engaged in team building. Although the trainer may be asked by someone else to do the team building, the contracting must be done with the actual team leader. The contracting process is a good way to build rapport with the team leader. It helps ensure that the manager actually wants the team building and is not doing it simply to satisfy his or her boss or for other political reasons.

SAMPLE CONTRACTING QUESTIONS

The following questions will help a trainer establish the team-building contract. It is helpful for managers to answer as many of these questions as possible before meeting with the trainer:

1. Why do you believe your team needs team building?

2. What role do you want me to play? (It is helpful if the trainer describes the options for the manager.)

3. What issues do you want me to focus on? If I uncover other problems, are you willing to address those issues as well?

4. What are your expectations of team building? What specific improvements do you expect to see?

5. Do you have a preference regarding how I go about gathering information from the team? Do you believe one-on-one interviews, focus group interviews, or some type of written questionnaire would work best?

6. What deliverables do you expect me to provide at the conclusion of the team building?

7. What role do you want to play? How do you believe you can best support the team and maximize the benefits of team building?

8. What's the schedule of activities? How soon do you want to conduct the team building?

9. What agreements do you need from me around confidentiality? What will I need to do to ensure the team feels comfortable talking with me?

10. How do you want to follow up on the team building? How will we evaluate progress after thirty days? three months? six months?

Contracting is most effective when both the manager and the trainer openly discuss their needs, preferences, and concerns. The responsibility to discuss these issues candidly resides with both parties. For example, the manager may have specific issues he or she wants to address through team building. The trainer may want to wait until the information gathering is completed before committing to a specific set of team-building goals. In other situations, managers may want to give the trainer their opinion about each team member. But the trainer wants to be unbiased when meeting with individuals. Discussing these issues provides an opportunity for the manager and trainer to work together and forge an effective partnership. The manager-trainer relationship should be one of openness and collaboration, in which responsibilities are shared, individual needs met, and expectations clear.

GETTING THE TEAM COMFORTABLE

Although a team may readily admit there are issues that need to be resolved, there is still a need to get their commitment to engage in team building. This is particularly true if team building is a new experience or if team members have had prior poor experiences with team building. The major commitment is the team's agreement to work together to address the issues, problems, or opportunities that have been identified.

There are several things the manager and/or trainer can do to gain the commitment of the team:

- Talk with the team about the advantages of conducting team building versus the disadvantages of not addressing the issues that have been identified.

- Review the overall purpose of the team-building session. Sometimes team members are reluctant because they are unclear about the purpose of the session. Understanding that team building is designed to address real life issues can help gain commitment.

- Begin to generate ground rules for the session as a way of helping the team feel safe talking about issues. Asking, What is the worst thing that can happen if we get together and talk about these issues? and then asking, What ground rules can we set up for the team-building session to prevent these things from happening? allows the team to create safety-building ground rules. The trainer can also talk with the team members about their hopes and concerns for the team-building session. This encourages participants to consider the advantages of team building as well as express their concerns. Using this technique provides insight into how to create a safe team-building environment.

- Simply talking about the issues with the team lets them know the trainer is sensitive to their needs. This alone helps encourage the team to engage in team building. Similarly, the fact that the manager and trainer are interested in gaining their commitment builds support for team building.

HANDLING RESISTANCE

Generally, the suggestions provided above will gain the team's commitment to team building. However, there are situations in which the team remains reluctant. The following suggestions present some other things the manager and trainer can do to overcome such resistance.

- Discuss the goals of the team building. Until an in-depth assessment is conducted, the goals will not be finalized. But the manager can talk about the general goals of team building and describe how team building can address the issues identified so far. Focusing on goals allows the team to visualize the tangible benefits of team building. Team members are more willing to invest their time and energy to gain tangible results.

- Give the team an idea of the results other teams have experienced as a result of team building. These success stories are a good way of encouraging the team to undertake team building. This is particularly powerful when the trainer shares examples of how teams with similar issues have used team building successfully.

- Explain the entire six-step process to the team. Sometimes teams are hesitant because they don't know what will happen once all the issues are brought up in a public forum. Teams are also concerned about how to move from discussion of issues to resolution. Helping the team understand the purpose of each step illustrates that there is a well-thought-out procedure guiding the team building.

- Sometimes the team is reluctant because the issues that need to be addressed involve other teams. If this is a problem, offer to facilitate a discussion that gets the commitment of these individuals to engage in team building. The trainer may even do this before talking with the hesitant team. Knowing that others believe team building is a good way to address issues helps the reluctant team make its commitment.

- Trainers may need to limit the number of issues that are addressed in team building. Teams are sometimes skeptical about the effectiveness of team building because there are so many issues to address. Feeling overwhelmed can cause teams to oppose team building. When this happens, the trainer can assure the team that, after the assessment, he or she will work with the manager to prioritize the issues that need to be addressed first. As an alternative, the trainer can work with the entire team to prioritize the issues that are most important to address in the team-building session.

- Propose that the initial team-building session deal with issues that are simpler to resolve, less sensitive, or not as controversial. This will give the team a sense of accomplishment and encourage its members to tackle tougher issues in subsequent sessions. In situations where the operating manager is reluctant to engage in team building, this approach makes it easier for him or her to commit to team building.

- The trainer may need to present the business case for team building. This is particularly important when the team needs to work on strategic issues, such as alignment with corporate goals, reengineering processes, integration after an acquisition, or similar issues. Teams may not understand that team building can be used to tackle these issues. Demonstrating the link between team-building outcomes and meeting business needs builds their enthusiasm for team building.

- Rather than conduct a full two-day team building, suggest the team begin to address issues at a staff meeting or another regularly scheduled meeting. This allows the team to initiate team building as part of its normal work activity. Sometimes this less intensive approach is more comfortable for the team. While this is difficult to do with complex issues, issues of lesser complexity can be handled in this way. When the team gains confidence in its ability to resolve issues, it may be ready to engage in a full-fledged team-building session.

GAIN THE SUPPORT OF STAKEHOLDERS OUTSIDE THE TEAM

In some situations, it is important to get the support of those who are not part of the immediate team. This includes situations in which any of the following conditions prevail:

- The operating manager wants to begin involving the team in strategic activities. Gaining the commitment of the higher level manager assures the operating manager and/or trainer that these individuals support the team's involvement in big-picture issues.

- Similarly, there are times when team building deals with issues that have broader organizational implications that reach beyond the immediate team. For example, issues such as rewards for teamwork, access to technology, cross-functional processes, and similar issues are beyond the scope of one team. These are issues that the team cannot solve by itself. Operating managers and trainers may need to talk with stakeholders to get their commitment to listen to the team's concerns. Without this commitment, the team may be more frustrated after the team-building session than before.

- Sometimes there is a need to share sensitive information as a part of team building. Examples of this include why a decision was made to shift responsibilities from one work unit to another, to delay the acquisition of new technology, or to fill higher level jobs through external recruiting rather than internal promotion. In order to address these issues, the operating manager must talk candidly about reasons for the decisions. Agreement from higher level stakeholders involved in these decisions needs to be secured before the manager talks with the team.

IDENTIFY ISSUES THAT MIGHT UNDERMINE SUCCESS

Gaining commitment also requires addressing issues that can undermine the success of team building. For example, the team leader is under pressure and it will be difficult to devote the time needed to team building. In other instances, travel schedules and other commitments make it difficult to get all the appropriate individuals together. These issues need to be resolved before going ahead with a commitment to do team building.

Upcoming organizational changes are important factors in gaining commitment. For example, if key roles are going to be filled in the next several weeks, team building should be delayed until the new individuals have joined the organization. The results of team building can be undermined when decisions and agreements are not endorsed or supported by new team members. Likewise, if major organizational changes are planned, it is best to delay team building. Team members' focus and energy will be on the organizational changes, even if they are minimally impacted by them.

Gaining commitment is the second step in the team-building process. It is one of the most critical. The effectiveness of all subsequent activities depends upon a solid commitment. Clear expectations, an explicit contract, and getting the team comfortable ensure you are ready to move on to the next step. It is better to delay team building than to skip or do a cursory job in gaining commitment.

Assess the Need

The goal of Step 3 is to determine the exact nature of the problems or issues that need to be addressed in the team-building session. It is essential to get beyond surface symptoms and identify the underlying causes. A team-building session based upon a systemic and explicit diagnosis of the issues has a much higher probability of success.

The assessment process involves investigation, compiling information, and processing information. The process of assessment can be broken down into a series of basic steps:

- Definition of objectives
- Selection of data-gathering or assessment method
- Gathering the data
- Analysis of the information
- Identification of the causative issues and themes

DEFINITION OF OBJECTIVES

The first step is to determine the objectives of the assessment. A clear under-standing of these broad goals clarifies what information is relevant, how much information you need to collect, and from whom. The objectives will vary depending upon whether the team building is designed to resolve issues that are impeding performance or to help the team meet a strategic challenge or prepare for change.

When team building is designed to address operational or interpersonal issues, the information gathering focuses on what's working well and what's not working well. When team building is designed to help a team deal with strategic issues or change, the information gathering focuses on how the team needs to position itself for future success. Sometimes, the information gathering explores both issues. For example, an information technology team was responsible for designing and implementing a new management information system. But in the course of their work, the team was experiencing conflict and role confusion. Also, they were grappling with how to meet the information-system needs of various stakeholders. Team building was used to help the group clarify roles, resolve interpersonal conflicts, and clarify the needs of each stakeholder group. Understanding stakeholder needs enabled the team to focus on information-technology solutions that supported global needs, not just domestic.

Generally, the data collection objectives will fall into one of three areas. *Operational and interpersonal factors* measure the extent to which the team is working well or not working well together. They assess the team's effectiveness in accomplishing its tasks and working well interpersonally. *Intergroup relations* indicate how the team is working with others, measuring the extent to which a team executes well cross-functionally or interorganizationally. *Strategic factors* assess the team's success in meeting broader organizational needs. They evaluate how well the team manages change, supports strategic objectives, meets customer needs, and similar factors.

Figure 4.1 provides a list of general questions that can be used to probe each category of issues.

TECHNIQUES FOR ASSESSMENT AND DATA GATHERING

The three most common ways of gathering data for team building are one-on-one interviews, small-group (also called focus-group) interviews, and questionnaires or other types of written assessments. It is important to consider the advantages and limitations of each technique. This enables the trainer and manager to select the most appropriate approach.

The interview is the most popular technique for data collection. It provides a rich source of information and is the most flexible and adaptable of all data-gathering techniques. The structure of the interview can vary from very little structure to a high degree of structure. Most interviews are somewhere in between and combine open-ended questions with those that require a simple yes or no response. There are at least three ways to conduct interviews: one-on-one in person, in small groups (focus groups), and by telephone. Each method has advantages and disadvantages.

You should consider the following when planning and implementing interviews to gather data. First, interviews with all team members may take a considerable amount of time. Logistics, setting up interview appointments, and coordinating schedules are all time-consuming activities. This becomes even more difficult if team members are dispersed geographically, even globally. Also, you must make sure you accurately record information during the interview process. This can be challenging if you are not an experienced note taker.

ASSESSMENT QUESTIONS

Operational and Interpersonal Issues

What types of problems is the team experiencing?

How long has the team been experiencing these problems?

What keeps individual team members from being as effective as they would like to be?

Are all team members experiencing these problems or are some more impacted than others?

What do people like best about the team?

How can the things that are working well be strengthened?

What needs to change to improve team effectiveness?

What does each team member need to do?

What does the team leader need to do?

Are there factors outside of the team that are hindering its effectiveness?

Intergroup Relations

What types of problems is the team experiencing working with other teams?

How long has the team been experiencing these problems?

Is the entire team having problems working with other teams or are some team members more impacted than others?

What is working well in your interaction with other teams?

How can this team work more effectively as part of a global team?

What needs to change in the way you are working with other teams?

What do members of your team need to do differently?

What do members of other teams need to do differently?

What can the leaders of both/other teams do to improve working relationships?

(continued)

Strategic or Change Issues

What is working well with respect to the merger or acquisition?

What types of problems is the team experiencing because of the merger or acquisition?

What does the team need to do in order to support the organization's strategy?

How does the team need to better align its goals and priorities to support the organization?

What can the team do to help the organization improve its:

profitability	quality
responsiveness	innovative approach
flexibility	customer satisfaction
execution	efficiency
speed	technology utilization

In what areas does the team do a good job meeting customer needs? How can the team continue to strengthen its performance in these areas?

What can the team do to improve customer satisfaction or retention?

How adaptive has the team been when required to make a major change? What does the team do well? What does it need to improve? In what areas has there been the greatest resistance to doing something new?

One-on-One Interviews

One-on-one interviews are one of the most effective ways to gather information. They provide an opportunity for each individual to talk confidentially and personally about the issues. Interviewing this way allows you to delve deeply into issues and understand each individual's full perspective. Finally, individual interviews offer an opportunity to build rapport with each team member before the team-building session. Likewise, this interviewing technique is of great benefit to trainers who are unfamiliar with the team. A personal interview tends to expose any resistance to or concerns about team building and gives the trainer an opportunity to address them before the session. A disadvantage of one-on-one interviews is the time it takes to talk with each individual.

Small-Group Interviews

Small-group interviews, often called focus groups, is a way to collect data from a group rather than individuals. This is done best when groups range from four to seven people. The same questions can be used that are used in individual interviews. It also has the advantage of eliciting different perspectives and allowing individuals to discuss, comparatively, how they see the issues. This makes it easier to begin sorting out the most important issues that need to be addressed during the team-building session. Focus groups generally take less time than one-on-one interviews. To be most effective two trainers need to conduct the focus-group interviews. One individual can ask the questions and the other can record the information on newsprint or a flip chart. This ensures the data is captured accurately.

There are several potential problems that can limit the effectiveness of focus groups as an assessment technique. Focus groups can have the disadvantage of different levels of participation. Thus, some individuals may talk a lot, others little. Also, it is a challenge to capture information accurately when several people are responding to the same question. Third, in some instances, team members may not be completely open and candid in front of their peers. Similarly, if team members are experiencing interpersonal problems with one another, it is doubtful they will raise the issue publicly. Finally, individuals may support or be influenced by the views of others, particularly if they are strongly expressed. In these instances, group-think can hamper individuals who hold different views from expressing their opinions.

Telephone Interviews

There are times when the interviewing has to be done over the telephone. This should be a fallback technique used only when it is not possible to conduct personal or focus-group interviews. For example, when team members are dispersed geographically or globally, telephone interviews may be the only way to gather data. When you have to rely on telephone interviews, it is important to send the interviewees the questions prior to the discussion. This helps the trainer and the interviewees make the best use of their time on the telephone. It is also a way to begin to build rapport. But, the trainer must be prepared to spend time talking with the individual, making sure he or she feels comfortable providing information. In other words, the same type of rapport building you would do face-to-face needs to be done for telephone interviews.

Questionnaires or Written Assessments

The major advantage of assessment instruments is that they allow simultaneous data collection from many individuals. This technique offers the convenience of gathering a lot of information with a minimal investment of time. Also, the fixed responses help the trainer analyze quantitative responses in a short period of time. Similarly, the trainer can compare the team's performance to normative data and thereby provide a richer perspective on the group's results relative to others. Assessments can be combined with interviewing techniques. This is probably the most effective way to gather data since you have both quantitative and qualitative data.

Like interviews, assessment questionnaires can be highly structured or more general. Highly structured assessments yield very specific information. As an added benefit, structured assessments or standardized questionnaires can be used to collect pre-team-building and post-team-building data. This is an effective way to evaluate a team's progress and identify issues that need to be addressed in a follow-up session. Lastly, a major advantage of questionnaires is confidentiality. They are the best way to guarantee anonymity.

However, like all techniques, there are disadvantages with questionnaires or assessments. First, team members may not take them seriously or may take the assessment hurriedly. Second, instructions must be very clear to avoid the problem of participants misinterpreting what to do and thereby completing the instrument incorrectly. Likewise, depending on how the instrument is designed, team members may give either extreme or neutral responses. In either case, the information is too skewed or too general to be useful. Finally, this technique does not provide a way to probe for a deeper understanding of issues. Thus, underlying causes are rarely identified using only written instruments.

The following chart (Figure 4.2) summarizes the advantages and disadvantages of the three data-gathering techniques just described.

OTHER SOURCES OF INFORMATION

Direct observations of the team provide another source of data. As a technique for data gathering, its value is sometimes overlooked. When done systemically, observations may provide information of comparable value to other techniques. The obvious problem is the bias of the observer, as well as the sensitivity of the observer. Also, the presence of the observer may have an effect on data collection that is not a problem with questionnaires, interviews, or focus groups. Thus, observation should be used to investigate specific aspects of team performance and supplement more formal data-gathering techniques. For example, if there are power, communication, conflict, or other issues, the

METHODS OF DATA COLLECTION

FIGURE 4.2

One-on-One Interviews		Standardized Questionnaires or Written Assessments		Focus Groups	
Advantages	Disadvantages	Advantages	Disadvantages	Advantages	Disadvantages
Rich source of data	Time consuming	Responses can be easily quantified and summarized	Unable to probe deeper issues raised by participants	Takes less time	Difficult to capture information accurately
Able to gather nonverbal feedback	Expensive	Able to gather comparative responses to the same questions	Predetermined questions may miss issues	Able to identify major themes more quickly	Inconsistent levels of participation
Builds rapport between interviewer and team members	Difficult to record responses	Easy to use with large numbers of people	Individuals may interpret questions differently	Able to see how team members relate to one another	Lack of candor or openness
Flexible, allowing data collection on a wide variety of topics	Difficult to quantify and summarize data	Relatively inexpensive	Easier for individuals to provide noncommittal responses	Easy to identify shared concerns or misunderstandings about team building	Acquiesce to strongly held views (group-think)
Easy to maintain	Skill of interviewer impacts effectiveness	Easy to use when individuals are widely dispersed geographically	Unable to gather nonverbal feedback	Able to gather nonverbal responses	Difficult to quantify and summarize data
	Difficult to use with large numbers of people	Able to gather data electronically	Does not build rapport between interviewer and team members	Able to probe more deeply into issues raised	Skill of interviewer impacts effectiveness
	Difficult to use when individuals are geographically dispersed	Easy to maintain confidentiality			Difficult to use when individuals are geographically dispersed
	Unable to gather data electronically	Able to obtain a large volume of data			Unable to gather data electronically
					Difficult to maintain confidentiality

trainer can better understand the nature of the problem by simply observing the team in action. Also, observation is very helpful when coaching the operating manager on how to interact with the team during the team building. Managerial behaviors that will undermine team building can be difficult to pinpoint unless directly observed in the context of leading the team. Similarly, dysfunctional interpersonal behaviors on the part of the team members or the team leader are easier to understand when observed directly.

Sometimes hard data is available and can be used. Again, this is a supplementary technique, not a primary technique for gathering information. These data include statistics on absenteeism, turnover, quality, customer complaints or compliments, goal achievement, profitability, and other information. A major advantage of this data is that it represents objective measures of success. Teams resistant to team building cannot argue with statistics that clearly show a need to improve their performance. These data also provide base-line measurements to which future measurements can be compared. The concrete, measurable nature of this data gives the team an immediate and important goal to work toward as an outcome of team building.

ESTABLISHING A DIAGNOSTIC RELATIONSHIP

The success of the data-collection process requires establishing a relationship between the trainer who gathers the information and those who provide it. Since the nature of that relationship affects the quality and quantity of information provided, it is essential that the trainer provide team members with a clear idea of who he or she is, why the data is being collected, how the data-gathering process will be conducted, and how the data will be used. Answering these questions allays fears and encourages individuals to provide candid and honest responses. The relationship trainers establish in the course of gathering data is important in building trust and confidence in them and the team-building process.

Establishing a diagnostic relationship is another form of contracting. The following exhibit provides guidelines and a structured process for establishing a diagnostic relationship with team members (Figure 4.3).

Taking time to establish a data-collection contract ensures the team members provide information that is honest, reliable, and complete. Effective relationship building in the data-gathering phase yields commitment to the team-building process and enthusiasm for doing the work necessary to address the issues raised. A good diagnostic relationship helps individuals begin to think about issues that concern the team and creates expectations and confidence that, working together, change is possible. Finally, data collection can contribute to the longer-term collaborative relationship between the trainer and the team. Team building is a process, and the initial two-day session is only the first step. A trusting trainer-team relationship facilitates the trainer's ability to continue working productively with the team throughout the process of change.

ESTABLISHING A DIAGNOSTIC RELATIONSHIP

1. **Who Am I?**—Let team members know who you are, and describe your role in the team-building process. Even when team members know you, your role in leading the team building needs to be clearly understood.

2. **Why Am I Talking with You?**—This second question describes the data-gathering activities. Define the goals of data gathering, why you chose this particular data-gathering method, and who else will participate in data gathering. Individuals often wonder if they have been specially selected to give information or if you are talking with everyone on the team. Often, individuals ask whether or not individuals outside the team, especially customers, will be part of the data-gathering process. Describing the process up front answers these questions.

3. **What Do I Need from You?**—You must explain how much time people will need to devote to the data-gathering process. This also provides an opportunity to clarify how the information will be used, who will have access to it, and answer similar questions. Team members want explicit answers about how the data will be collected, analyzed, and fed back. The quality and quantity of information gathered will be influenced by the extent to which individuals believe their information will be used responsibly.

4. **How Will I Protect Your Confidentiality?**—As in question 3, this issue is important to team members. Individuals providing information need to know who will see their responses and in what form. This is especially crucial when team members are asked to discuss sensitive or controversial issues. They will be concerned about protecting their privacy and fearful of being punished for their candor. In order to alleviate concern and increase the likelihood of obtaining honest responses, you need to assure team members that confidentiality will be maintained.

5. **Why Is This Diagnosis Beneficial?**—Talk openly with team members about the benefits of team building and the role data gathering plays in the team-building process. This helps individuals understand that the data gathered will be used to improve the team's performance and strengthen interpersonal relations.

(continued)

6. **Do You Have Any Concerns about Working with Me?**—The success of the diagnostic relationship depends on the trust established between you and those providing the data. You need to give team members an opportunity to ask questions about their involvement, background, or observations about the team. An open and honest exchange between you and team members encourages them to talk candidly and provide useful data. Be sure to allow enough time to discuss all questions raised by team members.

SETTING UP THE ASSESSMENT DISCUSSION

There are several things that you as a manager need to do to help ensure the success of the assessment process. First, planned assessments, either interviews or questionnaires, need to be announced by the team leader. This is also an effective way to introduce the team-building session. It alerts team members to the manager's intention to gather feedback and use it to address substantive issues. The announcement must also convey your commitment to team building. You may choose to announce the assessment session at a staff meeting, by memo, or by e-mail. It is important that the announcement inform team members about the purpose of the assessment, who will conduct it, approximately how long it will last, how it supports the team-building process, and what team members should expect to talk about during the discussion. If for some reason not everyone will take part in the assessment, clarify why certain team members have been chosen to participate. If assessments are going to be conducted with stakeholders outside the team, communicate this as well. Encourage individuals to be candid in their responses and stress the confidential nature in which their feedback will be handled. It is critical to remind team members that the team building will address the major themes or issues that emerge as opposed to individual concerns. Finally, let the team know how and when feedback will be provided. A sample announcement appears in Figure 4.4.

A written memo or e-mail is appropriate for teams that are familiar with team building. However, groups that are new to team building, who have conflict, or may have reservations about the team-building or the assessment process require a face-to-face meeting. In some instances, it is beneficial for the trainer to be present when the manager explains the purpose of team building, its goals as well as the assessment process. This gives team members an opportunity to express concerns and ask questions.

Second, the assessment meetings must be scheduled. The trainer or an administrative person who works closely with the team can do this. For interviews, there may be a preferred order to the interview schedule. For example, it may make sense to talk to senior people first. To ensure sufficient time is allocated it is advisable to schedule more time rather than less with each person. For example, if each interview is estimated to be an hour, schedule ninety minutes. It is easier to end the interview early than to ask individuals to stay longer. If possible, schedule time between interviews. This allows the trainer to complete interview notes and get set-up to talk with the next person.

Interviewing people in their offices gives the trainer a sense of the work environment. However, the primary concern is conducting the interview where the individual feels comfortable. Team members who work in an open office environment may not feel at ease talking there. In these situations, it is essential to arrange for a conference room or closed office for the interview.

SAMPLE ANNOUNCEMENT

To: (Team Members)

From: (Manager)   **CC:** (Trainer)

I have asked (Trainer's Name) to work with us and conduct a two-day team-building session.

I believe team building can help us achieve the following goals:

- Improve the effectiveness of our team in areas that are important to all of us.
- Provide an opportunity for us to evaluate how we are working as a team, both our strengths and weaknesses.
- Identify problem areas and corrective actions.

I have asked (Trainer's Name) to contact each of you and set up interviews. These will be one-on-one discussions designed to get your feedback about what the team is doing well and how we can improve. I have also asked (Trainer's Name) to gather feedback about me as a leader. Each interview will last approximately one hour.

Please be candid in your responses. (Trainer's Name) will analyze your feedback and identify the major themes that emerge. The feedback will be confidential; the team-building session will focus on major issues of most concern to the team, not on individual issues.

I want to thank you for your participation in this data-gathering process.

Please feel free to contact me or (Trainer's Name) if you have any questions about the upcoming team-building interviews.

INTERVIEWING GUIDELINES—ONE-ON-ONE INTERVIEWS AND FOCUS GROUPS

Most of the interviewing guidelines for one-on-one interviews are applicable for focus groups. However, because you are interviewing several people at once, there are some differences in preparation and technique. The first set of guidelines is for one-on-one interviews, the second for focus groups (Figures 4.5, 4.6). Figure 4.7 is an example of ground rules that are useful in conducting focus groups.

SAMPLE INTERVIEW QUESTIONS

Interviews can be structured, unstructured, or a combination of both. Structured interviews focus on specific aspects of team performance. Unstructured interviews are general inquiries and allow the participant to identify issues that need attention. The following are examples of twenty-five structured and twenty-five unstructured questions. Many of these questions are similar and overlap with one another. Any combination of these questions can be used and additional questions created. For a sixty-minute interview, eight to twelve questions are usually sufficient. This ensures you will have time to probe some responses more deeply (Figure 4.8).

QUESTIONNAIRES AND OTHER ASSESSMENT INSTRUMENTS

There are several team-building questionnaires available for you to use. Most are based on characteristics of team effectiveness derived from the work of leading management theorists. The following questionnaires are the most commonly used types of questionnaires. Many of the same guidelines that apply to interviews are also useful in administering questionnaires:

1. **Thoroughly explain the questionnaire or instrument.** You want to make sure individuals understand it. Ask them to read the instructions and solicit their questions.

2. **Administer the questionnaire.** Ask the individual(s) to complete the questionnaire.

3. **Thank the individual(s).** Thank each person for taking time to complete the questionnaire. You will also want to check to see if there are any questions.

4. **Explain the next steps.** Let the person know how you will use the data provided and explain the feedback process.

Two sample questionnaires are provided in Figures 4.9 and 4.13. The first incorporates the eight dimensions of team effectiveness explained on page 53. It is designed to assess where a team is in its growth from Work Group to High Performance Team. The second questionnaire includes the eight dimensions of effective teams and several others. It is a more general assessment and is not limited, specifically, to phases of team growth.

INTERVIEWING GUIDELINES: ONE-ON-ONE INTERVIEWS

The following guidelines will help you prepare for, conduct, and conclude interviews:

1. **Be prepared.** Be organized and prepared to conduct the interviews. This includes organizing and sequencing your questions, having a list of the team-building goals, planning how you will open the interview, and being familiar with each person on the interview schedule, i.e., who you are talking with, their position, length of service, etc. Think of questions to follow up on the ones you have prepared, probe deeper, and expose underlying issues.

2. **Open the interview.** Greet the team member and introduce yourself. Do one or more of the following things to begin building rapport: (1) Ask the person questions about himself or herself, e.g., how long they have been on the team, what their job is, how long they have been with the organization, etc. (2) If you are interviewing the individual in his or her office, open the discussion by commenting about a plaque, family pictures, desk mementos, or other items of interest. Talking about familiar and prized things relaxes the individual and builds rapport. This is particularly effective if you and the interviewee share a common interest, e.g., sports, sailing, skiing, etc. You also need to identify the individual's communication style and adapt to it. For example, some people will get to the point quickly, while others will think about their responses before answering. During the opening minutes of the interview, pay close attention to the person's communication style and pace yourself accordingly. (3) Explain how the interviews fit into the larger team-building process. Describe the purpose of the interview, what types of questions you are going to ask, how the data will be summarized and feedback given. Also, let the person know from whom you are gathering information. Stress the confidentiality of the information you are soliciting and reiterate that aggregate trends are your concern. Stop to give the team member an opportunity to ask questions. Next, tell the person you will be taking notes (or taping, with their permission). Let them know that if at any one time they feel uncomfortable with your doing this they only need to say so. This is also true if there is any question they don't want to answer.

3. **Conduct the interview.** Ask the questions you have prepared and, when needed, probe deeper for more information. The following questions are useful when you want to explore answers more deeply and identify underlying causes: Why do you believe this is true? How often has that happened? When did this problem first occur? Why do you feel this way? What's the most important issue for the team to address? Why do you believe this? What other things have happened to lead you to this conclusion?

You need to maintain control of the interview and not get diverted by extraneous issues that the individual may want to discuss. If the person begins to talk about things that appear off the topic, you can ask, How does that relate to the team?, Is this an example that pertains to what we're discussing? or Why is it important for me to know this? It is critical to get through the interview questions and discourage rambling.

If it appears you will run out of time, don't hurry or skip questions. If you need more time ask the individual if this is possible. You can also schedule a second meeting to complete the interviews if your schedule does not allow you to extend the allotted time. Optimally, you will want to keep the interviews from an hour to an hour and a half.

As the individual responds to the question, listen attentively while you make notes. Don't focus so much on taking notes that you lose emotional contact with the person. Make enough notes so that you understand the key messages and issues. You can complete the notes later. It is important that you pay enough attention to the individual to observe nonverbal feedback. There are times when you want to probe these cues as well. For example, if the person has been smiling and begins to frown when you pursue a certain line of questioning, you will want to ask why. For example, "I notice you frowned when I began to ask about information sharing. Why is that?" The following are other nonverbal cues you want to probe:

- Changes in tone or emphasis
- Minimal responses or shutting down after the individual has been open and talkative
- Refusal to make eye contact when certain questions are asked
- Displays of underlying feelings or emotion (frustration, anger, disapproval, etc.)
- Hesitancy to respond, or avoidance of a subject
- Nervousness, including rushing through the interview
- Defensiveness, or personalizing a question

4. **Solicit additional information.** Let the individual know you have finished your questions and give them an opportunity to provide any other

(continued)

information they want to share with you. Ask, "Is there anything else I should know about the team?" Or use a similar question to solicit final comments.

5. **Close the interview and thank the individual.** Thank the person for their time and information. Ask the team member if they have any questions about the next steps or any comments about the interview process. Often individuals are curious about how others are responding to your questions and will ask, "Are others saying the same thing?" Remembering that it is important to protect confidentiality, you can answer generally. For example, "Many common themes are emerging, although each interview is different." Even if the person does not ask, explain again that their information will remain anonymous and reiterate the next steps in the team-building process.

Sometimes, for whatever reason, you may not believe your note taking has been thorough. If you are concerned that all the salient information has not been captured or is not clear, you may ask the individual, "If I have any further questions about what you've told me, or need to clarify something, may I call you?" Thank the participant for his or her cooperation and end the interview.

INTERVIEWING GUIDELINES: FOCUS GROUPS

Most of the interviewing guidelines for one-on-one interviews are applicable for focus groups. However, because you are interviewing several people at once, there are some differences in preparation and technique:

1. **Be prepared.** Make sure you have a room that is conducive to the interviews. This means a room that seats all the interviewees comfortably, as well as you and the trainer who will be recording the participants' responses. You and the trainer need to agree on your roles. Only one of you should ask the questions and talk to the group. If there is a question about what to write on the newsprint or flip chart, the trainer should signal you. Finally, both of you need to know the order of the interview questions. Label or put headings on the flip chart or newsprint paper sheets. This will help the trainer-recorder keep the data organized.

2. **Open the interview.** Greet the participants and introduce yourself and the other trainer. It is important to start within five minutes of the scheduled time and not wait for participants who come late. You will want to do the following to begin building rapport:

   (1) Ask everyone to introduce themselves. Often team members know each other so the introductions do not need to be lengthy. If participants do not know each other, ask each person to identify their role on the team and how long they have been with the team.

   (2) Propose a set of ground rules for the interview session, similar to the following: [Figure 4.7] Make sure everyone understands the ground rules and agrees to comply with them. Remind participants that ground rules are intended to help everyone feel comfortable participating in the discussion. Ask participants, "Are there any other ground rules you want to propose?" Add to the ground rules, or edit them as needed. This is an important rapport-building step. You want to allow ten to fifteen minutes for establishing ground rules.

   (3) Explain how the interviews fit into the larger team-building process. Describe the purpose of the interviews, what types of questions you are going to ask, and how the data will be summarized and feedback given. You will also need to explain your role and the trainer's role. Stress

(continued)

47

again the confidentiality of the information you are soliciting and reiterate that your interest is in issues and concerns shared by most team members. Let participants know you will use a separate sheet of paper entitled "Other Issues" to capture comments that are of concern but not related to the interview topics. You will get agreement from the group on how to handle these issues at the conclusion of the meeting.

3. **Conduct the interviews.** As you ask each question, check to make sure everyone has an opportunity to respond. Instruct the trainer to mark with a ("✓") issues on which there is a lot of agreement. This will help you identify major themes later. Be sure you invite individuals who have been quiet into the discussion. You may also need to ask individuals who have been talking a lot to hold their comments. Managing time is usually a challenge. Keep track of time and let the group know when you need to move on to another question. During focus groups, you will also want to probe nonverbal cues. In particular, note issues where participants express feelings such as passion, apathy, frustration, anger, etc. Similarly, hesitancy to answer questions, avoidance, or silence need to be probed.

4. **Solicit additional information.** Ask the group if they have any other information they want to share that is important for you to understand.

5. **Close the interview and thank the participants.** Thank the group for their time and the information they have provided. Agree on how any issues captured on the Other Issues list will be handled.

FIGURE 4.7

GROUND RULES

- One person speaks at a time.

- Speak for yourself, using "I" statements.

- Respect different points of view and different perspectives.

- Make sure everyone participates in the discussion.

- Stay on the topic and don't digress.

- Express your views openly and honestly.

- Maintain the confidentiality of opinions expressed in this meeting.

- Focus on the issues that need to be addressed, not on individuals.

- Keep comments to the point and avoid lengthy stories or examples.

- Wait for one person to finish speaking and don't interrupt others.

SAMPLE INTERVIEW QUESTIONS

Structured Questions

1. Is the purpose or mission of the team clear?

2. Do you understand how this team's work contributes to the success of the overall organization?

3. Are you clear about your role on the team and the role of other team members?

4. Does the team have specific goals? Do you know what you are responsible for contributing to the success of the team?

5. Does the team have the skills it needs to do its work? Did you receive training as needed?

6. Does the team have the resources needed to do its work?

7. Are decision-making processes clear?

8. Is team communication open and is information shared widely or narrowly?

9. Is there mutual trust between team members? Do people respect one another?

10. Is there a sense of mutual accountability for the work of the team? Do people take personal responsibility for the team's performance?

11. Do people keep their commitments and follow through? Do they do what they say they are going to do?

12. Is work evenly distributed among team members?

13. Does the team interact well with other teams?

14. Is there enthusiasm for the work of the team?

15. Are people proud to be part of this team?

16. What are the three greatest challenges for the organization (or division, business unit)?

17. How will these challenges impact your team?

18. What are the biggest challenges confronting this team over the next three months (six months, year, etc.)?

19. What are the three things you are most proud of as a team member?

20. What are the most important three issues the team needs to address in order to improve its performance?

21. How does the team leader

- foster trust?
- facilitate open communication?
- involve others in decisions?
- respect individual talent, skills, and abilities?
- resolve problems?
- handle conflict?
- generate commitment?
- recognize accomplishments?
- deal with mistakes or failure?
- encourage new ideas and creativity?

22. In what ways does the team leader inhibit or fail to

- foster trust?
- facilitate open communication?
- involve others in decisions?
- respect individual talent, skills, and abilities?
- resolve problems?
- handle conflict?
- generate commitment?
- recognize accomplishments?
- deal with mistakes or failure?
- encourage new ideas and creativity?

23. Is continuous improvement a team value? How is it manifested?

24. Does the team learn from its mistakes? How is failure handled?

25. Does the team use lessons learned to improve its performance?

(continued)

Unstructured Questions

1. What does this team do well?

2. In what areas does the team need to improve?

3. How do others outside the team view this team? Do you work well together? Is there infighting?

4. If you could change one thing about this team, what would it be?

5. What should this team stop doing, start doing, and continue doing?

6. What are your greatest concerns as a member of this team? What are your greatest satisfactions?

7. What do you like most about this team? What do you like least?

8. When you talk to others about the team, what do you say?

9. What words would you use to describe this team?

10. What does this team contribute to the organization? Does it help the organization achieve its goals/strategy/vision? How?

11. What challenges does this team face over the next three to six months?

12. What are this team's top priorities over the next three to six months?

13. What are the strengths of your team?

14. What are the weaknesses of your team?

15. What do you believe to be the team's major problems?

16. Why is this team having the kind of problems it is experiencing?

17. What do you like best about this team?

18. On a personal level, what things make you an effective team member?

19. What keeps you from being a more effective team member?

20. What does the team leader do well?

21. What does the team leader need to improve?

22. What would make the team building successful for you?

23. What do you hope doesn't happen during or as a result of team building?

24.. How does this team work with other teams?

25. What can be improved about the way this team works with other teams?

TEAM-DEVELOPMENT QUESTIONNAIRE

Figure 4.9 is a team assessment that measures the extent to which a team is a true team, rather than a group, and identifies at what level the team is performing. The scoring continuum of development ranges from Work Group to High Performing and evaluates the following eight dimensions of team effectiveness:

1. **A shared and meaningful purpose**—A mission that is worth pursuing to which all team members commit. It is a purpose that is important and motivates and inspires team members to give their best. A team's shared purpose also supports the organization as a whole. By fulfilling its mission, a team helps the organization to accomplish its broader mission and goals.

2. **Specific goals**—The team's goals are derived from and support their shared purpose. These goals are unique to the team, but are linked to the organization's strategic objectives. A shared and meaningful purpose and specific performance goals form the foundation on which teams are built.

3. **Clear roles**—Role clarity ensures team members understand how their skills and expertise help the team achieve its goals and purpose. In this way, everyone plays a significant, though different, role in helping the team maximize its performance. Clear definition of roles does not mean team members don't share duties or tasks or that there is never overlap of responsibilities. But it does mean that everyone understands what has been entrusted to them and what the team is counting on them to contribute.

4. **A common and collaborative approach**—A common, collaborative approach has two aspects. First, teams must agree on *how* they will do their work—team processes. Thus, they agree on how to make decisions, solve problems, handle meetings, execute projects, etc. The second aspect of a common, collaborative approach is the *way* the team works together—team relationships. This includes all aspects of interpersonal relations, including communication, building trust, respecting differences, cooperation, etc.

5. **Mutual accountability**—In order to form a true team, team members must hold themselves and one another accountable for the team's performance. Accountability is a commitment team members make to themselves and fellow team members to be responsible for the attitudes and behaviors that promote team effectiveness. Mutual accountability is the basis of trust and respect and is foundational to shared leadership.

6. **Intergroup relations**—Effective teams work well with other teams. In organizations today teams do not work in isolation and every team is part of a larger structure comprised of many teams. A key dimension of team effectiveness is the extent to which a team supports other teams to jointly accomplish goals that are important for the entire organization.

7. **Passion**—Passion is the dimension of team effectiveness that describes the level of energy, confidence, and enthusiasm a team displays in all aspects of its work. This means team members share a passion for the team's work, and eagerly give their best. This passion is fueled by a shared conviction that the team has the power to do what is necessary to get the job done. It also means team members are proud to be part of the team.

8. **Skills and learning**—Teams must have the technical, functional, interpersonal, and other skills required to do their job and work well together as a team. This dimension also means that teams seek to learn, continuously improve, and grow. These teams ask, How can we do better tomorrow what we did today? They are successful in meeting new challenges because they are not afraid to critically evaluate themselves and change the way they do things.

TEAM-DEVELOPMENT QUESTIONNAIRE

On the following pages are a series of questions that describe various attributes of team effectiveness. Please indicate the extent to which each statement describes how my/our _____ team operates. Indicate your views by circling the *most accurate answer.* There are five possible answers for each question:

AS	Agree Strongly
A	Agree
N	Not Demonstrated Consistently
D	Disagree
DS	Disagree Strongly

	AS	**A**	**N**	**D**	**DS**
1. Our team has a meaningful, shared purpose.	5	4	3	2	1
2. Team members clearly understand their roles.	5	4	3	2	1
3. Team problem solving results in effective solutions.	5	4	3	2	1
4. Team members appreciate one another's unique capabilities.	5	4	3	2	1
5. We are able to resolve conflicts with other teams collaboratively.	5	4	3	2	1
6. Team members take personal responsibility for the effectiveness of our team.	5	4	3	2	1
7. Working on our team inspires people to do their best.	5	4	3	2	1
8. We have the skills we need to do our jobs effectively.	5	4	3	2	1
9. We are strongly committed to a shared mission.	5	4	3	2	1
10. When an individual's role changes, an intentional effort is made to clarify it for everyone on the team.	5	4	3	2	1
11. We address and resolve issues quickly.	5	4	3	2	1
12. Team members are effective listeners.	5	4	3	2	1
13. We seek to arrange our priorities to meet the needs of other work groups.	5	4	3	2	1
14. Team members maintain a can-do approach when they encounter frustrating situations.	5	4	3	2	1
15. My team has a strong sense of accomplishment relative to our work.	5	4	3	2	1

	AS	A	N	D	DS
16. We always ask ourselves, How can we do better tomorrow what we did today?	5	4	3	2	1
17. We focus on big-picture strategic issues as much as on day-to-day activities.	5	4	3	2	1
18. Team members understand one another's roles.	5	4	3	2	1
19. People on my team are rewarded for being team players.	5	4	3	2	1
20. Communication in our group is open and honest.	5	4	3	2	1
21. We communicate effectively with other groups.	5	4	3	2	1
22. Team members take initiative to resolve issues between themselves without involving the team leader.	5	4	3	2	1
23. People are proud to be part of our team.	5	4	3	2	1
24. As a team we are continuously working to improve cycle time, speed to market, customer responsiveness, or other key performance indicators.	5	4	3	2	1
25. We set and meet challenging goals.	5	4	3	2	1
26. Everyone values what each member contributes to the team.	5	4	3	2	1
27. Group meetings are very productive.	5	4	3	2	1
28. Members of my team trust each other.	5	4	3	2	1
29. Our team has established trusting and supportive relationships with other teams.	5	4	3	2	1
30. We spend very little time complaining about things we cannot control.	5	4	3	2	1
31. Team members frequently go beyond what is required and do not hesitate to take initiative.	5	4	3	2	1
32. We view everything, even mistakes, as opportunities for learning and growth.	5	4	3	2	1
33. We consistently produce strong, measurable results.	5	4	3	2	1
34. Team members avoid duplication of effort and make sure they are clear about who is doing what.	5	4	3	2	1
35. Our team has mechanisms in place to monitor its results.	5	4	3	2	1
36. Team members help one another deal with problems or resolve issues.	5	4	3	2	1
37. We work toward integrating our plans with those of other work groups.	5	4	3	2	1
38. Team members seek and give each other constructive feedback.	5	4	3	2	1
39. As a team, we work to attract and retain top performers.	5	4	3	2	1
40. We use various forms of training to keep our skills up-to-date.	5	4	3	2	1
41. We make sure our work helps the organization achieve its goals.	5	4	3	2	1

(continued)

		AS	A	N	D	DS
42.	When team members' roles change, specific plans are implemented to help them assume their new responsibilities.	5	4	3	2	1
43.	Our team works with a great deal of flexibility so that we can adapt to changing needs.	5	4	3	2	1
44.	We are able to work through differences of opinion without damaging relationships.	5	4	3	2	1
45.	Our collaborations with other teams are productive, worthwhile, and yield good results.	5	4	3	2	1
46.	Team members are sure about what is expected of them and take pride in a job well done.	5	4	3	2	1
47.	My team is excited about the contribution it is making to the organization's competitive viability.	5	4	3	2	1
48.	Team members embrace continuous improvement as a way of life.	5	4	3	2	1
49.	The mission and goals of my team are well aligned with the organization's mission and goals.	5	4	3	2	1
50.	Overlapping or shared tasks and responsibilities do not create problems for team members.	5	4	3	2	1
51.	When we choose consensus decision-making we do it effectively.	5	4	3	2	1
52.	Team members display high levels of cooperation and mutual support.	5	4	3	2	1
53.	The goals of our group support those of other groups.	5	4	3	2	1
54.	Team members consider how their actions will impact others when deciding what to do.	5	4	3	2	1
55.	My team is proud of its accomplishments and optimistic about the future.	5	4	3	2	1
56.	Team members work to ensure we are using best practice methods.	5	4	3	2	1

INTERPRETING THE RESULTS

Figure 4.10 shows the worksheet you need to score the profile once it has been administered. Figure 4.11 shows the first step of scoring a sample profile: the tallying of scores. Finally, Figure 4.12 demonstrates how to calculate averages for the eight dimensions of team effectiveness. Once you have completed your analysis, use these guidelines to interpret your results.

Work Groups—If the team scored 167 or below, they are in the Work Group category. What distinguishes a Work Group from an Authentic Team? In Work Groups, members interact primarily to share information and make decisions that help individual members perform better within their areas of responsibility. Beyond this, they do not have a shared purpose, team goals, well-defined roles, a common, collaborative approach, or any of the other attributes of an Authentic Team. Individual group members may work well with others and demonstrate a passion for their own work, seek continuous improvement and be accountable for their work. However, these characteristics are not generally true for all group members.

Work Groups can have a significant performance impact and may not need to become an Authentic Team. However, a Work Group that needs to become a team contributes less as a group than the individual members' potential. This is because their interactions detract from each member's individual performance without delivering joint benefits. Thus, the sum of the whole is less than the capabilities of the individual parts. For this reason, if the team scored in the Work Group category range, it needs to seriously ask whether it is time to become a real team.

- **Professed Teams**—Teams that scored between 168 and 195 are Professed Teams and are characterized by a lack of consistency. At times teams may exhibit several of the eight dimensions. But they qualify as "professed" because the dimensions of effectiveness are not part of the team culture. For example, sometimes they produce good results and sometimes they do not, sometimes team members work well together and sometimes they do not. Thus, although the team may have a shared purpose, it is not a meaningful one and team members have a hard time relating their work to the team's mission. In other situations, there is a lack of goal clarity and individual team members are focused on individual priorities. Roles may be unclear or there is no sense of mutual accountability. Professed Teams experience confusion and frustration because the organization, customers, and sometimes the team leader hold them accountable for demonstrating all the dimensions of team effectiveness. Like Work Groups, these teams contribute far less than their potential. Often morale is low because team members struggle to make the team concept work without understanding the need to address all dimensions of effectiveness. Team members expend considerable energy, and wonder why the team still has the same problems and does not produce results commensurate with team members' individual capabilities. Professed Teams are in a pivotal position. If the team does not meet the challenges of becoming an Authentic Team, it typically reverts to Work Group.

SCORING THE PROFILE

Directions: Using a blank questionnaire, tally the group's responses to each question and enter that total in the chart below. Add each column, and divide by the number of individuals who took the profile. Place the average scores in the boxes at the bottom. These are the team's average scores on each of the eight performance dimensions. Add all eight *total scores* and calculate the total average score. Place the composite average score in the box marked *Team Effectiveness Score*.

Team
Effectiveness
Score:

Purpose & Goals	Roles	Team Processes	Team Relationships	Intergroup Relations	Accountability	Passion	Skills & Learning
1] ___	2] ___	3] ___	4] ___	5] ___	6] ___	7] ___	8] ___
9] ___	10] ___	11] ___	12] ___	13] ___	14] ___	15] ___	16] ___
17] ___	18] ___	19] ___	20] ___	21] ___	22] ___	23] ___	24] ___
25] ___	26] ___	27] ___	28] ___	29] ___	30] ___	31] ___	32] ___
33] ___	34] ___	35] ___	36] ___	37] ___	38] ___	39] ___	40] ___
41] ___	42] ___	43] ___	44] ___	45] ___	46] ___	47] ___	48] ___
49] ___	50] ___	51] ___	52] ___	53] ___	54] ___	55] ___	56] ___
A	V	E	R	A	G	E	S

TEAM DEVELOPMENT INVENTORY
EXAMPLE OF HOW TO SCORE

On the following pages are a series of questions that describe various attributes of team effectiveness. Please indicate the extent to which each statement describes how my/our _____ team operates. Indicate your views by circling the *most accurate answer.* There are five possible answers for each question:

AS	Agree Strongly
A	Agree
N	Not Demonstrated Consistently
D	Disagree
DS	Disagree Strongly

	AS	A	N	D	DS
1. Our team has a meaningful, shared purpose.	$5_{[1]}$	$4_{[3]}$	$3_{[8]}$	2	1
2. Team members clearly understand their roles.	$5_{[2]}$	$4_{[8]}$	$3_{[2]}$	2	1
3. Team problem solving results in effective solutions.	5	4	$3_{[3]}$	$2_{[6]}$	$1_{[3]}$
4. Team members appreciate one another's unique capabilities.	5	4	3	$2_{[5]}$	$1_{[7]}$
5. We are able to resolve conflicts with other teams collaboratively.	5	4	$3_{[2]}$	$2_{[4]}$	$1_{[6]}$
6. Team members take personal responsibility for the effectiveness of our team.	5	$4_{[5]}$	$3_{[3]}$	$2_{[4]}$	1
7. Working on our team inspires people to do their best.	$5_{[1]}$	$4_{[6]}$	$3_{[2]}$	$2_{[3]}$	1
8. We have the skills we need to do our jobs effectively.	$5_{[6]}$	$4_{[5]}$	$3_{[1]}$	2	1
9. We are strongly committed to a shared mission.	$5_{[1]}$	$4_{[4]}$	$3_{[7]}$	2	1
10. When an individual's role changes, an intentional effort is made to clarify it for everyone on the team.	$5_{[3]}$	$4_{[6]}$	$3_{[3]}$	2	1
11. We address and resolve issues quickly.	5	4	$3_{[2]}$	$2_{[3]}$	$1_{[7]}$
12. Team members are effective listeners.	5	$4_{[6]}$	$3_{[6]}$	2	1
13. We seek to arrange our priorities to meet the needs of other work groups.	$5_{[2]}$	$4_{[5]}$	$3_{[2]}$	$2_{[3]}$	1
14. Team members maintain a can-do approach when they encounter frustrating situations.	$5_{[5]}$	$4_{[4]}$	$3_{[3]}$	2	1

	AS	A	N	D	DS
15. My team has a strong sense of accomplishment relative to our work.	5[4]	4[3]	3[2]	2[3]	1
16. We always ask ourselves, How can we do better tomorrow what we did today?	5[1]	4[2]	3[1]	2[6]	1[2]
17. We focus on big-picture strategic issues as much as on day-to-day activities.	5[4]	4[5]	3[2]	2[1]	1
18. Team members understand one another's roles.	5[2]	4[8]	3[1]	2[1]	1
19. People on my team are rewarded for being team players.	5[1]	4[1]	3[1]	2[4]	1[5]
20. Communication in our group is open and honest.	5[2]	4[2]	3[3]	2[5]	1
21. We communicate effectively with other groups.	5[2]	4[1]	3[1]	2[8]	1
22. Team members take initiative to resolve issues between themselves without involving the team leader.	5	4[1]	3[2]	2[1]	1[8]
23. People are proud to be part of our team.	5[3]	4[2]	3[2]	2[5]	1
24. As a team we are continuously working to improve cycle time, speed to market, customer responsiveness or other key performance indicators.	5	4	3[4]	2[4]	1[4]
25. We set and meet challenging goals.	5[3]	4[5]	3[4]	2	1
26. Everyone values what each member contributes to the team.	5	4	3	2[5]	1[7]
27. Group meetings are very productive.	5[2]	4[1]	3[9]	2	1
28. Members of my team trust each other.	5[1]	4[3]	3[8]	2	1
29. Our team has established trusting and supportive relationships with other teams.	5[2]	4[8]	3[2]	2	1
30. We spend very little time complaining about things we cannot control.	5	4	3[3]	2[6]	1[3]
31. Team members frequently go beyond what is required and do not hesitate to take initiative.	5	4	3	2[5]	1[7]
32. We view everything, even mistakes, as opportunities for learning and growth.	5	4	3[2]	2[4]	1[6]
33. We consistently produce strong, measurable results.	5	4[5]	3[3]	2[4]	1
34. Team members avoid duplication of effort and make sure they are clear about who is doing what.	5[1]	4[6]	3[2]	2[3]	1
35. Our team has mechanisms in place to monitor its results.	5[6]	4[5]	3[1]	2	1
36. Team members help one another deal with problems or resolve issues.	5[1]	4[4]	3[7]	2	1
37. We work toward integrating our plans with those of other work groups.	5[3]	4[6]	3[3]	2	1
38. Team members seek and give each other constructive feedback.	5	4	3[2]	2[3]	1[7]
39. As a team, we work to attract and retain top performers.	5	4[6]	3[6]	2	1
40. We use various forms of training to keep our skills up-to-date.	5[2]	4[5]	3[2]	2[3]	1

(continued)

	AS	A	N	D	DS
41. We make sure our work helps the organization achieve its goals.	5[5]	4[4]	3[3]	2	1
42. When team members' roles change, specific plans are implemented to help them assume their new responsibilities.	5[4]	4[3]	3[2]	2[3]	1
43. Our team works with a great deal of flexibility so that we can adapt to changing needs.	5[1]	4[2]	3[1]	2[6]	1[2]
44. We are able to work through differences of opinion without damaging relationships.	5[4]	4[5]	3[2]	2[1]	1
45. Our collaborations with other teams are productive, worthwhile, and yield good results.	5[2]	4[8]	3[1]	2[1]	1
46. Team members are sure about what is expected of them, and take pride in a job well done.	5[1]	4[1]	3[1]	2[4]	1[5]
47. My team is excited about the contribution it is making to the organization's competitive viability.	5[2]	4[2]	3[3]	2[5]	1
48. Team members embrace continuous improvement as a way of life.	5[2]	4[1]	3[1]	2[8]	1
49. The mission and goals of my team are well aligned with the organization's mission and goals.	5	4[1]	3[2]	2[1]	1[8]
50. Overlapping or shared tasks and responsibilities do not create problems for team members.	5[3]	4[2]	3[2]	2[5]	1
51. When we choose consensus decision-making we do it effectively.	5	4	3[4]	2[4]	1[4]
52. Team members display high levels of cooperation and mutual support.	5[3]	4[5]	3[4]	2	1
53. The goals of our group support those of other groups.	5	4	3	2[5]	1[7]
54. Team members consider how their actions will impact others when deciding what to do.	5[2]	4[1]	3[9]	2	1
55. My team is proud of its accomplishments and optimistic about the future.	5	4[5]	3[5]	2[2]	1
56. Team members work to ensure we are using best practice methods.	5	4[8]	3[1]	2[3]	1

SCORING THE PROFILE

Directions: Transfer the score from the Team Development Inventory sheets to the appropriate column. Add each column and divide by the number of individuals who took the profile. Place the average scores in the boxes at the bottom. These are the team's average scores on each of the eight performance dimensions. Add all eight *total scores* and calculate the total average score. Place the sum composite average score in the box marked Team Development Score.

Team Development Score: 168.7

Purpose & Goals	Roles	Team Processes	Team Relationships	Intergroup Relations	Accountability	Passion	Skills & Learning
1] 41	2] 48	3] 24	4] 17	5] 20	6] 37	7] 41	8] 53
9] 42	10] 48	11] 19	12] 42	13] 42	14] 50	15] 44	16] 30
17] 48	18] 47	19] 25	20] 37	21] 33	22] 16	23] 39	24] 24
25] 47	26] 17	27] 41	28] 41	29] 48	30] 24	31] 17	32] 20
33] 37	34] 41	35] 53	36] 42	37] 48	38] 19	39] 42	40] 42
41] 50	42] 44	43] 30	44] 48	45] 47	46] 25	47] 37	48] 33
49] 16	50] 39	51] 24	52] 47	53] 17	54] 41	55] 39	56] 41
281 ÷ 12	284 ÷ 12	216 ÷ 12	274 ÷ 12	255 ÷ 12	212 ÷ 12	259 ÷ 12	243 ÷ 12
23.4	**23.7**	**18.0**	**22.8**	**21.3**	**17.7**	**21.6**	**20.3**

A V E R A G E S

63

- **Emerging Teams**—Teams that scored between 196 and 223 are Emerging Teams. Typically there are two or three dimensions of effectiveness that need to be addressed. In Emerging Teams it is not unusual for team results to depend upon the performance of a few individuals rather than the contribution of everyone on the team. For this reason, some team members are strongly connected to the team's mission and goals while others are not. Likewise, some members exhibit passion and a desire to learn, and want to work collaboratively, but others do not. These teams are called "emerging" because, in a sense, everyone has not fully committed to the team in the same way. This is one reason why team performance will fluctuate greatly depending upon what is required. In general, Emerging Teams are more effective when tasks are routine or well known. They are less effective when challenged with more difficult tasks or new responsibilities, and in these situations they can become dysfunctional.

  Emerging Teams may have a difficult time distinguishing themselves from real teams. Thus, they can become very discouraged when the façade of being a real team breaks down and problems are exposed. This is why it is important to pinpoint what they must do to become an "Authentic Team."

- **Authentic Teams**—If the team scored between 224 and 251, it is an Authentic Team. This team exhibits all the dimensions of team effectiveness. Their performance is consistent and others outside the team view them as a real team. Authentic Teams produce excellent results. The team's energy level is high and there is a passion to contribute their best. Authentic Teams have established strong, supportive relationships with other teams. They are able to work together as a team or in subgroups to resolve issues. Leaders of Authentic Teams often comment, "My team resolves most of its issues and rarely involves me." Authentic Teams are not yet high performance because mutual accountability is limited to commitments made around work-related deliverables and relationships. Also, unlike High-Performance Teams, Authentic Teams spend less time focused on strategic and big picture issues.

- **High-Performance Teams**—Teams that scored 252 and above count as High Performance. They produce outstanding results and usually outperform all other like teams. The team flexibly anticipates and adapts quickly to change. This is a team whose members are deeply committed to one another's personal growth and success. This commitment typically transcends the team. Team meetings are focused, crisp, fun, and leadership is widely distributed. These teams spend a lot of time focused on strategic and big-picture issues, not in crisis management. High Performance Teams challenge themselves to exceed their own standards of performance. This keeps them at peak performance.

TEAM EFFECTIVENESS EVALUATIONS

Another sample questionnaire is the Team Effectiveness Evaluation (Figure 4.13). Unlike the prior inventory, it can be used to diagnose general

TEAM EFFECTIVENESS EVALUATION

Instructions: Indicate on the scales that follow your assessment of your team and the way it functions by circling the number you feel is most descriptive of your team.

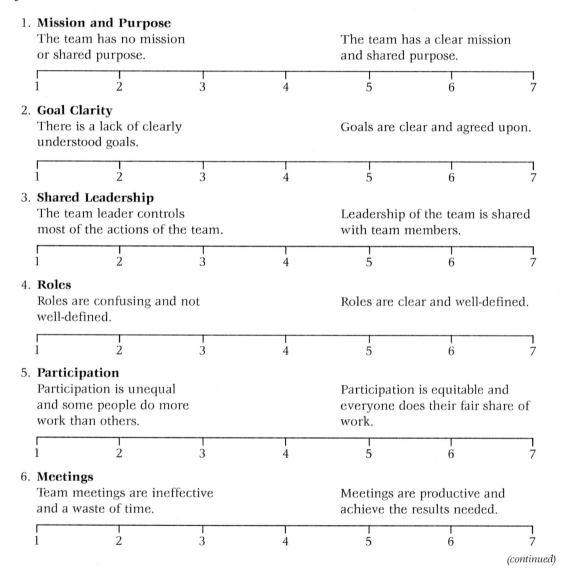

1. **Mission and Purpose**

   The team has no mission or shared purpose.

   The team has a clear mission and shared purpose.

   1   2   3   4   5   6   7

2. **Goal Clarity**

   There is a lack of clearly understood goals.

   Goals are clear and agreed upon.

   1   2   3   4   5   6   7

3. **Shared Leadership**

   The team leader controls most of the actions of the team.

   Leadership of the team is shared with team members.

   1   2   3   4   5   6   7

4. **Roles**

   Roles are confusing and not well-defined.

   Roles are clear and well-defined.

   1   2   3   4   5   6   7

5. **Participation**

   Participation is unequal and some people do more work than others.

   Participation is equitable and everyone does their fair share of work.

   1   2   3   4   5   6   7

6. **Meetings**

   Team meetings are ineffective and a waste of time.

   Meetings are productive and achieve the results needed.

   1   2   3   4   5   6   7

(continued)

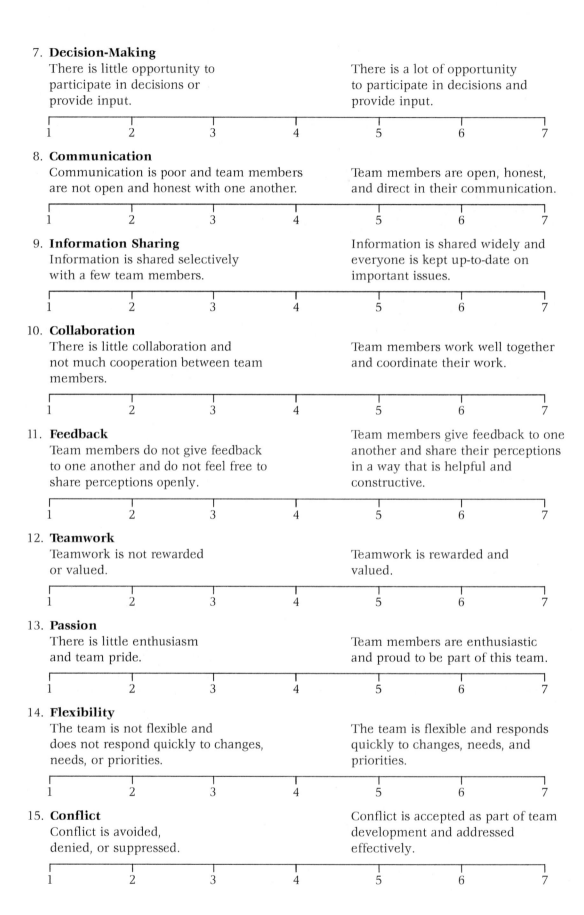

7. **Decision-Making**

There is little opportunity to participate in decisions or provide input.

There is a lot of opportunity to participate in decisions and provide input.

1   2   3   4   5   6   7

8. **Communication**

Communication is poor and team members are not open and honest with one another.

Team members are open, honest, and direct in their communication.

1   2   3   4   5   6   7

9. **Information Sharing**

Information is shared selectively with a few team members.

Information is shared widely and everyone is kept up-to-date on important issues.

1   2   3   4   5   6   7

10. **Collaboration**

There is little collaboration and not much cooperation between team members.

Team members work well together and coordinate their work.

1   2   3   4   5   6   7

11. **Feedback**

Team members do not give feedback to one another and do not feel free to share perceptions openly.

Team members give feedback to one another and share their perceptions in a way that is helpful and constructive.

1   2   3   4   5   6   7

12. **Teamwork**

Teamwork is not rewarded or valued.

Teamwork is rewarded and valued.

1   2   3   4   5   6   7

13. **Passion**

There is little enthusiasm and team pride.

Team members are enthusiastic and proud to be part of this team.

1   2   3   4   5   6   7

14. **Flexibility**

The team is not flexible and does not respond quickly to changes, needs, or priorities.

The team is flexible and responds quickly to changes, needs, and priorities.

1   2   3   4   5   6   7

15. **Conflict**

Conflict is avoided, denied, or suppressed.

Conflict is accepted as part of team development and addressed effectively.

1   2   3   4   5   6   7

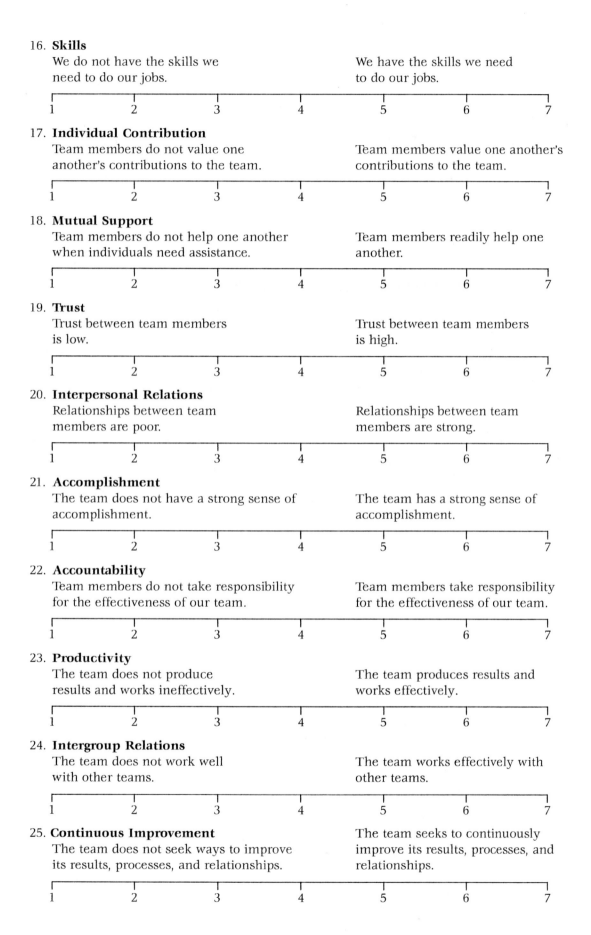

16. **Skills**

We do not have the skills we need to do our jobs.

We have the skills we need to do our jobs.

```
1     2     3     4     5     6     7
```

17. **Individual Contribution**

Team members do not value one another's contributions to the team.

Team members value one another's contributions to the team.

```
1     2     3     4     5     6     7
```

18. **Mutual Support**

Team members do not help one another when individuals need assistance.

Team members readily help one another.

```
1     2     3     4     5     6     7
```

19. **Trust**

Trust between team members is low.

Trust between team members is high.

```
1     2     3     4     5     6     7
```

20. **Interpersonal Relations**

Relationships between team members are poor.

Relationships between team members are strong.

```
1     2     3     4     5     6     7
```

21. **Accomplishment**

The team does not have a strong sense of accomplishment.

The team has a strong sense of accomplishment.

```
1     2     3     4     5     6     7
```

22. **Accountability**

Team members do not take responsibility for the effectiveness of our team.

Team members take responsibility for the effectiveness of our team.

```
1     2     3     4     5     6     7
```

23. **Productivity**

The team does not produce results and works ineffectively.

The team produces results and works effectively.

```
1     2     3     4     5     6     7
```

24. **Intergroup Relations**

The team does not work well with other teams.

The team works effectively with other teams.

```
1     2     3     4     5     6     7
```

25. **Continuous Improvement**

The team does not seek ways to improve its results, processes, and relationships.

The team seeks to continuously improve its results, processes, and relationships.

```
1     2     3     4     5     6     7
```

aspects of team effectiveness without linking it to specific stages of team development.

Figure 4.14 shows the worksheet you use to score the Effectiveness Evaluation (Figure 4.13). Refer to Figures 4.15 and 4.16 for examples of how to score this profile. Figure 4.16 indicates this team needs to focus on several performance dimensions. Since so many average scores are below 5.0, the trainer needs to look for themes or related items. For example, the low scores on Shared Leadership (2.4), Participation (1.6), and Collaboration (3.0) all point to a need to improve everyone's involvement in the team's activities, decisions, problem solving, etc. Low scores on Communication (2.5), and Information Sharing (1.6) clearly show an improvement in communication is required.

RELATING ASSESSMENTS TO TEAM EFFECTIVENESS

The Team Effectiveness Inventory and Team Effectiveness Evaluation reflect the eight dimensions of team effectiveness. Likewise, the Structured Interview Questions (Figure 4.8) explore all eight dimensions. The Unstructured Interview Questions are helpful when a trainer wants to probe a team's strengths and weaknesses in a way that does not limit responses to the eight performance dimensions. Unstructured Questions can also be used in combination with Structured Interview Questions.

Chapter 6 presents a two-day team-building session that helps teams address each aspect of effectiveness. This design can be modified if the trainer chooses interview questions or an assessment that explores different team effectiveness characteristics. However, in most situations, team building will need to address some if not all of the eight dimensions. This is particularly true for new teams or teams that are new to team building.

TEAM EFFECTIVENESS EVALUATION SCORE SHEET

Transfer each person's score to this tally sheet. Add each column and divide by the number of individuals who took the profile. These are the team's average scores on each performance dimension.

Dimension of Effectiveness	Total Score	Average Score
1. Mission and Purpose		
2. Goal Clarity		
3. Shared Leadership		
4. Roles		
5. Participation		
6. Meetings		
7. Decision Making		
8. Communication		
9. Information Sharing		
10. Collaboration		
11. Feedback		
12. Teamwork		
13. Passion		
14. Flexibility		
15. Conflict		
16. Skills		
17. Individual Contribution		
18. Mutual Support		
19. Trust		
20. Interpersonal Relations		
21. Accomplishment		
22. Accountability		
23. Productivity		
24. Intergroup Relations		
25. Continuous Improvement		

SAMPLE TEAM EFFECTIVENESS EVALUATION

Instructions: Indicate on the scales that follow your assessment of your team and the way it functions by circling the number you feel is most descriptive of your team.

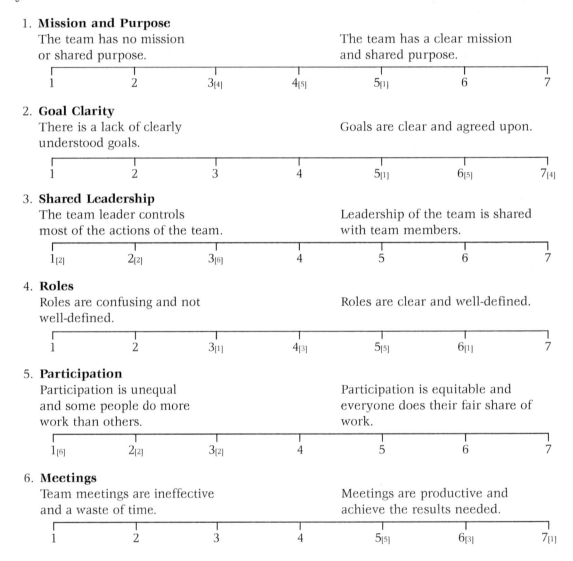

1. **Mission and Purpose**
   The team has no mission
   or shared purpose.

   The team has a clear mission
   and shared purpose.

   1   2   3[4]   4[5]   5[1]   6   7

2. **Goal Clarity**
   There is a lack of clearly
   understood goals.

   Goals are clear and agreed upon.

   1   2   3   4   5[1]   6[5]   7[4]

3. **Shared Leadership**
   The team leader controls
   most of the actions of the team.

   Leadership of the team is shared
   with team members.

   1[2]   2[2]   3[6]   4   5   6   7

4. **Roles**
   Roles are confusing and not
   well-defined.

   Roles are clear and well-defined.

   1   2   3[1]   4[3]   5[5]   6[1]   7

5. **Participation**
   Participation is unequal
   and some people do more
   work than others.

   Participation is equitable and
   everyone does their fair share of
   work.

   1[6]   2[2]   3[2]   4   5   6   7

6. **Meetings**
   Team meetings are ineffective
   and a waste of time.

   Meetings are productive and
   achieve the results needed.

   1   2   3   4   5[5]   6[3]   7[1]

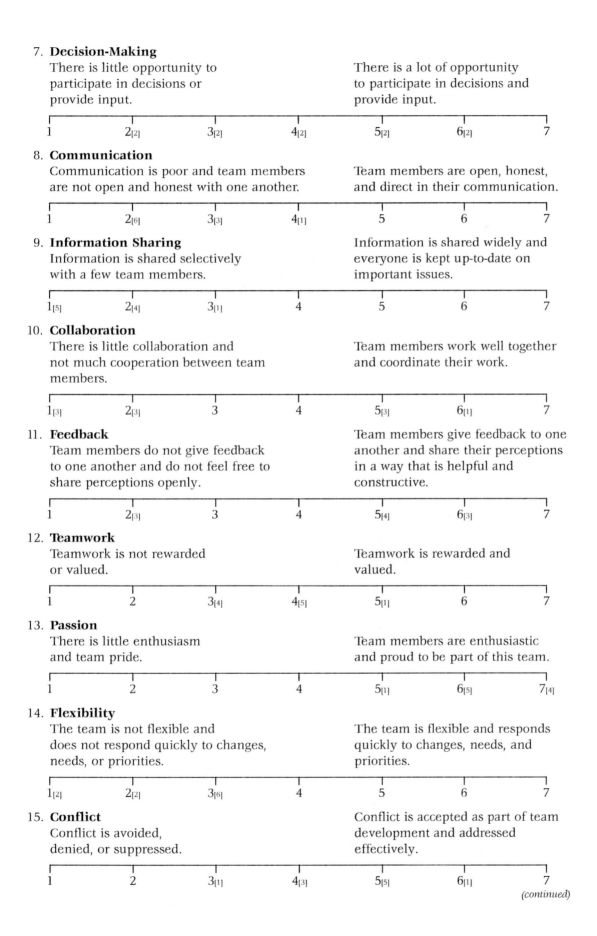

7. **Decision-Making**

There is little opportunity to participate in decisions or provide input.

There is a lot of opportunity to participate in decisions and provide input.

1   2[2]   3[2]   4[2]   5[2]   6[2]   7

8. **Communication**

Communication is poor and team members are not open and honest with one another.

Team members are open, honest, and direct in their communication.

1   2[6]   3[3]   4[1]   5   6   7

9. **Information Sharing**

Information is shared selectively with a few team members.

Information is shared widely and everyone is kept up-to-date on important issues.

1[5]   2[4]   3[1]   4   5   6   7

10. **Collaboration**

There is little collaboration and not much cooperation between team members.

Team members work well together and coordinate their work.

1[3]   2[3]   3   4   5[3]   6[1]   7

11. **Feedback**

Team members do not give feedback to one another and do not feel free to share perceptions openly.

Team members give feedback to one another and share their perceptions in a way that is helpful and constructive.

1   2[3]   3   4   5[4]   6[3]   7

12. **Teamwork**

Teamwork is not rewarded or valued.

Teamwork is rewarded and valued.

1   2   3[4]   4[5]   5[1]   6   7

13. **Passion**

There is little enthusiasm and team pride.

Team members are enthusiastic and proud to be part of this team.

1   2   3   4   5[1]   6[5]   7[4]

14. **Flexibility**

The team is not flexible and does not respond quickly to changes, needs, or priorities.

The team is flexible and responds quickly to changes, needs, and priorities.

1[2]   2[2]   3[6]   4   5   6   7

15. **Conflict**

Conflict is avoided, denied, or suppressed.

Conflict is accepted as part of team development and addressed effectively.

1   2   3[1]   4[3]   5[5]   6[1]   7

(continued)

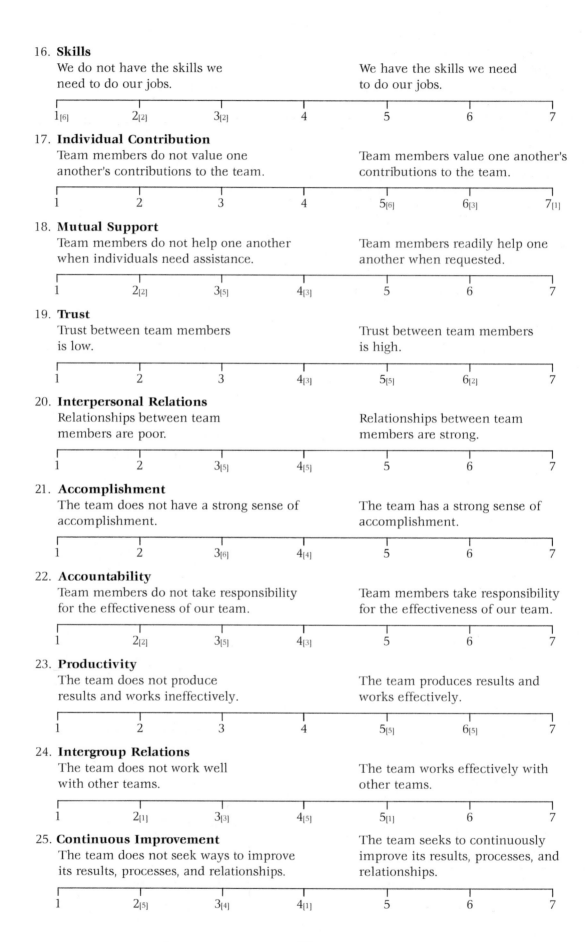

16. **Skills**

We do not have the skills we
need to do our jobs.

We have the skills we need
to do our jobs.

1[6]　　2[2]　　3[2]　　4　　5　　6　　7

17. **Individual Contribution**

Team members do not value one
another's contributions to the team.

Team members value one another's
contributions to the team.

1　　2　　3　　4　　5[6]　　6[3]　　7[1]

18. **Mutual Support**

Team members do not help one another
when individuals need assistance.

Team members readily help one
another when requested.

1　　2[2]　　3[5]　　4[3]　　5　　6　　7

19. **Trust**

Trust between team members
is low.

Trust between team members
is high.

1　　2　　3　　4[3]　　5[5]　　6[2]　　7

20. **Interpersonal Relations**

Relationships between team
members are poor.

Relationships between team
members are strong.

1　　2　　3[5]　　4[5]　　5　　6　　7

21. **Accomplishment**

The team does not have a strong sense of
accomplishment.

The team has a strong sense of
accomplishment.

1　　2　　3[6]　　4[4]　　5　　6　　7

22. **Accountability**

Team members do not take responsibility
for the effectiveness of our team.

Team members take responsibility
for the effectiveness of our team.

1　　2[2]　　3[5]　　4[3]　　5　　6　　7

23. **Productivity**

The team does not produce
results and works ineffectively.

The team produces results and
works effectively.

1　　2　　3　　4　　5[5]　　6[5]　　7

24. **Intergroup Relations**

The team does not work well
with other teams.

The team works effectively with
other teams.

1　　2[1]　　3[3]　　4[5]　　5[1]　　6　　7

25. **Continuous Improvement**

The team does not seek ways to improve
its results, processes, and relationships.

The team seeks to continuously
improve its results, processes, and
relationships.

1　　2[5]　　3[4]　　4[1]　　5　　6　　7

SAMPLE TEAM EFFECTIVENESS EVALUATION SCORE SHEET

Transfer each person's score to this tally sheet. Add each column and divide by the number of individuals who took the profile. These are the team's average scores on each performance dimension.

Dimension of Effectiveness	Total Score	Average Score
1. Mission and Purpose	37	3.7
2. Goal Clarity	63	6.3
3. Shared Leadership	24	2.4
4. Roles	46	4.6
5. Participation	16	1.6
6. Meetings	55	5.5
7. Decision Making	40	4.0
8. Communication	25	2.5
9. Information Sharing	16	1.6
10. Collaboration	30	3.0
11. Feedback	44	4.4
12. Teamwork	37	3.7
13. Passion	63	6.3
14. Flexibility	24	2.4
15. Conflict	46	4.6
16. Skills	16	1.6
17. Individual Contribution	55	5.5
18. Mutual Support	31	3.1
19. Trust	49	4.9
20. Interpersonal Relations	35	3.5
21. Accomplishment	34	3.4
22. Accountability	31	3.1
23. Productivity	55	5.5
24. Intergroup Relations	36	3.6
25. Continuous Improvement	26	2.6

Giving Feedback

After data have been collected, you need to analyze them and provide feedback to the team. There are two things the trainer wants to find out from the analysis: (1)What are the major issues that need to be addressed in the team-building session? (2) What are the underlying causes of the problems that have been identified?

An accurate analysis is important to providing valuable and reliable information to the team. Similarly, the extent to which the team building will be successful depends upon the team's ability to resolve issues everyone believes are important. An accurate and insightful analysis ensures the team will focus on the right issues and generate productive team-building outcomes. Consequently, an effective analysis is vital to the team's ability to begin the improvement process.

ANALYZING INTERVIEWS

A simple technique for analyzing interviews consists of looking at all team-member responses to a particular question and consolidating the statements that essentially make the same point. The trainer may also want to note (in brackets) the number of individuals who shared these views. An example of interview data summarized this way might look like the following:

Question 1: What are the team's strengths?

- We have the resources we need to do our job. (12)
- The team leader gives clear direction about priorities and goals. (9)
- We get a lot of information about what is happening throughout the organization. (8)

- Team members respect each other's skills. (8)
- People feel free to go to others for help. (7)

Question 2: In what areas does the team need to improve?

- We have a lot of conflict with other teams about project schedules. (12)
- People on this team are rewarded for their individual work, not teamwork. (9)
- Workloads are not evenly distributed; some people are always very busy and others don't have enough to do. (9)
- We have a lot of last minute crises because we don't do much planning. (8)
- There is a tendency to avoid conflict, and problems get magnified because we don't address them when they arise. (8)

In this example, the numbers in brackets represent the number of team members who identified each statement of strength or weakness. The five areas of strength and five areas of weakness are the major themes.

The trainer summarizes the feedback in some sort of report, usually of two to three pages. Specific statements or phrases that might identify team member(s) are avoided to maintain anonymity. If specific words from interviews capture shared views, those words should be used in the feedback summary. This ensures the trainer does not diminish the tone or intensity of the views expressed.

A second technique for analyzing interview data involves relating the data to organizational success criteria. For example, a large pharmaceutical organization used the McKinsey 7-S Framework to guide its reengineering initiative. This model examines an organization's structure, strategy, skills, staff, shared values, style, and systems as a framework for planning change or organizational improvement. Several months later, the top management of the new-products business group decided to do team building. The trainer, working with the team, used the 7-S model to structure interview questions and analyze the data. This helped the team evaluate how well they were performing on dimensions viewed as important organization-wide. Figure 5.1 presents an example of the interview analysis using a specific model or framework.

In a final way to analyze interviews, you identify major themes for each category of question. The categories are derived from common themes or trends in the data. The trainer identifies these by grouping similar responses into one category. For example, all responses that relate to Communcation are put into one category. This method of organizing the data reduces the volume of comments to a few major themes. Figure 5.2 shows what a sample analysis of major themes would look like.

FIGURE 5.1

SUMMARY OF INTERVIEWS

Each member of the management team was asked to evaluate the entire new-products business unit in seven areas:

- *Structure*   Is the division structured in a way that best enables achievement of corporate goals?
- *Strategy*   Does the division have a clearly articulated strategy?
- *Skills*   Does the division have the right skill mix?
- *Shared Values* How would you describe this division's shared values?
- *Staff*   Does this division have the people it needs, that is, are the key jobs filled with qualified people?
- *Style*   How would you describe the leadership style of the top leadership team?
- *Systems*   Does this organization have the systems in place to effectively execute its mission and goals?

A summary of the management team's feedback is as follows:

- *Strategy*   While the strategic goals are clear, specific tactical plans have not been developed. Without these plans, individual departments are pursuing their own priorities and are not yet aligned with the division's strategy.
- *Shared Values* As a leadership team, there is no consensus on shared values. Most team members feel there is a need to agree on values as a way of building a cohesive team and providing a clear statement to the organization about what's really important.
- *Structure*   There is concern that functional boundaries are too well-defined. Virtually all members of the management team want to organize in ways that allow for greater flexibility.
- *Skills and Staff* These two dimensions were viewed positively by every team member. The recruiting efforts over the past twelve months have resulted in filling critical jobs and acquiring technical specialists that have upgraded the group's skill level. This is viewed as a major accomplishment of the team.
- *Style*   The team described its style as high involvement and balanced between visionary and pragmatic. The group is comfortable with its style and believes it contributes to an open, participative, and high-energy environment.
- *Systems*   There is general agreement that the organization has systems in place to fulfill its goals and achieve its missions. Over the past several months considerable effort has been made to upgrade its information technology systems.

FIGURE 5.2

SAMPLE ANALYSIS: MARKETING TEAM

Overview

Team members believe there has been a lot of improvement in how individuals work together over the past six months. Overall, the team environment is positive and hopeful. Despite this, the team believes there are several areas in which improvement is needed.

Strengths

- Communication between team members is much improved and has become a strength. Everyone in the new building has helped this.
- New team members have brought needed skills to the team; this has enhanced the team's reputation in the organization.
- Everyone works hard and is dedicated; team members are willing to put in long hours to get the job done.
- The team celebrates its accomplishments. This helps avoid burnout, builds a sense of appreciation, and motivates people to give their best.
- The work is challenging and enjoyable. Team members like the diversified work they are given to do.

Areas of Improvement

Communication

Although communication has improved, most team members feel improvement must continue. The areas of concern are as follows:

- Some team members feel they are not consulted about decisions that impact their work.
- Customer feedback is only shared with a few people on the team.
- Information is not always provided in a timely way. For example, several team members did not find out about the recent product launch meeting until the day before the meeting. This happens a lot.

Project Coordination

- Everyone on the team is concerned about the lack of coordination of projects. There is no agreement about priorities. Supervisors take on new projects without considering workloads and commit to unrealistic deadlines.

Meetings

- The team rarely meets as a team. Although it is hard to coordinate schedules, there is a strong drive to have regular staff meetings and also project update meetings.

Procedures

- The team needs to standardize procedures for things such as using contract help, budgeting, and making customer visits. For example, a lot of time is spent discussing when a project can afford contract labor, whether it makes sense to visit a particular customer, or who should be involved in the visit, etc.

Challenges

The team identified the following as its major challenges over the next six months:

- Design materials and sales tools for the new products.
- Agree on a branding strategy.
- Identify the key messages that need to be highlighted in the new corporate brochure.

Success Criteria

The team believes the team-building session will be successful if:

- All the issues raised in the feedback are discussed openly and progress is made toward resolution.
- The team comes away with a list of specific actions designed to address major issues.
- Everyone participates nondefensively and cooperatively.
- Everything on the agenda is accomplished and team members feel good about what was accomplished.

ANALYZING QUESTIONNAIRES

Analysis of questionnaire data is easier than analyzing interview data since the instrument itself provides a conceptual frame of reference. Using a questionnaire that has a continuum for each item, ranging from *strongly agree* (or very characteristic) to *strongly disagree* (or very uncharacteristic), you can summarize the data by calculating (1) an average for each item; (2) the number of people who chose each point on the continuum; (3) standard deviation or the disparity between ratings on a single item. For example, three people agree communication is "good," two rate it as "needs improvement," and three rate it "poor."

If the questionnaire was related to a model of team growth such as 7-S framework discussed above, the composite score can be evaluated in terms of this framework.

CATEGORIZING THE DATA

In analyzing data, take care not to force data into specific categories. This is a danger when categorizing interview responses by theme. It is better to use a "miscellaneous" or "other themes" category to capture data that does not readily fit within the categories established. Many times, data can fit into more than one category. Sometimes trainers worry about putting the data into the "right" category. Remember that what's important is capturing the theme of the interviews accurately. For example, a theme such as concern that the right team members are not included in important decisions can be categorized as an inclusion or as a decision-making issue. Either category is appropriate.

Also, the trainer can recategorize the data if the categories initially established do not seem to work or if a major theme needs to be broken down into subthemes. Remember that the goal of this process is to help the team better understand the data. For example, if several issues are categorized under the topic of leadership, it may be helpful to identify subcategories such as communication, style, and conflict management under this general heading.

GUIDELINES FOR SUMMARIZING THE DATA

The most important guideline is *accuracy*. This is true whether you are summarizing questionnaires or interviews. Questionnaire averages or tallies by question must be checked for accuracy. The same is true when identifying major themes. Don't overstate or underrepresent the findings. Flawed data analysis will undermine the integrity of the team-building session and call into question the competence of the trainer.

Second, the data should be summarized and presented simply. Complex summaries or difficult-to-understand analyses will be rejected by the team. The data presentation needs to be user-friendly. Similarly, it is best to present the data in a manner that closely represents the information-gathering method. Interviewees must be able to relate the data you gave them to the questions they answered. When this happens individuals are confident that the trainer heard their views and trust the data's integrity.

For example, a trainer was working with a large foundation. She interviewed all of the managers and professionals on the team. In compiling the data, she decided to categorize the responses according to her favorite model of team development. Unfortunately, the team was not familiar with this model. Thus, when the feedback was delivered, there was a great deal of confusion. Participants could not relate the questions they answered to the major themes presented in the report. The trainer had to spend considerable time "translating" the report. This undermined the team's trust in the data and damaged the trainer's credibility.

Likewise, the data must be complete. All the feedback gathered must be accounted for in some way. This is easy with questionnaires where all responses are tabulated and reported back to the team. Sometimes it is more difficult with interview data. One way to do this is to present a list of "other issues" as part of the feedback report. During the team building, the group has an opportunity to decide whether it wants to address these issues and, if so, how.

GIVING FEEDBACK

Once the data are analyzed and summarized, you need to give the team leader and the team feedback. This is the first step in beginning to plan the actual team-building session. The team leader needs to understand the data, begin to own it, and then work with the trainer to formulate a plan of action. There are six guidelines that are important to follow in giving the feedback:

First, provide the team leader with basic demographic information. This includes advising him or her whether or not all team members participated in the data-gathering process. It is important that the leader knows the data is truly representative of the team's opinions.

Second, trainers often include their impressions as part of the feedback process. This is helpful and usually the team leader will want to know what conclusions the trainer has drawn while gathering data. But the trainer must distinguish the team's feedback from his or her observations, feelings, and impressions.

Third, keep in mind the psychological process of a manager who is about to receive feedback. It is very difficult for the team leader not to personalize the data at some level. He or she feels responsible for this team and may be anxious, hopeful, excited, or fearful about the feedback. Recognizing this, you should make sure there is enough time in the feedback meeting to discuss the data thoroughly. The leader must be able to process the information presented, both intellectually and emotionally, before beginning to plan the team-building session.

Fourth, the trainer needs to help the manager focus on the opportunity that team building provides to deal with the issues raised, strengthen team performance, and improve team member satisfaction. This is particularly critical when the trainer senses the manager is becoming discouraged or defensive. Statements such as "The team-building session is a good way to turn around these perceptions" or "Let's use the team building as a way to begin rebuilding trust" can encourage the manager to move forward with renewed commitment.

Fifth, the feedback session is an opportunity for the trainer to begin coaching the team leader. If the manager is disappointed by the feedback or disagrees with the feedback, coaching is essential. The trainer must help the team leader listen with an open mind and understand the issues raised, even if he or she disagrees with the team's opinion.

Finally, it is important to avoid data overload. If the feedback reveals a number of problem areas, the trainer needs to identify the most urgent ones first. Advising the team leader that there are five issues of greatest concern can help the manager work with the data and avoid overload. Trying to tackle too many issues can immobilize the manager and, subsequently, overwhelm the team with a feeling of hopelessness.

FEEDBACK MEETING WITH THE MANAGER

The initial meeting needs to be between the trainer and the manager. This ensures the manager hears the feedback first. Together, the manager and the trainer determine the best way to provide the feedback to the team. The meeting may take only an hour but more likely it will take longer.

The trainer should reiterate the context in which the data were collected, name the data collection method, and describe the overall mood of the team during the feedback meetings. For example, a trainer was gathering feedback from a team of union supervisors and leaders. She described to the manager their reluctance to participating in the data gathering. The interview sessions took twice as long because she had to spend considerable time building rapport and encouraging individuals to participate in the process.

The trainer must also explain how the data were analyzed. This ensures that the manager is acquainted with the techniques used and prepares the person for what he or she is about to see. Again, the trainer should stress that major themes were compiled.

It is helpful to give the manager a copy of the feedback report and go through it together. Taking the manager through page by page ensures he or she will not jump ahead. It also lets the manager assimilate the data at his or her own pace. Often, there are issues that are of particular concern while others of lesser interest.

The trainer may need to be firm in presenting the data. This is important if the manager disagrees with the information presented. In these instances, the trainer explains that sometimes a team's perceptions differ from the leader's. In these instances, team building provides an opportunity to explore these differences and better understand one another.

The trainer will want to get the manager's reaction to the data. Asking if the data are clear, make sense, and seem accurate is a way of gauging the individual's response to the information. This also provides an opportunity to explore why team members' responses may be different from the manager's and opens up topics such as the team's stage of development, the impact of leadership style, the influence of organizational factors, and other insightful areas of exploration.

Once the data are understood, the next steps are discussed. The trainer should come to the meeting ready to propose a team-building agenda. This includes a proposed set of goals, agenda topics, and the length of the team-building meeting. However, before sharing this, it is useful to get the manager's ideas about what needs to happen at the team building. This will help the trainer assess the extent to which the manager has understood, internalized, and is ready to act on the feedback. When the trainer and manager have different ideas about how to structure the team-building session, the pros and cons of each approach need to be thoroughly explored. In these instances, the trainer must be sensitive to the manager's readiness for change. What is important is initiating the team-building process and moving toward improvement. If the manager wants to proceed more cautiously, the trainer should honor this and get agreement on a limited-scope team-building effort.

Once agreement is reached, the trainer summarizes what has been agreed to and talks about next steps in setting up the team building. It is useful to document all of this in a follow-up memo or e-mail to the manager.

In some instances, the manager may need to think about the data before committing to the next steps. If this happens, the trainer needs to remind the manager not to share the data with any or all of the team. The trainer should set up another meeting with the manager within one or two days to make a decision on proceeding with team building. For example, the director of a small manufacturing organization wanted to use team building to strengthen several aspects of performance. Using focus groups, data were collected from all employees. The manager was shocked to learn that there were major problems with the leadership style of several of his key managers. In fact, this emerged as the most significant issue. The data were compelling and the trainer gave the manager two to three days to consider what to do. They agreed that the first team-building session would be conducted with only the manager and those who report directly to him. This provided an opportunity to talk about the findings with respect to leadership behaviors and commit to new ways of interacting with those managed. At the whole-group team building, the managers and his direct reports described the actions they had agreed to as a result of the team's feedback.

RECONTRACTING

Once the data have been discussed, the trainer and manager must review their initial contract. Often, there is a need to *recontract*. Recontracting provides the opportunity to reexamine the expectations, roles, deliverables, and similar agreements and to make changes as needed.

A part of recontracting is setting specific goals for the team-building session, agreeing on a detailed agenda, and deciding the length of the session. To do this, the trainer and the leader must decide how much time will be devoted to team building. For example, sometimes two full days are required but committing that much time is a problem. The trainer and manager need to agree on the time commitment as well as the issues that can be adequately addressed in that time frame. It is important to meet the team's needs without sacrificing the quality of the session.

Recontracting also includes discussing such logistical issues as the site of the team building, what dates are best, who will notify the participants, and whether or not there is prework. Usually, the administrative assistant who helped schedule the assessment sessions can help with several of these logistical issues.

THE FEEDBACK MEETING WITH THE TEAM

There are times when it is important for the trainer to present the feedback to the team in a meeting before the team-building session. This is useful in situations in which the manager wants to engage the team in identifying the specific issues which need to be addressed during the team building. It is also a strategy for building commitment to team building. Teams that are mistrustful or reluctant to engage in team building can gain confidence by being presented with the data, discussing it, and verifying that there is a need to work together to resolve the issues raised. Also, the manager may feel more comfortable if the team is presented with the feedback, knows the issues, and remains committed to go forward with the team building.

Keep in mind that even if, after data collection, there has been a decision *not* to do team building, the team still needs feedback on the data. This was part of the trainer's contract with the team and it must be upheld. Also, the reasons for not going ahead with the team building need to be explained. The manager and trainer can use this meeting to communicate the reasons for delaying or choosing not to do team building. The manager can also explain how the information gathered will be acted on in other ways.

For example, a marketing design team decided to engage in team building. The trainer interviewed each member of the team and provided the feedback to the team leader and her manager. Several of the team's concerns came from from issues that were beyond the team's control. These issues related to resource allocation, the ability to hire additional staff, and the long hours required preparing for major trade shows. The team leader and her manager agreed to work together and address these issues. A data feedback meeting was held and the feedback presented. The manager also distributed an action plan that outlined how she planned to work with her manager to resolve the issues raised. She committed to reexamine these issues again in six to nine months and get feedback about whether or not they were resolved.

LEADER'S GUIDE FOR THE DATA FEEDBACK MEETING

The data feedback meeting is designed to achieve the following objectives:

- Get agreement on the team's strengths and weaknesses.
- Identify the major issues that need to be addressed.
- Plan on the next steps.

DATA FEEDBACK MEETING AGENDA

Introduction (twenty to thirty minutes)

Put up overhead Objectives (Figure 5.3) and explain the meeting's goals. Then display and review the *meeting* Agenda overhead (Figure 5.4). The trainer explains the objectives and the agenda. Also, the trainer reviews the data-gathering process and explains how the data were summarized. It may be useful to establish ground rules for this meeting. A sample set of ground rules is listed in the overhead Data Gathering Meeting Ground Rules (Figure 5.5). Finally, the trainer checks to see if there are any questions.

Review the Feedback (thirty to forty minutes)

You can distribute copies of the feedback report prior to going through it. Overhead slides or flip charts should be used to display the data before the entire group. The overhead Data Discussion Questions (Figure 5.6) can help the team process the data. The trainer should decide which questions are most appropriate given the nature of the feedback. Encourage everyone to participate in the discussion. It is important to facilitate the team's ownership of the data.

Identify Major Themes (sixty to ninety minutes)

Suggest a process for identifying major themes and solicit other ideas from the team. Some teams will want to categorize the data in a certain way. Facilitate this discussion and agree on the procedure.

Keep the discussion focused on theme and issue identification. Sometimes teams want to begin working on issues during the feedback meeting. Remind them the team-building session is designed to resolve the issues raised. Allow enough discussion for the team to agree on the major themes or highest priority issues for the team-building meeting.

As an alternative, help the team sort the issues into: (1) issues that can be resolved immediately, (2) issues that need to be addressed in the team-building session, and (3) issues that should be addressed by others. This approach helps the team identify quick hits, that is, issues that can be resolved immediately as well as those which need to be handed off to other groups. Create an action plan that documents category 1 and category 3 issues. This plan

Objectives

The objectives of this data feedback meeting are the following:

- Agree on the team's strengths and weaknesses.

- Identify the major issues that need to be addressed.

- Plan the next steps.

Agenda

- Introduction
- Review the feedback.
- Identify major themes.
- Plan the next steps.
- Close the session.

Data Gathering Meeting Ground Rules

- Ask questions to clarify data, but don't criticize findings you don't agree with.

- Listen to others' perspective.

- Respect differences of opinion.

- Focus on the issues that are having the greatest impact on team performance.

- Participate actively in discussions.

Data Discussion Questions

- What major themes or issues do you see?

- What team strengths emerge?

- What are the major weaknesses of the team?

- In what areas do you agree with the data?

- In what areas do you disagree with the data?

- Are there any major issues the team needs to address that are not reflected in the data?

- Where should the team begin in order to improve its effectiveness?

- Which issues are the most important to address in the next three months?

- Can the team address all these issues or are some outside your control?

- What major categories could we group these issues into?

needs to specify which team members will either take the action to resolve the quick hits (category 1) or refer the issue to others for resolution (category 3).

Next Steps (ten to twenty minutes)

Get agreement on the next steps. This should be a commitment to go forward with team building. The trainer also gets agreement on the goals of the team building and a proposed agenda. You can also establish logistics, including dates and time.

Close the Session (five to ten minutes)

Thank participants for their time and willingness to process the feedback. Let the team know they will receive a written agenda and a confirmation of logistical arrangements prior to the actual team-building session.

Design and Lead the Team-Building Session

The outcome of the feedback meeting is a decision whether or not to go ahead with team building and, if so, agreement on goals and an agenda. From the data gathered it is now clear whether or not team building is appropriate and how it should be structured.

Conclude the feedback meeting with an agreement to prepare a final team-building agenda. In some instances, you may propose more than one alternative, and describe the advantages of each. It remains for the team leader and trainer to reach final agreement on which design is most appropriate.

There is no one right way to structure a team-building session. Every team is unique, with different problems, needs, and dynamics. For example, a new team may need to spend time getting to know one another as well as clarifying its purpose, goals, and roles. A short-term project team may need to concentrate on how team members will work together to get the task accomplished. Teams that are struggling will need to focus on issues such as conflict resolution.

This chapter describes how to lead a two-day team-building session that addresses the eight dimensions of effective teams. It is a template that can be modified for various situations. Subsequent chapters provide examples of how to lead team-building meetings devoted to specific needs, for example, resolving conflict, building trust, improving decision making, etc.

BUILDING THE ESSENTIALS OF TEAM EFFECTIVENESS

This workshop is designed to help a team address the basic essentials of team effectiveness. Effective teams share the following characteristics:

- A shared and meaningful purpose or mission
- Clear, measurable, and specific goals
- Well-defined roles and responsibilities
- A common and collaborative working approach
- A sense of mutual accountability
- Effective intergroup relations
- Passion and enthusiasm
- The skills required to do the job and commitment to continuous learning

The two-day team-building session provides an opportunity for the team to strengthen its performance on all eight dimensions. The overheads Objectives (Figure 6.1) and Agenda: Building the Essentials of Team Effectiveness (Figure 6.2) follow.

Materials Needed

- 1–2 flip charts and felt-tip markers
- Overhead projector
- Materials for the team-building activity you select
- Masking tape
- 10 × 14 index cards
- Post-It notes

Prework

Prior to the team-building session, you will want to do three things as prework:

- Distribute the objectives and agenda to team members.
- Select the team-building activity. Chapter 14 provides examples of team-building activities.
- Create Action Plan charts (Figure 6.3). Create several blank action plans and post one to two at the beginning of the session. This way you can record actions and decisions as they are agreed on. The What, Who, and When columns need to be completed by the conclusion of the team-building session. The action plan documents the next steps and agreements made during the team-building session. It is completed before the end of the meeting to clarify what action is to be taken (What), which team members are responsible for the action (Who), and when the action needs to be completed (When).

Objectives

- Review the characteristics of effective teams so that everyone understands what it takes to build a successful team.

- Discuss the team's feedback so that everyone understands how others perceive the team's strengths and weaknesses.

- Agree on the team's mission, that is, a shared, meaningful purpose.

- Agree on four to six specific, measurable team goals.

- Agree on the roles and responsibilities of each team member and the team leader.

- Agree on how the team will work together and create agreements to ensure individual and mutual accountability.

- Assess the team's skills and create a learning plan.

- Create an action plan that documents team agreements, decisions, and next steps.

- Evaluate the team-building session in order to identify ways to improve future team-building sessions.

Agenda: Building the Essentials of Team Effectiveness

DAY ONE

TOPIC	TIME
• Welcome and introduction	Five to ten minutes
• Review agenda and objectives	Five to ten minutes
• Expectations	Fifteen to twenty minutes
• Characteristics of teams	Fifteen to twenty minutes
• Review of feedback	Forty to sixty minutes
• Shared mission and purpose	Forty-five to sixty minutes
• Break	Ten minutes
• Team goals	Forty-five to seventy minutes

LUNCH

• Team-building activity	Forty-five to sixty minutes
• Roles and responsibilities	Ninety minutes to two hours
• Summarize day one action plan	Twenty to thirty minutes
• Close day one	Five to ten minutes

Agenda: Building the Essentials of Team Effectiveness

DAY TWO

TOPIC	TIME
• Introduction	Five to ten minutes
• Review day one	Twenty to thirty minutes
• Common, collaborative approach	Forty-five to sixty minutes
• Break	Fifteen minutes
• Accountability agreements	Ninety minutes to two hours

LUNCH

• Team-building activity	Forty-five to sixty minutes
• Skill assessment and plan	Sixty to ninety minutes
• Finalize action plans	Twenty to thirty minutes
• Next steps	Twenty to thirty minutes
• Evaluate team-building session	Ten to fifteen minutes
• Close day two	Five to ten minutes

SAMPLE ACTION PLAN FORMAT

What	Who	When	Status	Completed (X)

96

- Create an Issues chart or Bin list. This is used by the trainer to record issues that are not part of the agenda or that need to be discussed in another forum. You will review it at the end of each day and decide how to bring closure to these issues.
- Coordinate all the logistics (e.g., room, refreshments, etc.) for the session.

LEADER'S GUIDE FOR BUILDING TEAM EFFECTIVENESS
Welcome and Introduction—Day One (five to ten minutes)

Introduction: Welcome team members to the session. The team leader should do this. It is important that the team understand the leader's commitment to team building. The leader then introduces the trainer who will serve as the facilitator for the team building. You should also welcome the team.

Present and Review the Objectives and Agenda (five to ten minutes)

Put up the overhead 6.1, Objectives, and then the overhead 6.2, Agenda.

Present the Objectives and Agenda for day one and day two. Let the team know the workshop has been designed to address their feedback and the eight essential characteristics of effective teams. Check to see if there are any questions.

Expectations (fifteen to twenty minutes)

Distribute handout, Expectations (Figure 6.4).

Remind the team that this team-building session is an opportunity to improve team performance, both the results delivered and the way people work together. Ask the participants, What will success look like for you? Let the group know you want to gather their specific expectations. Give team members three to five minutes to write their expectations. Next, ask for a volunteer to share his/her expectations and chart them. Continue to gather expectations until everyone has had an opportunity to speak. Review the logistics: lunch times, how to handle messages, etc.

Characteristics of Effective Teams (fifteen to twenty minutes)

Introduce the concept of team effectiveness by defining a real team. "A team is a group of interdependent individuals who have complementary skills and are committed to a shared, meaningful purpose and specific goals. They have a common, collaborative work approach, clear roles and responsibilities, and hold themselves mutually accountable for the team's performance."

Put up the overhead What Is a Team (Figure 6.5).

Effective teams also display confidence, enthusiasm, and seek to continuously improve their performance. Put up the overhead Characteristics of

EXPECTATIONS

Team building is an opportunity to improve the team's performance.

Think about what you hope the team accomplishes as a result of this session. Answer the question:

"As a result of the team building, I hope we can _____."

Consider what is important to you personally, as well as the entire team.

Take five minutes to write your expectations.

What Is a Team?

A team is a group of interpendent individuals who have complementary skills and are committed to a shared, meaningful purpose and specific goals.

They have a common, collaborative work approach, clear roles and responsibilities, and hold themselves mutually accountable for the team's performance.

Effective teams display confidence, enthusiasm, and seek continuously to improve their performance.

Effective Teams (Figure 6.6). Let the team know you are going to explain each of the characteristics of effective teams:

- Effective teams have agreed on a shared and meaningful purpose or mission. The teams' mission builds a sense of personal responsibility for and commitment to the team's work.

- These teams have specific and measurable performance goals. Team goals describe the deliverables and the results they are expected to produce working together.

- Effective teams have agreed upon how they will work together to accomplish their purpose and goals. The team's approach is a collaborative one that integrates the skills and talents of every team member.

- Effective teams have well-defined roles and responsibilities. This means every team member knows what is expected and what he or she must contribute in order for the team to be successful.

- Effective teams have or develop the skills required, either individually or collectively, to achieve their mission and goals. This includes technical or functional expertise, problem-solving and decision-making skills and interpersonal skills. They are committed to continuous learning and improvement.

- Effective teams demonstrate mutual accountability. Mutual accountability means every team member holds himself or herself responsible for achieving the team's purpose and goals.

- Finally, these teams display passion, or confidence and enthusiasm. They are eager to give their best.

- Check to see if the team has any questions or comments.

Review the Feedback (forty to sixty minutes)

- Tell the team that you are going to review the feedback gathered prior to the team-building session. Remind team members that the interviews or questionnaire incorporated all dimensions of team effectiveness.

- Review the feedback with the team. If this has been done prior to team building, merely summarize what was discussed.

Team Mission (forty-five to sixty minutes)

Put up the overhead Components of Team Mission (Figure 6.7).

- Briefly describe the importance of agreeing on a shared, meaningful team mission and purpose. Explain that the mission describes what the team contributes to the organization and its customers. Advise the team that a good statement of mission or purpose succinctly summarizes what is expected of the team, the contributions it will make, and a common

Characteristics of Effective Teams

Real teams are characterized by the following:

- A shared, meaningful purpose or mission

- A set of specific and measurable goals

- A common and collaborative work approach

- Well-defined roles and responsibilities

- Mutual accountability for the team's response

- The skills required to do the job and a commitment to continuous learning and improvement

- Passion, as demonstrated by confidence and enthusiasm to do their best

Components of Team Mission

A team's shared and meaningful purpose describes what it is expected to contribute to the organization.

It describes the following:

- The common direction of the team and explanation of why it exists

- The customers the team serves and those who receive its outputs

- The team delivers the products and/or services it provides

- Its overall contribution to the organization and how it fits into larger picture

- Any other characteristics that are important to the team's success (e.g., quality, service and technology)

direction to guide goal setting. Factors that should be reflected in the mission statement include products, customers, quality, and services.

- Divide the group into two to three small groups. Ask each group to draft a mission statement and ask one person in each group to record the ideas. Give the groups ten to fifteen minutes. Select one of the team's to present their ideas first. Record on a chart the group's suggested mission statement. Next, ask each group to share their statement. Once all the mission statements are charted, help the team identify similar themes. Circle these words or phrases.

- When all the similar ideas have been identified, ask the group, How might we combine these into a mission statement? Record the proposed statement(s) and continue to edit it until the group believes it has a workable statement. Remind them that a good first draft is the goal of this exercise. Ask a few (two to three) team members to volunteer to finalize the statement for approval by the team. Write this on the Action Plan chart as the first action item in the What column.

Break (ten minutes)

- Give the team a ten-minute break. During the break make sure you have written a legible copy of the mission statement on a flip chart.

Team Goals (forty-five to seventy minutes)

- Show the group where you are on the Objectives and Agenda charts. Remind the team that there are several ways to approach setting goals. One way to do this is by getting every team member involved. Distribute the largest size of post-it notes or 10 × 14 index cards. Instruct each team member as follows:

  "Think about the team's statement of mission. Write down what you believe the team needs to accomplish over the next twelve months (or three months, six months, or nine months) to achieve its mission. I will give everyone three Post-Its/cards and a felt-tip marker to write your suggestions. Put one idea on each Post-It/card. Let's get agreement on three to five goals. Any questions?"

- Give everyone five minutes to write down their proposed team goals.

- Collect the Post-Its/cards. Display them at the front of the room by putting the flip charts side by side and post the Post-It notes/index cards on these charts. Group together similar ideas.

- Read each one and clarify any suggestions that need explanation. Check with the group and determine if any other ideas can be grouped together. Ask if there are any additional goals someone wants to propose before the selection process begins.

- Count the goals and let the team know how many have been proposed. Check with the team leader to confirm the number of goals he/she wants to commit to over the next twelve months or agreed upon time frame. If you need to reduce the list, work with the team to prioritize the goals. One way to do this is to ask each person to select their top three, four, or five goals. Go through each goal and, using a show of hands, ask team member to vote for their top choices. As an alternative to voting you can ask team members to:

1. Assign either 1, 3 or 5 points to their top three choices.

   or

2. Rank order from 1 to 5 their top five choices.

Put up overhead SMART Goals (Figure 6.8).

As a final review, use the SMART guidelines to evaluate the goals. Ask the team, Take a look at the goals we have agreed upon. Are each of them

S —Specific?
M—Measurable?
A —Attainable?
R —Results-oriented?
T —Time-based?

Work with the team and modify the goals as needed until each one meets the SMART criteria. Congratulate the team on its goals.

Lunch (sixty minutes)

- Adjourn for lunch. Let the team know that lunch will be one hour.

Team-Building Activity (forty-five to sixty minutes)

- Welcome the team as they come back from lunch. Conduct a team-building activity. Chapter 14 provides several examples.

Roles and Responsibilities (ninety minutes to two hours)

- Let the team know they are now going to clarify each member's role and responsibilities. Advise them this is an opportunity for each person to describe what he or she contributes to the team.
- Distribute two to three pieces of flip chart paper to each person. Ask them to take a piece of tape and felt-tip marker and to tape their paper on the wall. Give the following instructions:

Each person is going to write out his or her role and four to six major responsibilities. After you have done this, write down any questions you have about your role or responsibilities. This includes responsibilities about which you're not clear or that overlap with another team member's. You can also list

SMART Goals

Team goals need to meet the following "SMART" characteristics:

S–Specific

M–Measurable

A–Attainable

R–Results-oriented

T–Time-based

An example of an effective goal statement is the following:

"Improve customer responsiveness so that all requests are responded to within forty-eight hours."

"Upgrade every department's information technology system by installing the latest version of XPLS-WIN by June 30."

any responsibility you want to propose adding or eliminating. Identify these as recommendations you're proposing for changing your role.

Put up overhead Sample Roles and Responsibilities (Figure 6.9).

"Here is an example of what you are going to do. I have charted my role as a trainer in this meeting and the five things I am responsible for doing during this two-day session." Review the sample. You will have fifteen minutes to chart your role and responsibilities.

- Begin the discussion of roles and responsibilities with the leader or with team members. Whichever you choose, ask the individual to review what they have charted with the entire team. Next, review any questions or suggestions the individual has listed. Lead a team discussion and get agreement on whether or not to adopt the role changes recommended by the individual. For example, if an individual wanted to take on responsibility for tracking the status of team projects, write "Assume responsibility for project tracking" in the What column. Record the name of the individual who is taking on this responsibility in the Who column. Finally, record the date of transfer of responsibility in the When column. Write down any agreed upon changes on the posted Action Plan.

Put up overhead Clarification Questions (Figure 6.10). Then ask the entire team:

- ◆ Does anyone have any questions about this individual's role on the team?
- ◆ Are there any concerns about what this individual has presented?
- ◆ Do you feel something important has been omitted and needs to be added?
- ◆ Are there any changes you would suggest that would strengthen this individual's contribution to the team?
- Continue clarifying roles and responsibilities until each team member and the leader has had an opportunity to discuss their roles. Document all agreements and decisions made during this activity on the Action Plan.

Summarize Day One (twenty to thirty minutes)

- Refer to the Objectives and Agenda and review what has been accomplished. Review the Action Plan and confirm the decisions and agreements made throughout the day. Also, review all issues captured on the Issues list and decide how the group wants to bring them to closure.

Sample Roles and Responsibilities

Instructions:

- Describe your role on the team in one or two sentences.
- List your four to six major responsibilities. This list should represent how you spend ninety percent of your time.

Example:
Role:

- Plan, facilitate, and help implement the results of team-building session.

**Major
Responsibilities:**

- Collect feedback before the team-building session to determine how each person views the team's strengths and weaknesses
- Work with the team leader to design the two-day session and plan the agenda
- Coordinate all logistics required to make the team building successful
- Facilitate the team-building session and ensure all objectives are met
- Prepare a follow-up report that documents the results of the team building

Clarification Questions

- Does anyone have any question about this individual's role on the team?

- Are there any concerns about what this individual has presented?

- Do you feel something important has been omitted and needs to be added?

- Are there any changes you would suggest that would strengthen this individual's contribution to the team?

Close Day One (five to ten minutes)

Put up overhead Feedback Questions: Evaluating Day One (Figure 6.11).

- Close day one by getting feedback on the day. Ask the team:
  - ♦ What did you find helpful about today's team-building session?
  - ♦ Are there any issues discussed today that were not adequately addressed?
  - ♦ Is there anything about the way the session was conducted that you would like to see handled differently tomorrow?
- Record the positives and suggested changes on flip chart paper. Thank the team for their participation and adjourn the session.

Welcome and Introduction—Day Two (five to ten minutes)

- Welcome the team back for day two. Review the Objectives and Agenda for the second day.

Review Day One (twenty to thirty minutes)

- Briefly review what was accomplished on day one. You should also review the feedback from day one. Let the team know what you plan to do to address any suggested changes. Check to see if there are any questions about what happened on day one or the plans for day two.

A Common, Collaborative Approach (forty-five to sixty minutes)

- Refer to the feedback you gathered before the team-building session. Tell the team that they now need to agree on how they will work together to fulfill their mission, goals and responsibilities. This means getting agreement on things such as decision making, meetings, resolving conflicts, information sharing, supporting one another, etc. Agreement on a common, collaborative approach helps promote mutual trust and minimize destructive conflict. It ensures the team has developed its own unique processes for energizing and supporting one another and for keeping the team on track.

Put up overhead Common and Collaborative Approach (Figure 6.12).

- Review the major aspects of common and collaborative approach.
- Ask the team to look at this list and ask, "In what area does the team do a good job? Lead a discussion of these strengths. Next, ask the team to identify two to three ways in which it can build upon its strengths to make its performance even stronger. Again, use the actions to focus the discussion. List these actions on the Action Plan.
- Next, lead the team through a discussion of its improvement areas. List these on a separate chart. Tell the team that to address these improvements, you will help them make accountability agreements.

Feedback Questions: Evaluating Day One

- What did you find helpful about today's team-building session?

- Are there any issues discussed today that were not adequately addressed?

- Is there anything about the way the session was conducted that you would like to see handled differently tomorrow?

Common and Collaborative Approach

Effective teams reach agreement on how they will work together. This is their common approach. They also ensure that they work collaboratively, using the skills and talents of each team member.

The major aspects of common and collaborative approach are:

- making decisions
- conducting meetings
- providing opportunities for everyone to participate
- communicating within the team and sharing information
- valuing the contribution of each team member
- demonstrating mutual support, trust, and commitment
- working with other teams
- interacting interpersonally
- responding to changes with flexibility
- handling work agreements and utilizing skills
- encouraging innovation and new approaches
- resolving conflicts

Break (fifteen minutes)

Mutual Accountability (ninety minutes to two hours)

Put up the overheads Definition of Accountability and Mutual Accountability (Figures 6.13 and 6.14).

- Accountability is a commitment team members make to themselves and their team members to demonstrate attitudes, behaviors, and actions that promote team effectiveness. Advise the team that every team member must demonstrate mutual accountability for the team's performance. In addition, let the team know that effective teams create a culture of mutual accountability that builds confidence, trust, and commitment. Team members demonstrate mutual accountability by their attitude and behaviors. This means each person feels responsible to the others for everything that happens within the team. Commitments made to one another or the entire team are upheld. The team provides feedback and makes agreements in order to deal with problems and continuously improve its performance. For this reason, the team is going to make accountability agreements to address the weakness they have identified in the feedback.

- If the team has identified more than five areas of improvement, select the top five by prioritizing the list. Next, describe the process of contracting for accountability.

  Put up overhead Contracting for Accountability (Figure 6.15).
  Tell the team, "Accountability agreements are contracts between team members, including the team leader. They are designed to clarify specifically (1) what the team wants to do in order to improve some aspect of its performance and (2) what each team member will do to support the agreement. Accountability agreements are different from team norms, or ground rules. These agreements are designed to help the team handle issues that are blocking team effectiveness, or impeding team growth." Let the team know that starting with each of the top five issues, you will facilitate an agreement that describes what team members will do to improve the team's performance.
  Put up overhead The Four Principles of Accountability Agreements (Figure 6.16).
  Discuss the Four Principles of Accountability Agreements.
  Put up overhead Sample Team Agreement (Figure 6.17a, b, c).
  Provide a couple of illustrations of sample agreements.

- Identify the issue the team wants to address first. Let the team make the selection even if you believe the one chosen is not the most important issue. Ask a question to get the discussion started: "What do team members have to do in order to demonstrate effective _____?"
  Write down the essence of the response and use accountability-based language. For example, if you ask, "What would team members have to do to demonstrate effective communication?," a response of, "Stop talking

Definition of Accountability

Accountability is a commitment team members make to themselves and their team members to demonstrate attitudes, behaviors, and actions that promote team effectiveness.

Accountable team members fully accept their membership in the team and feel personally responsible for the team's results.

A second aspect of accountability is mutual accountability. This means team members feel responsible to one another for everything that happens within the team. Commitments made to the team are important and upheld. The team provides feedback and makes agreements in order to deal with problems that arise and continuously improve its performance.

Mutual Accountability

Team members demonstrate mutual accountability when they:

- Hold themselves accountable for everything that happens within the team, rather than expecting the team leader to hold them accountable.

- Are willing to take personal responsibility for what they have or have not contributed to the team.

- Represent the team accurately to others.

- Accept the team's feedback and modify their behaviors based on that feedback.

- Believe it is important for each member to understand how his or her personal choices affect the team.

- Consider how their actions will impact other members of the team and do what is in the best interest of the team.

Contracting for Accountability

Accountability agreements are contracts team members make with each other. They are designed to clarify:

(1) What the team wants to do in order to improve some aspect of its performance.

(2) What each team member will do to uphold the agreement.

Accountability agreements are different from team norms or ground rules. These agreements are designed to help the team handle issues that are blocking team effectiveness or impeding team growth. They require thorough discussion by all team members.

The Four Principles of Accountability Agreements

1. Team members agree to hold themselves accountable for keeping the agreements.

2. Team members agree to hold one another accountable for keeping the agreements.

3. The team agrees to use regular feedback to keep themselves and others accountable.

4. Team members work together to help one another fulfill the accountability agreements.

Sample Team Agreement

Issue: Keeping commitments and meeting deadlines.

Agreement

Team members will keep their commitments to one another.

Clarifications

1. Speak up if you can't do something you've been asked to do.
2. If you cannot meet a commitment, give the other person as much advance notice as possible.
3. Put team commitments and priorities first.

(continued)

Sample Team Agreement

Issue: Involving others in special projects.

Agreement

Team members will look for ways to involve others in special projects.

Clarifications

1. Talk to others to see if they have the skills required and don't assume they have nothing to contribute.

2. Explain what you need from others so they can make an informed decison about whether or not they can help.

Sample Team Agreement

Issue: Handling conflicts and disagreements.

Agreement

Team members will work with one another to resolve conflicts or disagreements.

Clarifications

1. Talk directly to the person with whom you have the disagreement or conflict before you involve the team leader.

2. State your view of the issue and listen to the other's view.

3. Be willing to compromise and work toward a solution both parties can agree to.

4. Don't get other team members involved in the discussion who are not part of the conflict or disagreement.

behind our backs to other people," should be made. "Discuss issues face-to-face with the people involved." This accountability-based language clearly specifies the desired new behavior, not what isn't working.

- Make sure each statement of desired behavior is clear. Then, ask anyone if they have a problem with the initial statement. You may need to modify the wording a bit to get everyone's agreement. If someone suggests a rewording that changes the meaning of the statement, that is, introducing a new idea, record it as a new statement. The group can address it subsequently.

- Solicit input from team members that will further clarify what is expected or identify what is needed in order to fulfill the agreement. To solicit these clarifications ask questions such as:
  - Is there anything we need to add to this statement to clarify what is expected?
  - What will keep you from upholding this agreement; what do you need to add to the agreement to make it workable?
  - Is there anything that will keep you from fulfilling this agreement?
  - Are there any exceptions for you in keeping this agreement?
  - Is the agreement clear?

- Write out clarifications/conditions underneath the agreement. These make the agreement practical and further specify what the team needs to do to make the agreement work. Check to make sure there are no individual constraints. This is important if a few team members have been quiet during the agreement-building process. Also, if you are doing this with a cross-functional team, some individuals may need special conditions.

- You want to get consensus on the agreement. Ask each person individually if he/she agrees to:
  - Be accountable for keeping the agreement.
  - Hold others accountable for keeping the agreement.
  - Encourage the group to make no more than 4–6 agreements.

Team-Building Activity (forty-five to sixty minutes)

Conduct a team-building activity. Chapter 14 provides several examples of team-building activities.

Skill Assessment and Learning Plan (sixty to ninety minutes)

- Advise the team you are going to look at the final aspect of team effectiveness: skills and learning. Review the Characteristics of Effective Teams to remind the team that effective teams either have, or develop, the skills required to do the work that needs to be done. This includes technical or functional expertise, problem solving, decision-making and interpersonal skills. They also exhibit a commitment to continuous learning and improvement.

Put up the overhead Skills Assessment and Plan (Figure 6.18).

Skills Assessment and Plan

Skill Assessment Questions

- Are there any skills critical to achieving the team's mission and goals missing or underrepresented on the team?

- Are there others outside the team who can provide these skills?

- Does the team need to upgrade its technical or functional expertise in any area?

- Is there a need for training in any of the following skills:
  - problem solving
  - decision making
  - communication, that is, feedback, listening, speaking up, etc.

- Are there any other areas in which the team needs training in order to fulfill its mission and achieve its goals?

- Put the team into small groups to do the assessment exercise. Present the questions each group will be asked to discuss.
  - Are there any skills critical to the team's performance of its mission and goals missing or underrepresented?
  - Does the team need to upgrade its technical or functional expertise in any area?
  - Is there a need for training in: (1) problem solving, (2) decision making (3) communication? or in any other related skill areas?
- Remind the team that they are evaluating the skills needs of the entire team. Individual skill-building needs are not part of this exercise. Give each group fifteen to twenty minutes to discuss and answer each question. Next, select one group to report their assessment and recommendations. Chart any recommendations for skill building, or training.
- Solicit responses from each of the other groups and continue adding to the list of training recommendations. If there are several recommendations, ask the team to prioritize and categorize the list. For example, ask, "What training needs to happen over the next three months?" "What training needs to happen by year end, etc.?" Chart the training that needs to happen over the next three months under a First Priority Training Needs. Chart the training that needs to happen over the next time period, for example, by year-end, such as Second Priority Training Needs, and so forth.
- Review the final categorized/prioritized list with the team and ask, "How does this look?" "Is this a good training plan?"
- To conclude this discussion, ask the team, in what ways can the team use the skills acquired to improve its performance? Ask them to think about how this training can benefit customers and other key stakeholders. Generate a list of ideas and make these part of the action plan.

Finalize Action Plan (twenty to thirty minutes)

- Review the entire Action Plan. Make sure that, for each action, all the columns have been filled in:
  - What—Describe the agreed upon action and check to make sure it is clear.
  - Who—Reconfirm the individual(s) who are responsible for the action. If more than one person has volunteered, assign a "Lead."
  - When—Make sure there is a completion date for each activity. Check with the individuals who are responsible and with the team leader to confirm the feasibility of getting this action accomplished by the projected completion date.
- You will also review the Accountability Agreements.

- Finally, decide how the team wants to handle the issues on its Issues list. During the two days it's likely some have been resolved. Get the team's agreement on how to address those that remain.

Next Steps (twenty to thirty minutes)

- Summarize the session into a team-building report. This will document the results of the team-building session.
- Ask the team to plan the following as next steps:
  - How often will you review the Action Plan in order to evaluate progress?
  - How often will you review your Accountability Agreements?
  - When should we have a follow-up team-building session to evaluate progress?
- Record all these next steps. They will be part of the summary report.

Evaluate the Team-Building Session (ten to fifteen minutes)

- You need to give the team an opportunity to evaluate the two-day team-building session. Begin this by reviewing the Objectives and Expectations. Ask the team for feedback. For example, "Do you feel we met the Objectives?", "Have your expectations been met?"
- Next, ask the team to think about future team-building sessions. Ask the team, "Is there anything we could do to make future team-building sessions better?" Record their suggestions. This will also be part of the team-building report.

Close Team-Building Session (five to ten minutes)

- Thank the group for their participation.

Implementing the Results

INTRODUCTION

Effective team building results in agreements, decisions, and other actions. The success of the team building depends on the implementation of these actions in a timely and thorough manner.

As noted earlier, the trainer must clarify his or her responsibility for documenting the results of team building and helping to implement the action plan. Sometimes the trainer assumes this as a sole responsibility; at other times various team members and the team leader share these duties.

OVERVIEW OF TEAM-BUILDING REPORT AND IMPLEMENTATION PLAN

This chapter provides a sample of a team-building implementation plan. It illustrates some or all of the information that needs to be documented. This sample document includes the following:

- **Executive Summary**—A one- to two-page synopsis of the team-building session. This is helpful for stakeholders outside the team as well as for those who participated in the session. It is a short overview of the highlights of the two-day team building.

- **Team's Feedback**—A summary of the team's feedback documents and forms a baseline for the team performance at the time of the team building.

- **Mission, Roles, and Agreements**—The document should include everything the team created during team building. This includes mission statement, role agreements, accountability agreements, and similar items.

- **Action Plans**—The action plan is the team's major tracking mechanism. There are various ways to create action plans. This chapter illustrates categorized action plans.

As you will see in the figures, these plans are designed to address three areas of performance improvement. They are to (1) strengthen execution of team mission and functional roles, (2) clarify team member roles and responsibilities, and (3) improve communication between functions.

- **Next Steps**—These were documented separately during the team-building session, but alternatively they can be part of the action plan.

- **Evaluation**—The team's feedback about the team building needs to be part of the summary report.

GUIDING IMPLEMENTATION ACTIVITIES

The trainer and team leader can help ensure effective implementation of team-building results by:

- Documenting the results and distributing the follow-up report within five to ten days after the team-building session. This helps maintain momentum and initiate improvement actions quickly. This responsiveness helps teams realize value for the time invested.

- Working with the team to manage commitments. The sample report in this chapter includes several action items. The trainer helped the team prioritize those that needed to be done immediately and those that required more time. Thus, the action commitments span a six-month period. Team building generates enthusiasm, and sometimes teams tend to overcommit, for example, by believing that all improvement actions can be accomplished in the next thirty days. It is important to make realistic commitments. A team will feel a great sense of accomplishment if they complete three action items within thirty days; they will be discouraged if in the same period they commit to ten and don't achieve any.

- Making sure everyone on the team has a role in the implementation plan. An important team-building outcome is greater sharing of responsibility for the team's performance. To do this, everyone on the team needs to take responsibility for helping implement action items. The trainer must ensure some individuals do not overcommit and others undercommit. It is also essential that the team leader balance his or her involvement in implementation activities.

- Checking on progress after thirty days. The trainer needs to see how well the team is executing its implementation plan. A thirty-day check-in is a good way to calibrate whether the team is on track or struggling. Coaching the team and team leader helps the struggling team identify barriers to implementation and work through them. It also is an opportunity to encourage the team to keep pursuing implementation of commitments.

THE TEAM-BUILDING REPORT

CONTENTS

EXECUTIVE SUMMARY

The marketing leadership team participated in a two-day team building on January 6 and 7. The team provided feedback prior to the meeting. The two-day objectives were established to address the issues of greatest concern and the agenda was designed to support these objectives.

The objectives for the team building were as follows:

Day 1

- Understand the characteristics of effective teams.
- Review the team's feedback and identify areas of strengths and improvement.
- Create a clear definition of marketing's mission and corporate role.
- Agree on a clear definition of functional, and team members' role and responsibilities.

Day 2

- Agree on how the various marketing functions will work together and share responsibility for marketing activities.
- Create accountability agreements that address areas of concern identified in the feedback.
- Agree on how to use the skills of team members.
- Create a finalized action plan and a list of next steps.

The feedback gathered prior to the team building was presented. The team discussed the major themes and agreed that the list of strengths and areas of improvement was accurate.

The team developed a Mission Statement that describes marketing's mission and purpose.

Next, the team spent time clarifying each function's corporate role and individual team members roles and responsibilities. Recent organizational changes were discussed.

The team agreed on several actions designed to improve the following:

- Execution of its mission and corporate responsibilities.
- Execution and coordination of functional roles and responsibilities.
- Team communication.

Skill utilization was discussed and the team agreed that the role clarification activity addressed these issues.

Three accountability agreements were put in place to address concerns about meeting commitments and supporting one another.

The team finalized its action plan and evaluated the team-building session. It agreed to do a follow-up one-day session in three months.

Team's Feedback

Prior to the team building, the team provided feedback about its strengths and areas for improvement.

Team Strengths

- Cohesive team environment
- Talented people who know what they are doing
- Team members are communicating better than before team building
- Fun group to work with
- Complementary skill sets
- Everyone enjoys working with each other
- Our jobs provide a variety of responsibilities
- Hard-working, creative, friendly, intelligent group; go-getters
- Collaborative, not confrontational, in discussing problems
- Commitment to learning and growth

Team Improvement Areas

- The team needs to agree on the scope of marketing's responsibilities and its corporate mission.
- Roles and responsibilities require several areas of clarification:
  - each team member's role
  - the boundaries and scope of shared duties
  - overlap between new-product marketing and marketing services
- Improve communication between the marketing functions, especially with respect to keeping each other up-to-date.
- Improve several work processes and procedures:
  - find a better way to archive shared materials
  - find a better way to jointly develop materials used by the United States and Europe
  - develop a project planning process
- Improve mutual accountability in the areas of:
  - meeting commitments and deadlines
  - willingness to help others when they are overloaded

TEAM MISSION

Educate customers in order to promote our products to current and potential customers. We do this in a way that generates revenue and profits, while using customer feedback for future product development.

Marketing's Corporate Role

Marketing is responsible for:

- increasing the organization's visibility to customers, investors, employees, and shareholders.
- providing proactive and responsive sales support through:
  - sales tools
  - training and development
  - competitive analysis
  - tradeshow planning and coordination
  - public relations
- creating a successful new product strategy and guiding new product launches.

Functional Roles

- *Public Relations Communications*—conducts activities to ensure that key stakeholder groups understand our mission, marketing strategy, products, culture, and people. We are responsible for all PR activities and formulating consistent worldwide messaging.

- *Marketing Services*—develops tradeshow, event, and exhibit materials. We produce advertisements, literature, and other materials. We are also responsible for translation of materials into several languages.

- *Sales Support*—supports the sales department by developing sales support material, sales training, sales tools and kits, and product support packages. We support all of our sales people on a worldwide basis.

- *New Product Marketing*—supports product launches, provides competitive analysis, and conducts market research, etc. We work with research and development to help formulate new products and price new products.

Roles and Responsibilities

Mike

Role:
- Manage marketing efforts to meet or exceed management's and shareholders expectations.

Responsibilities:
- Oversee marketing of our products and brands to maximize perceived value.

- Spearhead the use of customer interaction to develop better products and increase revenue.

Issues:
- Clarify worldwide scope of responsibility.

Donna

Role:
- Support and assist Mike, helping to leverage his time so he can work more on broader marketing initiatives.

- Support the marketing department in coordinating and overseeing special events that help promote our products and attract new customers.

Responsibilities:
- Coordinate tradeshows and other events

  a) take the lead in confirming attendee's registration

  b) coordinate all planning and logistics

  c) find methods to improve/streamline process, and implement it as is appropriate

- Provide support for Mike when he travels.

Rick

Role: • Develop, implement, and communicate marketing strategy.

Responsibilities: • Design and help create sales and marketing tools.

• Communicate product development, features, positioning, and pricing to customers.

• Work with customers to create and implement sales promotions, product pricing, product training, etc.

• Address and resolve day-to-day tactical issues with customers.

Gwen

Role: • Support needs of customers to promote our products.

Responsibilities: • Develop and coordinate production of marketing materials.

• Develop and produce material for training events.

• Facilitate communication to field sales and marketing in support of our products.

Issues: • Upgrading equipment and software support.

Lisa

Role: • Run marketing services.

Responsibilities: • Create and produce materials that promote our products.

• Ensure consistent, high-quality look and feel for all materials.

• Organize and manage tradeshows and events to raise awareness and visibility for company.

• Schedule and manage internal designers, outside contractors, and vendors to meet deadlines.

Issues: • Clarify overlap of responsibility with sales support.

Bill

Role:
- Support major accounts.

Responsibilities:
- Support sales team in development of marketing strategy and tactics designed to increase market share with existing customers.
- Work with customers to develop specific programs.
- Assist team in setting up major marketing opportunities.

Jeff

Role:
- Manage new product launches through and ensure we have an effective product launch strategy.

Responsibilities:
- Teach customers the features/functionality of our products through sales tools/communication.
- Help customers introduce new products.
- Act as liaison with field roles.

Issues:
- Develop collateral.
- Develop new technologies.
- Improve feedback with other marketing functions to help gather new product ideas from customers.

Sue

Role:
- Coordinate customer training from conception to completion.

Responsibilities:
- Handle equipment and event logistics.
- Supervise setup and tear-down of events.
- Work with vendors—rentals, Audio/Visual, etc.

Issue:
- It is unclear who has responsibility for staffing events to ensure people are available for setup and tear-down when needed.

Gina:

Role: • Marketing new products.

Responsibilities: • Responsible for all aspects of product launches for Signa products

• Responsible for defining new product features and keeping on top of competitive landscape.

• Responsible for communicating and educating customers and promoting use/visibility of new products.

Issue: • Where does my role stop and the business development group's start?

Larry

Role: • Lead communication and public relations.

Responsibilities: • Help develop core messages for presentations, annual reports, and other communications.

• Collect and distribute, company-wide, competitive and market data.

• Manage external communication with media, analysts, etc.

Issue: • What is the most efficient separation of my duties and those of marketing services?

Accountability Agreements

1. Team members will meet deadlines, schedules, and commitments to one another.

Clarifications

a. Commit to dates that are realistic.

b. Let others know when you can't commit to the schedule they propose and offer an alternative.

c. Keep everyone who is involved in the project up-to-date on the status of your deliverables.

d. Let others know as soon as possible if you are going to miss a deadline.

2. Team members will be sensitive to one another's workloads, multiple priorities, and demands.

Clarifications

    a. Ask a team member if they can participate on your project team rather than assuming they can.

    b. Talk to the manager first when you want to to use one of his/her employees on your project.

    c. Be honest with others about what you can and cannot do.

3. Team members will help one another when someone is overloaded and needs help.

Clarifications

    a. Let others know as soon as possible when you need help rather than waiting until there is a crisis.

    b. If you notice someone seems overloaded and you can help, volunteer to do so.

Action Plan

What	Who	When	Status	Completed (X)
Explore more co-marketing opportunities with largest customers as a way to do more pull marketing.	Bill—Lead Mike	March 1		
Provide ready-made materials for the upcoming launch and produce materials on time.	Gina—Lead Lisa	April 10		
Provide sales and account people with information that helps them better address key issues of concern to customers.	Jeff—Lead Gina	June 1		
Compile a CD with a list that identifies when press releases were issued, tools, and background materials.	Larry	February 1		
Create a European archiving system for material and develop a method of distributing this material.	Donna—Lead Lisa Larry	May 10		
Create a centralized way to capture competitive analysis information and develop a process to disseminate it appropriately. Provide instruction so field personnel will know how to use competitive information.	Larry			

What	Who	When	Status	Completed (X)
Clarify worldwide scope of responsibilities.	Mike Helen	June 1		
Identify the need to upgrade computer and software support for the entire marketing department.	Rick—Lead Gwen	March 15		
Clarify overlap of responsibilities with sales support.	Lisa—Lead Jeff	June 1 and ongoing		
Put in place guidelines to get more thorough and accurate feedback from customers about new products.	Rick—Lead Team	February 1		
Get agreement with business development on who is responsible for projecting new product life cycles.	Mike—Lead Gina Will Dan	June 1 and ongoing		
Communications will be responsible for creating messages and copy for public relations material. Marketing services will be responsible for producing public relations materials.	Lisa—Lead Larry	Immediate and ongoing		
Sue has responsibility for getting equipment and handling event logistics. Marketing support and human resources recruit and assign people to work at events.	Sue—Lead Mike Donna Jessica	Immediate and ongoing		

Action Plan

What	Who	When	Status	Completed (X)
Evaluate the feasibility of putting the product launch guide on the Web.	Dan—Lead Jeff	February 15		
Take responsibility for asking counterparts the right questions, e.g., —"How can I help you?" —"What's coming up?"	All	Immediate and ongoing		
Conduct two-hour staff meetings once a month to provide an opportunity to discuss issues and solve problems as a team.	Mike—Lead Team	Begin in February		
Exchange notes from staff meetings.	Team	Weekly		
Standardize sales support tools. Get input from marketing services, field sales, and new product marketing.	Gwen Lisa Bill	May 15		
Begin e-mailing presentations to field sales and major account managers.	Larry	Immediate and ongoing		
Keep the team up-to-date on public relations issues, activities, etc. on a regular basis.	Larry	Weekly		

Next Steps

- Document the results of the team building and distribute the report — Mike/Donna
- Track all action items and complete them according to schedule — Mike/Team
- Check with the team in thirty days to see how they are doing — Donna
- Plan and conduct a follow-up team-building session in three months — Mike/Donna/Team

Evaluation of Team-Building Session

+	▲
• We met all objectives. • We took breaks when discussions got intense or nonproductive • Everyone participated. • People opened up and shared their true feelings. • Mike listened and did not dominate or try to solve everyone's problem. • We turned off all our phones and let ourselves be interrupted only for true emergencies. • Everyone volunteered for action items.	• Two team-building activities were too much and the second one was not a good use of time. • We need to plan to have dinner together on the evening of the first day. • It would have been helpful to have the agenda sooner than two days before the meeting • Let's start each day earlier and end a little earlier.

Evaluating the Team-Building Session

Evaluation is the final step in the team-building process. It is important because it allows the trainer and the team to examine the effectiveness of team building over time. The immediate evaluation at the end of the meeting provides feedback about the quality of the workshop, the attainment or nonattainment of all of the objectives, and the participants' feelings about the usefulness of the session. But after three to six months, the evaluation focuses on the extent to which team building has actually helped improve team performance. The trainer and team should not expect all issues to be resolved completely after six months or that new issues may not emerge during that time. Rather, the three- to six-month evaluation provides an opportunity to look at both progress to date and to identify how subsequent team building—or other interventions—can help the team continue to strengthen performance.

The evaluation needs to be done by the trainer, team leader, and the team. Together, they examine the following issues.

First, all parties need to assess the status of action plan implementation. The first check-in with the team needs to be thirty days after the conclusion of the team-building session. This ensures that the team is on track and has begun implementing team-building agreements, decisions, and action items.

After three months, the trainer works with the team to identify any problems or obstacles that have been encountered. Typically, some things have been implemented but in other areas the team is struggling. The three-month discussion is an opportunity for the trainer to provide coaching about how to overcome obstacles and barriers. Use an Implementation Planning Guide to identify the most common roadblocks and guide the development of a plan to overcome them. See the example in Figure 8.1.

FIGURE 8.1

SAMPLE IMPLEMENTATION PLANNING GUIDE

The following planning guide helps you identify potential obstacles to implementing the results of team building. For each problem area, a few actions are recommended to deal with the obstacles.

Problem or Obstacle	Recommendations
Mission and Goals	*Mission and Goals*
The team's role undergoes a major change due to reorganization or some other organizational shift.	Review the team's mission and make the changes that reflect its new purpose and direction.
The team is focused exclusively on day-to-day priorities rather than strategic goals.	Work with the team to help it allocate its time and balance day-to-day activities with strategic goals.
The team's goals are too ambitious and team members are having trouble meeting them.	Revisit the goals and adjust them as necessary. This may require reprioritizing the goals and/or revising completion dates.
The team's goals are not well aligned with the organization's strategy and goals.	Review the goals and determine if they can be modified to align them better with the organization's strategy. Work with the team and set one to two additional goals that support the organization's strategy. In so doing, the team can continue to pursue its other goals but also begin working on strategic initiatives.
Roles	*Roles*
There is actual or perceived role confusion because of new team members, work reassignments, new projects, or other reasons.	Reclarify team member roles. Remind the team that changes such as new members, new projects, or other shifts in responsibilities usually require reexamining roles. Encourage them to do this whenever changes occur.

Problem or Obstacle	Recommendations
Team Processes	*Team Processes*
Team members remain reluctant to provide input to decisions despite the leader's encouragement	Encourage the leader to look for opportunities to delegate decisions to team members.
Group meetings are not productive and don't achieve the intended results.	Facilitate a discussion of team meetings. Identify what is working well and what needs to be changed. For immediate improvement, coach the team about the need to establish clear meeting objectives and put together well-planned agendas.
The team isn't doing a good job monitoring its results, including the status of projects.	Suggest the team take time during staff meetings or similar forums to review progress against goals, project status, etc. Doing this on a regular basis helps the team get into the habit of monitoring its progress.
Team Relationships	*Team Relationships*
Most of the work is done by a few team members and the team is not capitalizing on the expertise and skills of every team member.	Encourage the leader to look for opportunities to redistribute work and make specific work assignments. These adjustments are designed to better capitalize on skills and expertise.
The team demonstrates poor listening, feedback, or other communication skills.	Suggest appropriate training to build skills.
Team members bring issues and problems to the team leader that they could resolve between themselves.	Check with the leader and discuss how he or she is handling these situations. Recommend that the leader *require* individuals to work with one another to resolve issues before bringing the issues to him or her. Tell the leader to make it clear he or she will only get involved in issues that cannot be resolved by team members.
Intergroup Relations	*Intergroup Relations*

The team is having problems working with other teams. This may include:
    conflicts with other teams
    poor communication
    lack of trust and support
    lack of poor cooperation
    conflicting plans, goals or priorities
	This is an opportunity to do team building with the other team. Both groups can work to identify underlying problems and jointly develop solutions.

(continued)

Problem or Obstacle	Recommendations
Accountability	*Accountability*
Team members don't take personal responsibility for the team's results and are only concerned with their individual responsibilities.	Suggest the leader examine the team's goals, projects, and work assignments. He or she should look for ways to assign projects and other work so that interdependency is maximized.
Team members complain and blame others rather than taking responsibility to resolve problems, deal with obstacles, etc.	Coach the leader and encourage him or her to stress the importance of taking responsibility rather than blaming and complaining. Suggest the leader use responses like, "What can we do to improve the situation?," "Let's focus on things that are within our control," or "How can we deal with this situation and resolve these issues?" Replies such as these shift the focus from powerlessness or blame to empowerment and accountability.
Team members are reluctant to give one another feedback and complain privately to the leader about others.	Work with the team and set up ground rules or new accountability agreements. This allows the team to establish a mechanism for giving feedback to one another that is comfortable for team members.
Passion	*Passion*
The team does not take pride in its work or have a sense of accomplishment.	Identify ways the leader can recognize and reward accomplishments. For example, the leader can take every opportunity to link the team's work to larger organizational goals. This lets the team know how their work helps meet major competitive challenges.
Team members do not take initiative but do only what is required.	Encourage the leader to look for ways to reward initiative.
Skills and Learning	*Skills and Learning*
The team is satisfied with the status quo and doesn't look for ways to improve, learn, or grow.	Ask the leader to use team goals to challenge the team to improve some aspect of its performance. For example, select an area in which the team is doing well and set a "stretch" goal. Let the team know it is an ambitious goal designed to encourage continuous improvement.
Team members are afraid of making mistakes and don't take risks.	The leader needs to make sure team members know risk-taking is supported. Giving team members examples of how they can do this encourages risk-taking behavior. It is also important that the leader use failure as a coaching-learning opportunity and not respond punitively.

Second, the trainer works with the team and team leader to identify issues that need to be addressed in subsequent team-building sessions. Re-administering the initial assessment does this best.

There are two follow-up assessments in this chapter (Figures 8.2 and 8.8). These are adaptations of the questionnaires in Chapter 4. They are designed specifically for the purpose of evaluating the team's progress since team building. The first assessment (Figure 8.2) is completed and scored by each team member (Figure 8.3). Examples of how an individual would score and tally the assessment are provided in Figure 8.4 and Figure 8.5. Next, the trainer tallies the individual score sheets and compiles the group's evaluation of the effectiveness of the team-building session. Figure 8.6 is a team composite worksheet and Figure 8.7 is an example of a completed team composite worksheet with an interpretation of results. The second assessment (Figure 8.8) also requires team members to score their results but the scoring is more qualitative. After taking the assessment, each person examines their results and is asked to list the areas in which they believe:

- The team has shown the most improvement since team building.
- The team still needs to improve.
- The follow-up team-building session should focus.

Figure 8.9 is the summary sheet each person completes after taking the assessment. The trainer compiles this feedback and uses it to plan the next team-building session.

Similarly, Chapter 4 interview questions can be modified to evaluate the impact of team building. For example, questions such as "What is the team doing better since it engaged in team building?", "What has not changed since team building?", and "In what areas is the team still struggling?" help assess the impact of team building.

There are a few guidelines trainers need to follow in conducting Step 6 of the team-building process. First, the evaluation must be a collaborative effort. Sometimes trainers independently evaluate the results of team building based on casual observations of the team. Things *seem* to be better. A few team members may believe team performance has improved. Unfortunately, the trainer cannot determine if the team building has really made a difference without a collaborative assessment of results.

Second, the evaluation process offers a learning opportunity for the trainer, the leader, and team. Learning is an important attribute of personal and team effectiveness. The evaluation step facilitates learning because the team examines how well it has performed against its team-building commitments. Thus, the team gains insight into why it has performed well in certain areas and, perhaps, poorly in others.

On a personal level, the trainer learns how well the session met the team's needs and how effectively he or she led the workshop. For example, a team of advertising professionals participated in a two-day team-building session. The pre-team-building assessment indicated a need to address all aspects of team

MEASURING THE EFFECTIVENESS OF TEAM BUILDING

Directions: On the following pages are a series of questions designed to measure the effectiveness of the team-building session. The questions are the same ones you answered in the pre-team-building feedback questionnaire.

Please indicate the extent to which each statement describes how the team is now working together. Indicate your answer by circling the *most accurate answer.*

There are three possible choices:

I = Improved since the team-building session

NI = No improvement since the team-building session

NC = No change required because performance was good prior to and after the team-building session

This assessment helps identify the ways in which team building has enhanced team performance. It will also identify areas in which further team-building sessions can continue to improve performance.

Questions	Scale		
1. Our team has a meaningful, shared purpose.	I	NI	NC
2. Team members clearly understand their roles.	I	NI	NC
3. Team problem solving results in effective solutions.	I	NI	NC
4. Team members appreciate one another's unique capabilities.	I	NI	NC
5. We are able to resolve conflicts with other teams collaboratively.	I	NI	NC
6. Team members take personal responsibility for the effectiveness of our team.	I	NI	NC
7. Working on our team inspires people to do their best.	I	NI	NC
8. We have the skills we need to do our jobs effectively.	I	NI	NC
9. We are strongly committed to a shared mission.	I	NI	NC
10. When an individual's role changes, an intentional effort is made to clarify it for everyone on the team.	I	NI	NC
11. We address and resolve issues quickly.	I	NI	NC
12. Team members are effective listeners.	I	NI	NC

Questions		Scale	
13. We seek to arrange our priorities to meet the needs of other work groups.	I	NI	NC
14. Team members maintain a can-do approach when they encounter frustrating situations.	I	NI	NC
15. My team has a strong sense of accomplishment relative to our work.	I	NI	NC
16. We always ask ourselves, "How can we do better tomorrow what we did today?"	I	NI	NC
17. We focus on big-picture strategic issues as much as on day-to-day activities.	I	NI	NC
18. Team members understand one another's roles.	I	NI	NC
19. People on my team are rewarded for being team players.	I	NI	NC
20. Communication in our group is open and honest.	I	NI	NC
21. We communicate effectively with other groups.	I	NI	NC
22. Team members take initiative to resolve issues between themselves without involving the team leader.	I	NI	NC
23. People are proud to be part of our team.	I	NI	NC
24. As a team, we are continually working to improve cycle time, speed to market, customer responsiveness, or other key performance indicators.	I	NI	NC
25. We set and meet challenging goals.	I	NI	NC
26. Everyone values what each member contributes to the team.	I	NI	NC
27. Group meetings are very productive.	I	NI	NC
28. Members of our team trust each other.	I	NI	NC
29. Our team has established trusting and supportive relationships with other teams.	I	NI	NC
30. We spend very little time complaining about things we cannot control.	I	NI	NC
31. Team members frequently go beyond what is required and do not hesitate to take initiative.	I	NI	NC
32. We view everything, even mistakes, as opportunities for learning and growth.	I	NI	NC
33. We consistently produce strong, measurable results.	I	NI	NC
34. Team members avoid duplication of effort and make sure they are clear about who is doing what.	I	NI	NC
35. Our team has mechanisms in place to monitor its results.	I	NI	NC
36. Team members help one another deal with problems or resolve issues.	I	NI	NC

(continued)

Questions		Scale	
37. We work toward integrating our plans with those of other work groups.	I	NI	NC
38. Team members seek and give each other constructive feedback.	I	NI	NC
39. As a team, we work to attract and retain top performers.	I	NI	NC
40. We use various forms of training to keep our skills up-to-date.	I	NI	NC
41. We make sure our work helps the organization achieve its goals.	I	NI	NC
42. When team members' roles change, specific plans are implemented to help them assume their new responsibilities.	I	NI	NC
43. Our team works with a great deal of flexibility so that we can adapt to changing needs.	I	NI	NC
44. We are able to work through differences of opinion without damaging relationships.	I	NI	NC
45. Our collaborations with other teams are productive, worthwhile, and yield good results.	I	NI	NC
46. Team members are sure about what is expected of them and take pride in a job well done.	I	NI	NC
47. Our team is excited about the contribution it is making to the organization's competitive viability.	I	NI	NC
48. Team members embrace continuous improvement as a way of life.	I	NI	NC
49. The mission and goals of my team are well aligned with the organization's mission and goals.	I	NI	NC
50. Overlapping or shared tasks and responsibilities do not create problems for team members.	I	NI	NC
51. When we choose consensus decision-making, we do it effectively.	I	NI	NC
52. Team members display high levels of cooperation and mutual support.	I	NI	NC
53. The goals of our group support those of other groups.	I	NI	NC
54. Team members consider how their actions will impact others when deciding what to do.	I	NI	NC
55. My team is proud of its accomplishments and optimistic about the future.	I	NI	NC
56. Team members work to ensure we are using best-practice methods.	I	NI	NC

INDIVIDUAL SCORE SHEET

Directions: Transfer the score from the Team Building Effectiveness Inventory to the appropriate column. Total the number of I, NI and NC scores in the box below each category. Each Total column should add up to 7.

Purpose and Goals

1 _____
9 _____
17 _____
25 _____
33 _____
41 _____
49 _____

Totals:	I	NI	NC
	___	___	___

Roles

2 _____
10 _____
18 _____
26 _____
34 _____
42 _____
50 _____

Totals:	I	NI	NC
	___	___	___

Team Processes

3 _____
11 _____
19 _____
27 _____
35 _____
43 _____
51 _____

Totals:	I	NI	NC
	___	___	___

Team Relationships

4 _____
12 _____
20 _____
28 _____
36 _____
44 _____
52 _____

Totals:	I	NI	NC
	___	___	___

Intergroup Relations

5 _____
13 _____
21 _____
29 _____
37 _____
45 _____
53 _____

Totals:	I	NI	NC
	___	___	___

Accountability

6 _____
14 _____
22 _____
30 _____
38 _____
46 _____
54 _____

Totals:	I	NI	NC
	___	___	___

Passion

7 _____
15 _____
23 _____
31 _____
39 _____
47 _____
55 _____

Totals:	I	NI	NC
	___	___	___

Skills & Learning

8 _____
16 _____
24 _____
32 _____
40 _____
48 _____
56 _____

Totals:	I	NI	NC
	___	___	___

FIGURE 8.4

MEASURING THE EFFECTIVENESS OF TEAM BUILDING EXAMPLE

Directions: On the following pages are a series of questions designed to measure the effectiveness of the team-building session. The questions are the same ones you answered in the pre-team-building feedback questionnaire.

Please indicate the extent to which each statement describes how the team is now working together. Indicate your answer by circling the *most accurate answer.*

There are three possible choices:

I	=	Improved since the team-building session
NI	=	No improvement since the team-building session
NC	=	No change required because performance was good prior to and after the team-building session

This assessment helps identify the ways in which team building has enhanced team performance. It will also identify areas in which further team-building sessions can continue to improve performance.

Questions	Evaluation of Team Building Impact Scale		
1. Our team has a meaningful, shared purpose.	(I)	NI	NC
2. Team members clearly understand their roles.	(I)	NI	NC
3. Team problem solving results in effective solutions.	I	(NI)	NC
4. Team members appreciate one another's unique capabilities.	(I)	NI	NC
5. We are able to resolve conflicts with other teams collaboratively.	(I)	NI	NC
6. Team members take personal responsibility for the effectiveness of our team.	(I)	NI	NC
7. Working on our team inspires people to do their best.	I	(NI)	NC
8. We have the skills we need to do our jobs effectively.	(I)	NI	NC
9. We are strongly committed to a shared mission.	(I)	NI	NC
10. When an individual's role changes, an intentional effort is made to clarify it for everyone on the team.	(I)	NI	NC
11. We address and resolve issues quickly.	I	(NI)	NC
12. Team members are effective listeners.	(I)	NI	NC
13. We seek to arrange our priorities to meet the needs of other work groups.	(I)	NI	NC
14. Team members maintain a can-do approach when they encounter frustrating situations.	(I)	NI	NC
15. Our team has a strong sense of accomplishment relative to our work.	I	(NI)	NC

Questions		**Scale**	
16. We always ask ourselves, "How can we do better tomorrow what we did today?"	(I)	NI	NC
17. We focus on big-picture strategic issues as much as on day-to-day activities.	I	(NI)	NC
18. Team members understand one another's role.	(I)	NI	NC
19. People on my team are rewarded for being team players.	(I)	NI	NC
20. Communication in our group is open and honest.	(I)	NI	NC
21. We communicate effectively with other groups.	I	(NI)	NC
22. Team members take initiative to resolve issues between themselves without involving the team leader.	(I)	NI	NC
23. People are proud to be part of our team.	(I)	NI	NC
24. As a team, we are continuously working to improve cycle time, speed to market, customer responsiveness, or other key performance indicators.	(I)	NI	NC
25. We set and meet challenging goals.	(I)	NI	NC
26. Everyone values what each member contributes to the team.	(I)	NI	NC
27. Group meetings are very productive.	(I)	NI	NC
28. Members of my team trust each other.	I	NI	(NC)
29. Our team has established trusting and supportive relationships with other teams.	I	(NI)	NC
30. We spend very little time complaining about things we cannot control.	(I)	NI	NC
31. Team members frequently go beyond what is required and do not hesitate to take initiative.	(I)	NI	NC
32. We view everything, even mistakes, as opportunities for learning and growth.	(I)	NI	NC
33. We consistently produce strong, measurable results.	(I)	NI	NC
34. Team members avoid duplication of effort and make sure they are clear about who is doing what.	(I)	NI	NC
35. Our team has mechanisms in place to monitor its results.	(I)	NI	NC
36. Team members help one another deal with problems or resolve issues.	I	NI	(NC)
37. We work toward integrating our plans with those of other work groups.	I	(NI)	NC
38. Team members seek and give each other constructive feedback.	(I)	NI	NC
39. As a team, we work to attract and retain top performers.	(I)	NI	NC

(continued)

Questions		Scale	
40. We use various forms of training to keep our skills up-to-date.	I	NI	(NC)
41. We make sure our work helps the organization achieve its goals.	(I)	NI	NC
42. When team members' roles change, specific plans are implemented to help them assume their new responsibilities.	I	(NI)	NC
43. Our team works with a great deal of flexibility so that we can adapt to changing needs.	(I)	NI	NC
44. We are able to work through differences of opinion without damaging relationships.	I	(NI)	NC
45. Our collaborations with other teams are productive, worthwhile, and yield good results.	(I)	NI	NC
46. Team members are sure about what is expected of them, and take pride in a job well done.	(I)	NI	NC
47. My team is excited about the contribution it is making to the organization's competitive viability.	(I)	NI	NC
48. Team members embrace continuous improvement as a way of life.	I	NI	(NC)
49. The mission and goals of my team are well aligned with the organization's mission and goals.	I	(NI)	NC
50. Overlapping or shared tasks and responsibilities do not create problems for team members.	I	NI	(NC)
51. When we choose consensus decision-making, we do it effectively.	I	(NI)	NC
52. Team members display high levels of cooperation and mutual support.	I	(NI)	NC
53. The goals of our group support those of other groups.	I	(NI)	NC
54. Team members consider how their actions will impact others when deciding what to do.	(I)	NI	NC
55. My team is proud of its accomplishments and optimistic about the future.	(I)	NI	NC
56. Team members work to ensure we are using best practice methods.	I	NI	(NC)

FIGURE 8.5

INDIVIDUAL SCORE
SHEET—EXAMPLE

Directions: Transfer the score from the Team Building Effectiveness Inventory to the appropriate column. Total the number of I, NI and NC scores in the box below each category. Each Totals column should add up to 7.

Purpose and Goals

1   I
9   I
17 NI
25 I
33 I
41 I
49 NI

Totals:	I	NI	NC
7	5	2	0

Roles

2   I
10 I
18 I
26 I
34 I
42 NI
50 NC

Totals:	I	NI	NC
7	5	1	1

Team Processes

3   NI
11 NI
19 I
27 I
35 I
43 I
51 NI

Totals:	I	NI	NC
7	4	3	0

Team Relationships

4   I
12 I
20 I
28 NC
36 NC
44 NI
52 NI

Totals:	I	NI	NC
7	3	2	2

Intergroup Relations

5   I
13 I
21 NI
29 NI
37 NI
45 NI
53 NI

Totals:	I	NI	NC
7	2	5	0

Accountability

6   I
14 I
22 I
30 I
38 I
46 I
54 I

Totals:	I	NI	NC
7	7	0	0

Passion

7   NI
15 NI
23 I
31 I
39 I
47 I
55 I

Totals:	I	NI	NC
7	5	2	0

Skills & Learning

8   I
16 I
24 I
32 I
40 NC
48 NC
56 NC

Totals:	I	NI	NC
7	4	0	3

TOTALING THE TEAM'S SCORE

Directions: Collect each person's score sheet. Add the total of I, NI, and NC scores for each
of the eight performance dimensions. The total scores for each dimension should
equal the number of respondents.

Purpose and Goals

I _____

NI _____

NC _____

Roles

I _____

NI _____

NC _____

Team Processes

I _____

NI _____

NC _____

Team Relationships

I _____

NI _____

NC _____

Totals:	I	NI	NC
	___	___	___

Totals:	I	NI	NC
	___	___	___

Totals:	I	NI	NC
	___	___	___

Totals:	I	NI	NC
	___	___	___

Intergroup Relations

I _____

NI _____

NC _____

Accountability

I _____

NI _____

NC _____

Passion

I _____

NI _____

NC _____

Skills & Learning

I _____

NI _____

NC _____

Totals:	I	NI	NC
	___	___	___

Totals:	I	NI	NC
	___	___	___

Totals:	I	NI	NC
	___	___	___

Totals:	I	NI	NC
	___	___	___

FIGURE 8.7

TOTALING THE TEAM'S
SCORE—EXAMPLE

Directions: Collect each person's score sheet. Add the total number of I, NI, and NC scores for each of the eight performance dimensions. The total scores for each dimension should equal the number of respondents.

Purpose and Goals

I   50

NI 20

NC 0

Roles

I   50

NI 10

NC 10

Team Processes

I   40

NI 30

NC 0

Team Relationships

I   30

NI 20

NC 20

Totals:	I	NI	NC
70	50	20	0

Totals:	I	NI	NC
70	50	10	10

Totals:	I	NI	NC
70	40	30	0

Totals:	I	NI	NC
70	30	20	20

Inter-Group Relations

I   20

NI 50

NC 0

Accountability

I   70

NI 0

NC 0

Passion

I   50

NI 20

NC 0

Skills & Learning

I   40

NI 0

NC 30

Totals:	I	NI	NC
70	20	50	0

Totals:	I	NI	NC
70	70	0	0

Totals:	I	NI	NC
70	50	20	0

Totals:	I	NI	NC
70	40	0	30

Interpretation of Results

The assessment was administered to ten team members. Everyone on the team (100%) feels there has been an improvement in mutual accountability. This is the most positive result derived from the team-building session. Second, at least 70% of the team feels there has been improvement in clarity of the team's purpose and goals, role definition, and that team members displayed a greater sense of passion about the team and its work together.

The trainer needs to focus the follow-up team-building session on several dimensions, including team processes, team relationships, and skills and learning. The team's feedback indicates that about half the group feels there has been improvement in these three areas but that the other half feels there has been either no improvement or no change since the team-building session. In addition, over 70% of the team feels there has been no improvement in working with other teams (Intergroup Relations). This appears to be the dimension that was least impacted by team building. The follow-up session needs to address this issue as well.

MEASURING THE EFFECTIVENESS OF TEAM BUILDING

Evaluation of Team-Building Impact

Mission and Purpose
  1. The team has a clear and shared purpose.   I   NI   NC

Goal Clarity
  2. Goals are clear and agreed upon.   I   NI   NC

Shared Leadership
  3. Leadership of the team is shared with   I   NI   NC
     team members.

Roles
  4. Roles are clear and well-defined.   I   NI   NC

Participation
  5. Participation is equitable and everyone   I   NI   NC
     does their fair share of work.

Meetings
  6. Meetings are productive and achieve the   I   NI   NC
     results needed.

Decision Making
  7. There is a lot of opportunity to participate   I   NI   NC
     in decisions and provide input.

Communication
  8. Team members are open, honest, and   I   NI   NC
     direct in their communication.

Information Sharing
  9. Information is shared widely and   I   NI   NC
     everyone is kept up-to-date on important
     issues.

Collaboration
  10. Team members work well together and   I   NI   NC
      coordinate their work.

Feedback
  11. Team members give feedback to one   I   NI   NC
      another and share their perceptions in a
      way that is helpful and constructive.

Teamwork
12. Teamwork is rewarded and valued.   I   NI   NC

Passion
13. Team members are enthusiastic and   I   NI   NC
    proud to be part of the team.

Flexibility
14. The team is flexible and responds quickly   I   NI   NC
    to changes, needs, and priorities.

Conflict
15. Conflict is accepted as part of team   I   NI   NC
    development and addressed effectively.

Skills
16. We have the skills we need to do our jobs.   I   NI   NC

Individual Contribution
17. Team members value one another's   I   NI   NC
    contribution to the team.

Mutual Support
18. Team members readily help one another   I   NI   NC
    when requested.

Trust
19. Trust between team members is high.   I   NI   NC

Interpersonal Relations
20. Interpersonal relationships between team   I   NI   NC
    members is good.

Accomplishment
21. The team has a strong sense of   I   NI   NC
    accomplishment.

Accountability
22. Team members take responsibility for the   I   NI   NC
    effectiveness of our team.

Productivity
23. The team works productively and   I   NI   NC
    effectively.

Intergroup Relations
24. The team works effectively with   I   NI   NC
    other teams.

Continuous Improvement
25. The team seeks to continuously improve   I   NI   NC
    its results, processes, and relationships.

SUMMARY: MEASURING THE EFFECTIVENESS OF TEAM BUILDING

Evaluation of Team-building Impact

1. For the items you marked as I (Improved), list the five to eight areas in which you believe the team has demonstrated the most improvement since the team-building workshop.

   - _____   - _____
   - _____   - _____
   - _____   - _____
   - _____   - _____

2. Are there any other improvements you have observed as a result of the team-building session?

   - _____
   - _____
   - _____
   - _____

3. For the items you marked as NI (Needs Improvement), list the three to five areas you believe the team needs to address in the next three months.

   _____

   _____

   _____

   _____

   _____

4. Are there any areas not included in this survey that you believe the team needs to address in a follow-up team-building session?

   _____

   _____

   _____

   _____

5. Other comments:

   _____

   _____

   _____

effectiveness: shared purpose, goals, roles, etc. The team was enthusiastic after the session and believed they had taken a major step forward in their growth as a team. The thirty-day check-in indicated that only a few of the actions planned had been implemented. The team recommitted to its plan and momentum remained high. At the end of three months, the team was doing some things well but was having trouble meeting its goals and executing planned training. The evaluation brought out the team leader's ambivalence about the practicality of some of the goals and training commitments. It became clear she felt too many goals were focused on personal development and not enough on improving customer service and quality. This adversely impacted her commitment to training. The trainer facilitated a discussion of the leader and her team to address these concerns. There was agreement to modify the goals and delay training until the team was up to speed in meeting customer needs and quality standards. After the follow-up session, the trainer reflected on the issues raised by the leader. The trainer had sensed concern on her part during the team-building session but had been reluctant to address it. The results of the follow-up session taught him to be more sensitive to potential problems and not ignore warning signals.

Also, the trainer must be realistic about the impact of team building. Teams often use team building as only one means of improving their performance. This means that other activities are going on concurrently that help strengthen the team. Consequently, it is important not to overstate the results of team building but to help the leader and team evaluate them in the broader context of everything the team is doing. All team interventions aim at encouraging the team to use a variety of methods to stimulate better performance. In fact, the follow-up evaluation often generates ideas for other things a team can do in addition to team building.

Finally, the trainer needs to coach the team leader on how day-to-day leadership facilitates team development. Helping team members seize opportunities to share leadership, coaching individuals, giving feedback, and other activities all encourage team and individual growth.

9

FAST STARTS FOR CROSS-FUNCTIONAL PROJECT TEAMS

INTRODUCTION

Today's thriving organizations ensure their continued growth from the successful development of projects that generate new products or services, improve key processes, and solve critical problems. The project teams that set and meet these goals enable organizations to respond effectively to competitive demands and are essential to implementing change and growth strategies. Organizations typically bring together seven or more disciplines to bring a new product to market, develop the next-generation information technology system, design new manufacturing processes, reduce cycle time in processing customer orders, prepare a strategic plan, or implement a new procedure to upgrade quality.

Successful project teams face three challenges. First, in order to be successful, there must be strong organizational support. Second, they must utilize good project management techniques. Third, these teams need to work effectively with key stakeholders by managing boundaries and interfaces.

Strong organizational support means creating a team-based organization that is organized for project management and rewards effective cross-functional teamwork and execution. In addition, project goals must be linked to the broader organizational strategy and objectives. A project support system that includes information technology, upper management sponsorship, and training is also required. Finally, there must be a plan to develop the skills of current and future project managers.

This chapter describes how to use team building to help newly formed cross-functional teams meet a major challenge—getting off to a fast, strong start.

DEVELOPING A CROSS-FUNCTIONAL PROJECT TEAM

The six-step team-building process can be used to enhance project team success. In fact, team building is an essential first step in creating a successful project team. Complex projects require multidiscipline teams who work together for several months—and sometimes more than a year. For more complex projects, the team must learn a good deal as it executes each step of the project. The interdependency this collaboration entails requires that a variety of people with a wide range of skills work together as a well-functioning and cohesive team.

Individuals selected for the project team may not be accustomed to working with each other but bring to the team the norms and behaviors of their home departments. This collection of different expectations, work approaches, and behaviors can be counterproductive. Also, the project team must begin to function effectively in a short period of time. This is a daunting challenge.

Developing a cohesive team begins with team building. The team-building session provides an opportunity for team members to agree on:

- The team's charter
- The team's mission, goals, and vision of success
- Team member roles and responsibilities and other key stakeholders' roles
- Work approach and agreements for mutual accountability
- Project phases and key milestones
- A learning and resource plan
- A stakeholder-communication and relationship-building plan

Engaging in team building soon after the team's formation helps the team address all of these dimensions of team effectiveness.

THE TEAM-BUILDING PROCESS

The six-step team-building process for project teams is as follows:

Step 1—Gain the commitment.

Step 2—Clarify the team charter.

Step 3—Collect information from team members.

Step 4—Design and conduct a two-day team-building session.

Step 5—Implement the results.

Step 6—Evaluate the impact of team building.

STEP 1—GAIN THE COMMITMENT

For project teams, the trainer needs to gain the commitment of the team leader and other key stakeholders. Similar to the steps discussed in Chapter 3, the decision to engage in team building begins with a contract or agreement. The same contracting process can be used with cross-functional project teams. Once the contract is established with the team leader, the trainer needs to work with any other key stakeholders to get support for team building. Generally, this is not required. However, these stakeholders should know that a team-building session will be conducted. They may provide useful input about what the team needs to accomplish in team building. In this way, their perspective is helpful because they can identify special challenges or obstacles of which the team leader is not aware.

STEP 2—CLARIFY THE TEAM CHARTER

The team sponsor and project-team leader create the charter. It is important to get input from other key stakeholders. The charter addresses the questions the team leader can expect individuals to ask about their participation on their team.

Figure 9.1 is an example of the Team Charter Worksheet. It lists the questions to be addressed in order to create a good charter. The sponsor and team leader should consider the charter they create to be a final draft. It is important to present it to the team as such and then allow them to ask questions and offer their input. In so doing, the project leader and team work together to finalize it. Presenting the charter to the team as a draft gives them the opportunity to provide input and modify it. It is the opportunity to contribute to the design of the charter that builds the team's commitment to it.

STEP 3—COLLECT INFORMATION FROM TEAM MEMBERS

The trainer who facilitates the team-building session reviews the final draft of the charter with the team leader. The team leader also needs to send a copy of the drafted charter to each team member. This provides an opportunity for them to review it prior to the trainer's interviews.

The Team Member Interview Worksheet (Figure 9.2) is a guideline for talking with each team member.

The trainer summarizes the feedback gathered from the team. The following issues are important to discuss during the team-building session.

- The extent to which team members understand how the project supports the organization's strategy and goals.

- Questions or concerns about the reason for forming the team, the team's purpose, and mission.

TEAM CHARTER

The project team leader works with the team sponsor and other key stakeholders to get agreement on all aspects of the project. The trainer and the project leader discuss the worksheet once it has been completed. This charter worksheet forms the basis of the trainer's discussion with each project team member.

Organizational Alignment

1. What strategic goals of the organization does this project support?

_____

_____

_____

2. Why is this team being formed?

_____

_____

_____

3. What are the sponsor's expectations about what this team needs to accomplish?

_____

_____

_____

4. Do other stakeholders have different expectations?

_____

_____

_____

(continued)

5. How will the team's success be measured?

_____

_____

_____

Team Information

1. What is the team's purpose and mission?

_____

_____

_____

2. What are the goals for this team?

_____

_____

_____

3. What is the time frame for meeting these goals?

_____

_____

_____

4. Where can the team go for the information it needs?

_____

_____

_____

5. What resources will be available to the team?

_____

_____

_____

(continued)

6. What are the roles and responsibilities of the team sponsor?

_____

_____

_____

7. What are the roles and responsibilities of the team leader?

_____

_____

_____

8. What are team members' roles and responsibilities?

_____

_____

_____

9. What training and/or orientation will be provided?

_____

_____

_____

10. How often will the team be expected to report progress and results?

_____

_____

_____

11. What processes will be used to communicate with the sponsor and other key stakeholders?

_____

_____

_____

(continued)

12. What are the limits of the team's decision-making authority?

_____

_____

_____

13. Who approves decisions that lie outside the team's limits of authority?

_____

_____

_____

14. What other constraints and boundaries does the team need to be aware of?

_____

_____

_____

15. When will the team disband?

_____

_____

_____

TEAM MEMBER INTERVIEW

The trainer/facilitator should plan to talk with each project team member before the team-building session. The purpose of these discussions is to review the proposed team charter and identify any issues, questions, or concerns that need to be discussed—and resolved—at the two-day team-building session. The interviews will be most effective if team members have an opportunity to review the charter prior to talking to the trainer.

Organizational Alignment

1. Do you have any questions about how the team's output will support the organization's strategic goals?

   _____

   _____

   _____

2. Do you know why the team was formed? Do you have any questions about why the team was formed?

   _____

   _____

   _____

3. How do you believe the team's success should be measured?

   _____

   _____

   _____

(continued)

Team Information

1. Do you have questions about the team's proposed purpose and mission? Is there anything you would change or add?

_____

_____

_____

2. How do the goals look to you? Is there anything you would change or add?

_____

_____

_____

3. Do you have any questions or concerns about resources? Are there any other resources you feel the team needs?

_____

_____

_____

4. What do you believe are the role and responsibilities of the team sponsor?

_____

_____

_____

5. What do you believe are the roles and responsibilities of the team leader?

_____

_____

_____

6. What do you believe are your roles and responsibilities as a team member?

_____

_____

_____

(continued)

7. Is there any training or orientation you feel the team needs?

_____

_____

_____

8. Do you have any questions or concerns about communicating with the sponsor and key stakeholders?

_____

_____

_____

9. What kind of communication will your manager expect?

_____

_____

_____

10. Are the decision-making guidelines clear?

_____

_____

_____

11. Do you feel the team has sufficient decision-making authority?

_____

_____

_____

12. Are the team boundaries clear? Do you believe the team has been empowered sufficiently to do what it has been chartered to do?

_____

_____

_____

Comments: Is there anything else you feel we need to discuss during the team-building session?

_____

_____

_____

- Ideas about how success should be measured that are different from or supplement those proposed in the charter. Also, it is particularly important to identify concerns about meeting expectations.

- Everyone's role and responsibilities must be clearly understood and agreed to.

- Resource and training concerns need to be thoroughly discussed. Team members' commitment is either enhanced or diminished depending on whether or not they feel they will be provided with everything required to execute the project successfully. This includes the scope of its authority and its boundaries.

- Finally, capture any other questions or concerns team members want to discuss during the team-building session. You must decide which issues are appropriate for discussion by the entire team and which issues need to be resolved between a particular team member and project leader. In general, all the questions covered in the Team Member Interview Worksheet represent issues that are appropriate for discussion during the team-building session. But if, for example, a team member is concerned about his or her ability to devote the time required to the project, this needs to be discussed one-on-one with the leader.

STEP 4—DESIGN AND CONDUCT A TWO-DAY TEAM-BUILDING SESSION

The trainers and team leader work together and plan the team-building session. The first step is reviewing the information collected from team members. This will provide a good indication of how much time needs to be devoted to each topic.

The Leader's Guide for Building Team Effectiveness in Chapter 6 can be used for project teams. The following modifications to that guide need to be made for project teams. Figure 9.3 displays the Agenda and Objectives for the team-building session.

Definition of a Team (fifteen to twenty minutes)

Put up overhead Definition of a Project Team (Figure 9.4)

Introduce the concept of team effectiveness by defining a project team. Let the group know that a project team is a short-term team that comes together only for the life of the project. It brings together people with complementary skills and is chartered to achieve a shared purpose or mission and specific project goals. Like all teams, they must agree on a collaborative work approach, roles, and mechanisms to hold one another mutually accountable.

Characteristics of Effective Cross Functional Project Teams (fifteen to twenty minutes)

To introduce this discussion, make the point that to be effective short-term project teams must put in place the eight characteristics of team effectiveness.

Agenda: Project Teams

Day One

Topic

- Introduction
- Expectations
- Definition of a team
- Characteristics of effective cross-functional project teams
- Review charter and team feedback
- Team vision of success

Time

Five to ten minutes

Five to ten minutes

Fifteen to twenty minutes

Fifteen to twenty minutes

One and a half to two hours

Sixty to ninety minutes

LUNCH

- Team-building activity
- Team leader and team member roles and responsibilities
- Summarize day one
- Close day one

Sixty to ninety minutes

Sixty to ninety minutes

Twenty to thirty minutes

Ten to fifteen minutes

Agenda: Project Teams

Day Two

Topic	**Time**
• Introduction	Ten to fifteen minutes
• Review day one	Fifteen to twenty minutes
• Project phases and key milestones	Sixty to ninety minutes
• Common approach and accountability agreements	Sixty to ninety minutes

LUNCH

• Stakeholder analysis and plan	Sixty to ninety minutes
• Skill resource assessment	Sixty to ninety minutes
• Finalize action plan and agreements	Thirty to forty minutes
• Next steps	Ten to fifteen minutes
• Evaluate team building	Ten to fifteen minutes
• Close two-day session	Five to ten minutes

(continued)

Objectives: Project Teams

- Understand the characteristics of effective project teams so that everyone has a shared picture of success.

- Review the team's charter so that all team members understand what is expected.

- Agree on the team's vision of success.

- Agree on team member, team leader, and sponsor roles and responsibilities.

- Create accountability agreements in order to clarify mutual expectations about how the team will work together.

- Plan major project phases and identify key milestones.

- Design a stakeholder plan based on a stakeholder analysis.

- Assess skills and resources in order to identify what the team requires in order to be successful.

- Create an action plan that documents actions, agreements, and next steps.

Definition of a Project Team

Cross-functional project teams come together only for the life of a project. They bring together individuals with complementary skills from various disciplines or functions and are chartered to achieve a specific mission and project goals. To be effective they must agree on a collaborative work approach, roles, and mechanisms to hold one another accountable, and have the skills and resources required.

This begins by creating a well-defined charter that is agreed upon by the project sponsor, the team, and key stakeholders. Let the team know that the charter describes the team's mission, goals, boundaries, and all other expectations critical to the team's success.

Review the Charter and Team Feedback (one and a half to two hours)

The trainer leads the group through a discussion of the team's charter. The goal of this discussion is to resolve all questions and concerns. This is an opportunity to resolve issues or questions raised by team members prior to the team-building session. The charter needs to be displayed on an overhead projector and, ideally, each team member should have a copy of it. The issues identified during the one-on-one interviews need to be listed on a flip chart stationed at the front of the room next to the overhead. This allows everyone to examine the charter and issues in parallel. On a separate chart, document proposed modifications to the charter. The leader lets the team know which charter elements they can change and which ones need to be discussed with the sponsor. Those requiring sponsor approval must be documented as open action items. To conclude this activity the trainer summarizes the charter elements that have been agreed to, the proposed changes, and the issues that need to be resolved.

Team Vision of Success (sixty to ninety minutes)

Project teams can benefit from discussing their vision of success. The team mission reflected in the charter is proposed by the project sponsor and agreed to, often with modifications, by the project team. However, creating a team vision helps generate enthusiasm and momentum on the part of team members.

The Leader's Guide for Creating a Team Vision guide describes the process for conducting this activity (Figure 9.5).

Team-Building Activity (sixty to ninety minutes)
Team Leader and Team Member Roles and Responsibilities

The charter defines the general roles and responsibilities of the team leader, sponsor, and team members.

Use the procedure described in Chapter 6 to agree on the specific role and responsibilities of each team member. This activity confirms the functional or technical expertise each person brings to the team and how they are expected to use that expertise for project success. Also, it gives individuals an opportunity to discuss how shared and overlapping functional or technical responsibilities will be handled.

You may use the R.A.C.I. (responsibility, accountability, consultation, informing) chart rather than the process described in Chapter 6. The R.A.C.I. responsibility charting process is described in Figure 9.6. You should use a

FIGURE 9.5

LEADER'S GUIDE FOR CREATING A TEAM VISION

OBJECTIVES

- Generate an image and list of characteristics that describe the project team at its most successful.
- Identify characteristics that guide the team's work together.

DESCRIPTION OF THE PROCESS

Describe the purpose of creating a team vision as follows:

> We have just agreed on the team's charter. The charter describes the team's mission and goals. These clarify our direction, purpose, and deliverables. We want to take this sense of purpose to the next level and create a vision of success. The vision describes the team's ideal, unique, and shared image of this project's success. It is your picture of what the team will achieve by executing project expectations at the highest level. Vision allows you to express your highest standards and values. It allows the team to set this project apart and make it a special experience for everyone on the team. Vision helps teams realize a key characteristic of team effectiveness—passion for your work together.

Next, break the team into pairs or small groups. Ask the groups to discuss and answer two or three of the following questions:

- What do you want most to accomplish on this project?
- What would ideal project execution look like?
- What will the organization be able to do that it has not been able to do as a result of this project?
- What is your dream for this project?

Ask each group to chart their responses to each question and to select someone in their group to present their responses.

Allow each group to present its vision statement. To get agreement on a team vision you can:

- Take all this information, identify common themes, and create a short vision statement of twenty-five words or less.
- As an alternative, identify common themes and create a list of statements that express the team's vision.

Finally, allow team members to add to or modify the vision statement or list of statements until they are pleased with their vision.

R.A.C.I. RESPONSIBILITY CHARTING

R.A.C.I. Charting clarifies roles and responsibilities in a way that fosters greater ownership and more supportive sharing of duties.

Each individual uses a sheet of flip chart paper and creates the following chart:

Major Responsibilities	R	A	C	I

The chart is to be completed as follows:

Major Responsibilities—list your four to six major responsibilities on this team. These describe how you will use your expertise to ensure the team fulfills its charter or vision.

R, A, C, I—For each responsibility area, indicate with a check (✓) whether you are:

R—solely responsible for executing this activity. If you believe you share responsibility with other team members, write SR. Also, write in the name of the individual with whom the responsibility is shared.

A—accountable to ensure the responsibility is executed. In most instances, an individual will be both responsible or accountable. However, in some instances, the team leader will be accountable for responsibilities that are executed by others. For example, on a project chartered to upgrade software on all existing products, the engineers assigned were responsible for designing software applications that meet specifications. The project leader was accountable to ensure all software applications meet specifications and standards. Only one person should have an A for each responsibility listed.

C—expected or required to consult with others in executing a responsibility. For example, using the software project example, an individual responsible for creating training sessions for the new software applications will need to consult various users to get input on the content of the training. Responsibilities marked with a C should also list by name those with whom the team member plans to consult.

I—planning to inform others after the responsibility has been completed. Since not everything needs to be communicated to everyone, use I when it is important for others to know the status of a particular activity. Again indicate the individuals or groups you plan to inform.

Each individual presents his or her chart. Team members discuss each person's chart and suggest changes in the R, A, C, or I delineation. In particular, the trainer helps team members identify areas in which they want to be consulted or informed. Project teams often experience problems because individuals feel excluded from key decisions. Making sure the team identifies those who want to be consulted is crucial. Similarly, informing those who believe they need to be in the information chain is important.

R.A.C.I. chart when there are overlapping responsibilities or in situations when there is a great deal of role confusion. R.A.C.I. charting helps team members clarify, specifically, who is responsible for executing shared duties and who is accountable for making sure the work is done. Individuals also have an opportunity to identify when they want to be consulted or informed about specific team activities.

Project Phases and Key Milestones (sixty to ninety minutes)

Project teams will use several techniques for planning projects and tracking performance. During the two-day team building, the trainer guides the team through a simple planning process. This plan is designed to get everyone's agreement on the project phases, deliverables for each phase, and key milestones throughout the life of the project. It also identifies when and with whom the team needs to communicate during the project. Figure 9.7 provides a format for creating this project plan.

The Project Planning Format helps the team plan the following:

- Phases—Projects typically have four or five phases from initiation to implementation. The name under each phase asks the team to identify its phases.

- Goals—Each project phase has at least one goal. For example, goals of the initiation phase include completing the project charter and ensuring that the project has all the resources required to execute its charter.

- Deliverables—List the products or outputs the team is expected to deliver in each phase. These represent the key milestones. The date these deliverables are due is also stipulated.

- Stakeholder communication—The team needs to identify which stakeholders they need to communicate with during each project phase by indicating Who to communicate with, What to communicate, and When the communication needs to take place.

The trainer can guide the team through the planning process by:

- Posting the Project Planning Format (Figure 9.7) and facilitating a discussion of each project phase. Post-It notes should be used to record project phases, deliverables, and so on. This way it will be easy to shift information as the team deliberates.

- Dividing the team up into two or three groups and asking each group to create a project plan. You can then post the plans and work with the team to merge them and create a final project plan.

Stakeholder Analysis and Plan (sixty to ninety minutes)

The success of cross-functional project teams depends in large part on how well the team manager works with key stakeholders external to the team. All teams need to establish good interteam relations with other teams across the

PROJECT PLANNING FORMAT

Phase 1	Phase 2	Phase 3	Phase 4	Phase 5
Name:	Name:	Name:	Name:	Name:
Goals:	Goals:	Goals:	Goals:	Goals:
Deliverables and Dates:	Deliverables and Dates:	Deliverables and Dates:	Deliverables and Dates:	Deliverables and Dates:
Stakeholder Communication: Who: What: When:	Stakeholder Communication: Who: What: When:	Stakeholder Communication: Who: What: When:	Stakeholder Communication: Who: What: When:	Stakeholder Communication: Who: What: When:

organization. Because of their interdisciplinary nature, cross-functional project teams are required to develop strong, supportive relationships with key stakeholders across the organization.

The two-day team-building session provides an opportunity for the team to:

- Clarify the team's key stakeholders and do a stakeholder analysis
- Develop a plan to work effectively with stakeholders and to manage boundary relationships
- Develop a stakeholder communication plan

The team charter identifies key stakeholders and documents their expectations. Key stakeholder groups typically include:

- The functional managers to whom cross-functional team members report
- Internal and external customers
- Senior management decision-makers, including the team's sponsor
- Groups who:
  - Must implement or help implement the team's output, for example, new-product service, process improvement, procedure, and so on.
  - Have information, expertise, or other resources that can help the team do its work.
  - Can provide informal support that will help the team execute the project and gain organizational acceptance.

Stakeholder Analysis Worksheets (Figures 9.8 and 9.9) are two alternative approaches to stakeholder analysis. The analysis should be facilitated by first examining how the stakeholder analysis will be done. Do this by reviewing the directions on Figures 9.8 and 9.9. Then

- Separate team members into groups of three or four and ask each group to do a stakeholder analysis. As an alternative, the entire team can work together and complete the analysis.
- Bring the team back together (if subgroups were used to do the analysis) and discuss each group's evaluation of stakeholder support and their issues.
- Transfer the Key Actions Needed from Figure 9.8 to the action plan and document what the team is going to do to build relationships with key stakeholders. If Figure 9.9 was used, summarize planned actions on an action plan.

If stakeholder issues are complex and there are several things that need to be resolved, the trainer may want the team to do a complete stakeholder plan. The Stakeholder Plan (Figure 9.10) allows the team to develop a strategy for increasing stakeholders' support and decreasing potential resistance.

STAKEHOLDER ANALYSIS WORKSHEET

Purpose

The purpose of the Stakeholder Analysis is to identify which stakeholders are likely to support or resist the team's output or recommendations. It guides the team in planning the actions needed to gain everyone's buy-in.

Instructions

1. List all key stakeholders. A stakeholder is any person (or group of people) who is likely to be affected by the team's output or solution. Individuals or groups that may have a stake in the project include those who:

   - need to approve or implement the team's work
   - must supply something the team needs for their work
   - are depending on the team to provide something they need to do their work or achieve their goals
   - can block or delay a decision or implementation of the team's output or solution

2. Rate each stakeholder with one of the symbols in the right-hand column based on their anticipated:

support of the team's output or solution	+
neutrality	=
resistance to the team's output or solution	–

3. Evaluate the potential gain/loss to each stakeholder group. Ask yourself, What do they feel they have to gain and/or lose? Next, rate the gain/loss to the team. This clarifies how each stakeholder's support or lack of it can impact the project positively or negatively.

4. List the key issues based on the evaluation of gain/loss to each stakeholder or stakeholder group.

5. List the key actions recommended to gain stakeholders' support and ensure positive stakeholders continue their support.

(continued)

STAKEHOLDER ANALYSIS WORKSHEET

Project: _____

Stakeholder name: (group or person)	Rating +, =, −	Gain to stakeholder Loss to stakeholder	Gain to team Loss to team

Summary of key issues:

Key actions needed:

STAKEHOLDER ANALYSIS WORKSHEET

Source: Glenn Parker, Cross-Functional Teams. (San Francisco: Jossey-Bass 1994), Exhibit 7.1, p. 97.

1. Identify an individual, department, or other team your team needs to be successful.

2. List the specific types of help you need from this stakeholder.

3. What is this stakeholder expecting from the team? What kind of assistance or help does he or she need from this team?

4. Identify a common objective you share with the stakeholder.

5. What potential barriers may prevent the stakeholder and your team from working together effectively?

6. What can you do to overcome these barriers?

7. Which team member is the most appropriate person to work with the stakeholder?

8. What specific actions can the team take to develop a supportive relationship with the stakeholder?

STAKEHOLDER PLAN

Purpose

A stakeholder plan helps teams manage stakeholder relationships in such a way that the project is successfully supported and implemented. The stakeholder plan is a proactive approach that gives teams a strategy for increasing stakeholders' support for the project and/or decreasing their opposition.

Instructions

1. The stakeholder plan is used in conjunction with a stakeholder analysis. In the first column, write down the list of stakeholders or stakeholder groups identified in the stakeholder analysis.

2. Define the influence objective. If the team is successful in influencing the stakeholder, what will it gain? Be specific about the outcome the team desires as a result of influencing this stakeholder or stakeholder group.

3. Increase benefits to stakeholder. Review the stakeholder analysis and list the things the team can do to make the project more beneficial to the stakeholder.

4. Reduce cost to stakeholder. Review the stakeholder analysis and list things the team can do to make their potential output or solution less costly to the stakeholder.

5. Plan the team's strategy. List the actions the team believes will achieve the influence objective. Identify who on the team will meet with the stakeholder and when the meeting needs to occur. In some instances, someone who is not on the team might be the right person to meet with the stakeholder. This individual should be recommended as the Who on the stakeholder plan, and the team member who will ask this individual to take the action identified.

Key Stakeholder(s)	Influence Objective	Increase Benefit	Reduce Cost	ACTION PLAN		
				WHAT	WHO	WHEN

Figure 9.11 is an example of a Stakeholder Plan. A cross-functional team, chartered to reduce the time it took their division to develop and launch new computer products, developed this plan. The team successfully reengineered the new product development process, reducing the time from conception to product launch by 30 percent. This Stakeholder Plan is the team's strategy for working with stakeholder groups to get agreement on adopting the new process.

STEP 5—IMPLEMENT THE RESULTS

Projects can be very complex and groundbreaking. When these projects are also large and involve considerable financial investment, their success is critical. Even with up-front team building, projects often encounter obstacles to success. This chapter includes two checklists. The first describes common pitfalls that cross-functional teams often experience (Figure 9.12). Obstacles to Project Success (Figure 9.13) describes common obstacles to project success. Both checklists identify issues the team leader and sponsor need to pay attention to as the project moves forward. Many of them have been addressed in the charter. However, as project execution begins, things sometimes change. This list reminds the leader and sponsor of how cross-functional teams and/or projects can get derailed.

STEP 6—EVALUATE THE IMPACT OF TEAM BUILDING

The trainer needs to check in with the project team thirty days after the team-building session. Rather than a three-month or six-month follow-up, evaluating team progress every forty-five days is recommended. Quick intervention and recovery is essential for cross-functional project teams. The checklists described in Step 5 (Figures 9.12 and 9.13) can help pinpoint problem areas.

STAKEHOLDER PLAN—EXAMPLE

FIGURE 9.11

Key Stakeholder(s)	Influence Objective	Increase Benefit	Reduce Cost	ACTION PLAN		
				WHAT	WHO	WHEN
Marketing	Get agreement to upgrade product launch materials.	• Offer better marketing to support introductions of new products.	• No cost to marketing to get product launch guide completed sooner.	Get agreement to upgrade quality of product launch guide.	A1	April 1
Manufacturing	Get agreement not to duplicate quality checks.	• Eliminate duplication of effort.	• Time saved in avoiding duplication will offset cost of changing manufacturing process.	Pilot process in manufacturing and finalized the changes they need to make.	Tim	April 1
Quality	Present new guidelines and processes and get agreement.	• Improve processes. • Simplified process and clear quality guidelines.	• Time saved in streamlining and clarifying processes will offset cost of changes.	Ask quality manager to review guidelines and provide final edits	Carol	April 30
Sofware Engineering	Get agreement to complete final version of software sooner.	• Better schedule execution.	• New product development process will not require additional engineers.	Present new process to software supervisors. Get agreement on how they will plan and monitor software development projects.	Ann	May 30
Hardware Engineering	Get buy-in on simplified hardware design.	• Improved design of hardware.	• New product development process will not require additional engineers.	Review proposed process and simplified design with hardware managers for final approval.	Jim	May 30

COMMON PITFALLS FOR CROSS-FUNCTIONAL TEAMS

This checklist identifies the major problems that undermine cross-functional teams. Both the team sponsor and team leader need to be aware of these potential problem areas. Many of the issues can be dealt with through effective chartering. Others need to be monitored throughout the life of the project.

❏ **Unclear Sponsorship**—It is not clear who is sponsoring the team and as a result there is no senior leadership support.

❏ **Unclear Resourcing**—The team either does not understand what resources it has or resource commitments fluctuate.

❏ **Key Stakeholders Are Not Committed**—There is a failure to gain the support of key stakeholders or retain their support through appropriate involvement in key decisions, plans, etc.

❏ **Team's Work is Not Linked to Business Strategy or Goals**—The team loses momentum because its work is not linked to strategic priorities. This pitfall may also impede implementation of the team's output or solution due to lack of alignment with business objectives.

❏ **Level of Empowerment is Not Clear or Disputed**—Confusion or disagreement about the team's decision-making latitude creates problems for the team, particularly in working with the sponsor and other key stakeholders.

❏ **Roles Unclear or Disputed**—The team-building session should clarify general expectations of all team members. Throughout the project, role boundaries and expectations need to be reclarified or redefined as required.

❏ **Pressure from the Home Team Introduces Other Agendas**—This can be a major problem if team members are assigned to the project on a part-time basis. The team leader needs to work with team members' managers to ensure individuals can devote the time required to the project.

❏ **The Team Reflects Problems in the Hierarchy**—Cross-functional project teams must not work in a traditional, hierarchical manner. To prevent this, the team leader must continuously look for opportunities to share leadership.

❏ **Individuals Do Not Value Others' Perspective or Expertise**—The team-building session is designed to encourage a supportive and mutually

(continued)

respectful team environment. It is important to foster this attitude on an ongoing basis by appropriately involving team members in decisions, problem solving, etc.

❏ **Functional Elitism Undermines Team Unity**—Team members must feel their participation is valued regardless of their function. The team leader needs to be sensitive to potential issues in this area and ensure the ideas and contributions of everyone are respected.

❏ **Team Meetings Are Unproductive**—If individuals consider team meetings to be a waste of time, it robs the team of the valuable opportunities to work collaboratively. Efficient, well-conducted meetings that achieve specific objectives are essential to team effectiveness.

❏ **Communication and Information Sharing Are Selective and Not Inclusive**—Everyone on the team needs to be part of the communication channel and kept up-to-date about relevant information.

❏ **Team Members Do Not Represent the Team Accurately to Others**—It is important that, as team members talk with their home team and other key stakeholders, that they accurately represent the team's decisions, plans, etc.

❏ **Lack of Accountability for Team Performance**—All team members need to be accountable for the team's performance and share responsibility for ensuring the team's success.

OBSTACLES TO PROJECT SUCCESS

This checklist identifies common pitfalls that lead to project failure. Awareness of these obstacles can help team leaders anticipate and avoid these problems.

- ❏ Sufficient time is not allocated to the project.
- ❏ The organization does not allocate sufficient financial resources.
- ❏ Teams react to pressure from the sponsor or other key stakeholders and commit to unrealistic deadlines.
- ❏ Team members are too optimistic about how long it will take to complete activities.
- ❏ The schedule starts to slip one day at a time.
- ❏ Team members begin pointing fingers at other team members and accuse one another of delaying the project.
- ❏ The project manager decides to add more people to the project when it begins to fall behind schedule.
- ❏ The project begins to exceed its budget.
- ❏ Conflicts arise over team member time and resource requirements.
- ❏ Cooperation between the team and other organizational units begins to erode.
- ❏ The team leader has little or no power.
- ❏ Conflicts and other problems are not resolved in a timely manner and, as a result, team members lose enthusiasm.

Resolving Team Conflict

INTRODUCTION

Building trust and resolving conflict are two of the most challenging aspects of creating an effective team.

Team building can be used to help teams diagnose the underlying causes of conflict and develop mechanisms for resolving these differences. Before participants engage in this type of team building, the team needs to determine whether they are experiencing destructive or constructive conflict. Second, the team should exhibit a desire to tackle the issues and work collaboratively to resolve their differences. Finally, if the conflict involves only one or two team members, the trainer needs to work with the team leader on individual conflict-resolution strategies rather than engaging the entire team.

A team's ability to understand conflict and manage it effectively are essential for its growth and development. Every aspect of team performance is jeopardized when conflict is unresolved

The six-step team-building process can be used to help teams deal with conflict.

STEP 1—IDENTIFY THE NEED

The trainer and team leader discuss the leader's perception about the team's conflictive issues or differences. It is important in Step 1 to differentiate constructive from destructive conflict. Destructive conflict polarizes a team and deepens differences. It destroys morale and can result in irresponsible behavior, for example, name calling, shouting, etc. Constructive conflict is generated when teams work together to solve problems, generate new ideas, or tackle tough issues. Unlike destructive conflict, individuals are attacking the problem or issue, not one another. Although team members have differences of opinion, they are working together to find the best solution and solve the problem. Team building is designed to help groups resolve destructive conflict. Constructive conflict—which results in breakthroughs, innovation, and creativity—needs to be encouraged. The Outcomes of Conflict Worksheet (Figure 10.1) can help you lead this discussion.

In general, if more than six of the items in the Constructive Conflict list are checked, it is probable that conflict is helping the team grow, learn, and mature. Similarly, if more than six of the items on the Destructive Conflict list are checked, team building is appropriate. When assessing whether the team needs help, the trainer should talk with the leader about how and when conflict manifests itself, whether the entire team is involved or only certain individuals, and what happens as a result of the conflict, that is, does it get resolved quickly or does it fester for weeks? This discussion, along with the Outcomes of Conflict Worksheet, ensures a good decision is made about whether team building is appropriate.

STEP 2—GAIN THE COMMITMENT

This step is conducted in the same way as described in Chapter 3.

STEP 3—COLLECT INFORMATION AND IDENTIFY ISSUES

The Outcomes of Conflict Worksheet can be used to identify whether the team's views of constructive and destructive conflict are compatible with the team leader's. In addition, if team building is required, this worksheet identifies the team's strengths in managing conflict as well as the problem areas that need to be addressed. If the team's view of constructive versus destructive conflict is different from the leader's, the trainer and the leader need to discuss this. The leader must understand how the team is experiencing conflict and its impact.

The trainer also needs to profile the team leader's and team members' conflict management style by evaluating the results of the Conflict Style Profile and Scoring the Profile (Figure 10.2). For planning purposes, it is best to have each person complete the assessment prior to team building. This allows the trainer to assess style preferences and the various ways in which individuals prefer to deal with conflict. If for some reason team members cannot complete the profile before the session, it is short enough to do during the team-building workshop.

OUTCOME OF CONFLICT WORKSHEET

The following questions help you identify whether the conflict the team is experiencing is constructive or destructive.

Constructive Conflict

When the team disagrees, expresses differences of opinion, or argues divergent points of view, does the outcome:

❏ Open up and clarify the issues.

❏ Help resolve the problem and gain closure.

❏ Release new information and perspectives.

❏ Help individuals share information.

❏ Increase the involvement of the individuals needed to solve the problem.

❏ Release emotions and allow authentic communication to occur.

❏ Help build cohesiveness.

❏ Affirm direction, priorities, and plans.

❏ Promote growth of individuals and the team.

❏ Provide learning opportunities.

❏ Result in breakthroughs, creativity, or innovative ideas.

Destructive Conflict

When the team disagrees, expresses differences of opinion, or argues divergent points of view, does the outcome:

❏ Divert energy for a prolonged period of time, making it difficult to get work done.

❏ Destroy morale.

❏ Polarize the team.

❏ Deepen differences.

❏ Produce irresponsible interpersonal behavior.

❏ Usually not solve the problem.

❏ Undermine team spirit and cohesiveness.

(continued)

❏ Cause individuals to withhold information and ideas to avoid disagreements.

❏ Suppress open and authentic communication.

❏ Discourage breakthrough thinking, creativity, or innovative ideas.

❏ Cause team members to avoid engaging in problem solving or abdicate responsibility for helping to address important issues.

The following questions may be used as a way of getting deeper insight into the team's conflict management issues:

1. What is the team's greatest strength in handling conflict?

2. What is the team's greatest weakness in handling conflict?

3. What kinds of issues or situations usually trigger team conflict?

4. When conflict first arises, what do team members usually do?

5. Does everyone on the team get involved in the discussion and work toward resolution?

6. What could the team do to be more effective in dealing with conflict?

CONFLICT STYLE PROFILE

Instructions: For each statement in the inventory, choose the one that most closely reflects the way you prefer to deal with conflict. Sometimes you will find that more than one statement is appropriate. In that case, choose the one that most closely represents what you would do. After you have answered all the questions, score the profile.

1. When I am in an angry discussion, I prefer to:
   a. talk face-to-face.
   b. find out what the other person wants.
   c. wait until tempers cool.
   d. explore various alternatives to resolve the issue.

2. When someone on the team is hostile toward me, I tend to:
   a. stay away from that person.
   b. seek an open exchange to clear the air.
   c. confront the individual about their attitude.
   d. listen to the other person's concerns.

3. When I observe others in the midst of a conflict, I usually:
   a. attempt to help if I can.
   b. leave as quickly as possible.
   c. become involved and take a position.
   d. observe what's going on and see what happens.

4. When someone puts personal needs ahead of what's best for the team, I am apt to:
   a. tell them what I think about their behavior.
   b. try to understand why they feel a need to do this.
   c. seek the other person's help in finding a solution.
   d. let others on the team take responsibility for solving the problem.

5. When I am involved in an interpersonal dispute, I like to:
   a. stress the things we agree on and minimize our differences.
   b. reduce tension by not discussing areas of disagreement.
   c. encourage both of us to get our issues and concerns out immediately.
   d. dismiss it when it impacts my ability to do my job effectively.

(continued)

6. A team's ability to resolve conflict depends most on:
   a. accepting different points of view.
   b. openness and candor.
   c. a willingness to work through differences.
   d. a patient, nonjudgmental approach.

7. When I am upset with someone I tend to:
   a. wait until my anger subsides before I decide what to do.
   b. let the person know how I feel right away.
   c. make sure I don't react in a way that will damage our relationship.
   d. focus on the issue we need to resolve rather than personalities.

8. The phrase that best describes my approach to dealing with conflict is:
   a. attack it head on.
   b. look for a win-win solution.
   c. let it work itself out.
   d. try to understand others' point-of-view.

9. I believe a team can minimize conflict by:
   a. letting the team leader resolve controversial issues.
   b. being willing to yield to others' point of view.
   c. expressing opinions and letting the best argument win.
   d. seeking creative solutions and alternatives.

10. When I communicate with someone with whom I have a conflict, I:
    a. speak rapidly and forcibly, with power.
    b. find an alternative to face-to-face discussion, for example, voice mail or e-mail.
    c. focus the discussion on what's important to both of us.
    d. let the other person talk first before I speak.

11. The word others would use to describe my approach to conflict is:
    a. mediator.
    b. yielding.
    c. tough.
    d. retreat.

12. When someone does something that irritates me, my tendency is to:
    a. tell them to stop.
    b. do nothing and hope they stop.
    c. speak gently and let the individual know my feelings.
    d. try to persuade the person to stop.

13. The quality that I value most in dealing with conflict is:
    a. understanding and empathy.
    b. examination of the real issues and creative resolution.
    c. strength and certainty.
    d. calmness and tranquility.

14. When others seek my help in resolving conflict, they can count on me to:
    a. discourage strong emotions.
    b. encourage listening and mutual respect.
    c. propose solutions and tell them what to do.
    d. help them understand what all parties need to reach a workable solution.

15. When conflict polarizes the team, I tend to:
    a. avoid taking sides and remain neutral.
    b. try to find out what we agree on before tackling the disagreements.
    c. make my position clear so that everyone knows where I stand.
    d. encourage my peers to listen to one another and avoid jumping to conclusions.

16. When others challenge my competence or abilities, I usually respond by:
    a. accepting it as a difference of opinion.
    b. changing the subject and not reacting to the challenge.
    c. a strong rebuttal and, sometimes, counterattack.
    d. encouraging a discussion that explores why our viewpoints differ.

17. When work-related stress causes conflict, it is best to:
    a. deal with it quickly and keep the team focused on our goals.
    b. let people deal with stress as best they can.
    c. help one another deal with the stress-causing issues.
    d. try to soothe others' feelings and make people feel better.

18. The best approach to take when people have different ideas about what needs to be done is to:
    a. take the approach most people agree with.
    b. look for an integrative solution rather than making a quick compromise.
    c. insist on the right course of action even if it's unpopular with some team members.
    d. not make a decision right away because it could make things worse.

19. When teamwork breaks down because of conflict, the team leader should:
    a. do whatever is necessary to avoid needless tension.
    b. send a clear message that personal feelings must not hinder teamwork.
    c. encourage those involved to work together and rebuild their relationship.
    d. help those involved work through their differences.

20. The best way to uncover underlying issues that are causing conflict is to:
    a. tell people it is the only way for everyone to try and get what they want.
    b. wait until people are ready to talk about what's really bothering them.
    c. encourage people to work hard to resolve the deeper issues.
    d. help people feel comfortable opening up with one another.

(continued)

SCORING THE PROFILE

Directions: Circle the answer you selected for each question. Then add the number of items circled in each column. The column with the highest score indicates your preferred conflict management style.

Direct	Avoidance	Collaborate	Accommodate
1a	1c	1d	1b
2c	2a	2b	2d
3c	3b	3a	3d
4a	4d	4c	4b
5d	5b	5c	5a
6b	6d	6c	6a
7b	7a	7d	7c
8a	8c	8b	8d
9c	9a	9d	9b
10a	10b	10c	10d
11c	11d	11a	11b
12a	12b	12d	12c
13c	13d	13b	13a
14c	14a	14d	14b
15c	15a	15b	15d
16c	16b	16d	16a
17a	17b	17c	17d
18c	18d	18b	18a
19b	19a	19d	19c
20a	20b	20c	20d

Totals:

STEP 4—DESIGN AND CONDUCT THE TEAM-BUILDING SESSION

Figure 10.3 presents the Objectives and Agenda for the conflict-resolution team-building session.

The following Leader's Guide can help you conduct the conflict resolution team building.

LEADER'S GUIDE FOR CONFLICT RESOLUTION

Introduction (five to ten minutes)

Welcome participants and review the Objectives and Agenda. Explain that learning to manage conflict effectively enables the team to do a better job in all aspects of its work. To make this point it is also helpful to review the outcomes of constructive versus destructive conflict.

Put up overheads Outcomes of Destructive Conflict and Outcomes of Constructive Conflict (Figure 10.4).

Hopes and Concerns (twenty to thirty minutes)

Ask the participants to think about their hopes for the team building and any concerns they may have. You can state the purpose of this activity as follows: "Before we begin the team-building session, I'd like to gather your hopes and concerns. Please pair up with the person next to you and answer these two questions:

- What are your hopes for this team-building session? What do you hope we can accomplish during these two days?

- What are your concerns about this team-building session? What do you want to make sure does not happen during these two days?

Take five minutes to discuss these questions. Then I will chart your responses." After five minutes, gather the Hopes and Concerns from each pair. Let the participants know these responses will be used to establish ground rules for the team-building session.

Ground Rules (fifteen to twenty minutes)

Ask the team to look at the list of Hopes and Concerns. Explain the following: "Ground Rules are behavior norms that describe how the team will work together during the two-day team-building. These ground rules are intended to help us realize the hopes and prevent the concerns." Lead the group in a brainstorming session and create a list of ground rules. Make sure the ground rules are clearly understood and that everyone agrees to them.

Objectives

- Gain a clear understanding of the nature of conflict.

- Review the team's feedback and identify the issues that need to be resolved.

- Understand personal styles of handling conflict.

- Learn techniques for conflict resolution.

- Create accountability agreements that will serve as conflict resolution guidelines.

- Agree on the next steps.

AGENDA
Resolving Team Conflict

Day One

Topic	**Time**
• Introduction	Five to ten minutes
• Hopes and concerns	Twenty to thirty minutes
• Ground rules	Fifteen to twenty minutes
• Defining conflict	Thirty to forty minutes
• Review of feedback	Thirty to forty minutes
• Conflict management styles	Sixty to ninety minutes

LUNCH

• Team-building activity	Forty-five to sixty minutes
• Healthy conflict resolution in team	Sixty to ninety minutes
• Conflict management ground rules	Thirty to forty-five minutes
• Summarize day one	Twenty to thirty minutes
• Close day one	Ten to fifteen minutes

(continued)

AGENDA
Resolving Team Conflict

Day Two

Topic	Time
• Review day one	Fifteen to twenty minutes
• Assertive messages techniques	Forty-five to sixty minutes
• Team-building activity	Forty to sixty minutes
• Accountability agreements	Sixty to ninety minutes
• Evaluate team-building session	Ten to fifteen minutes
• Close session	Five to ten minutes

Outcomes of Destructive Conflict

Conflict is *destructive* when it:

- Diverts energy for a prolonged period of time, making it difficult to get work done.

- Destroys morale.

- Polarizes and divides the team.

- Deepens differences.

- Produces irresponsible interpersonal behavior.

- Does not result in new behaviors.

- Suppresses open and authentic communication.

- Causes team members to avoid addressing issues.

- Discourages creativity or breakthrough thinking.

- Undermines team spirit and cohesion.

- Causes individuals to withhold information or ideas.

(continued)

Potential Outcomes of Constructive Conflict

Conflict is *constructive* when it:

- Opens up and clarifies issues.

- Helps resolve problems and gain closure.

- Releases new information and perspectives.

- Helps individuals share information and ideas.

- Increases involvement of individuals needed to solve the problem.

- Allows authentic communication to occur.

- Builds cohesiveness.

- Affirms direction, priorities, and plans.

- Promotes team and individual growth.

- Facilitates team learning.

- Results in breakthroughs, creativity, or innovative ideas.

Definitions of Conflict (thirty to forty minutes)

This activity is designed to help each person think through the topic of conflict on a personal level. Distribute the Personal Definition of Conflict worksheets (Figure 10.5) and ask participants to spend ten minutes writing brief responses to each question. Encourage participants to give their first response and not spend a lot of time deliberating on their answers. Remind them there are no right or wrong answers.

The purpose of this activity is to begin exploring the topic of conflict from each team members' viewpoint. When each person has completed the worksheet, divide the team into groups of three or four and ask them to take turns reading their responses to one another. Allow fifteen to twenty minutes for the reading and discussion.

To summarize the small group discussions, assemble the entire team and ask the following questions:

- What did they learn about others' views of conflict?

- What similarities and differences were found?

Review of Feedback (thirty to forty minutes)

This activity can be handled the same way as described in Chapter 6.

Conflict Management Styles (sixty to ninety minutes)

Introduce the Conflict Style Profile. If participants have not completed it prior to team building, distribute the profile to each participant. Let participants know this instrument provides insight into how each person prefers to handle conflict. It also helps the team develop appropriate mechanisms for handling conflict. After the profiles are completed, distribute Interpreting Your Profile (Figure 10.6) and allow five to seven minutes for reading the interpretation. Briefly review the chief characteristics of each style (Figure 10.7). Check to see if there are any questions about the conflict management styles. Pair up the participants and ask them to discuss their style with their partners using the following questions:

- What are the strengths of your style?

- What are the potential weaknesses of your style?

Allow ten minutes for this discussion.

Put up overheads Team Profile Grid and Conflict Management Styles (Figures 10.8 and 10.9).

PERSONAL DEFINITION
OF CONFLICT WORKSHEET

Instructions: Please read each of the open-ended statements on this worksheet. These statements are intended to help you think about and discuss with others your views about conflict. Complete each sentence as quickly as you can.

1. My personal definition of conflict is:

2. I believe a team is experiencing conflict when the following things occur:

3. My strategies for dealing with conflict are as follows:

4. The strengths of my conflict management strategies are:

5. The weaknesses of my conflict management strategies are:

INTERPRETING YOUR PROFILE

This profile is designed to assess an individual's behavior in conflict situations. The following are descriptions of each of the four conflict management styles:

Direct Style—High scores indicate a strong need to control people or situations. There is an emphasis in overcoming opposition and pursuing one's own interests and needs. Individuals who have high direct scores approach conflict situations by:

- Defending their position
- Trying to win
- Seeking an immediate resolution
- Taking charge
- Taking authority to resolve differences
- Making quick decisions about what needs to be done
- Arguing their position forcefully

Avoidance Style—High scores indicate a tendency toward passivity and withdrawal in conflict situations. These individuals do not address the conflict, tend to sidestep issues, or postpone confronting issues. Individuals who have high avoid scores approach conflict situations by:

- Trying to avoid creating unpleasant situations
- Letting others take responsibility for resolving conflict
- Encouraging others to delay direct confrontation
- Accepting the situation
- Suppressing their own needs and feelings
- Denying there is a problem
- Looking for ways to avoid taking a stand or expressing an opinion that might create disagreement

Collaborative Style—High scores indicate a desire to stand up for one's own needs in conflict situations while using a proactive approach to engage in collaboration. Individuals with the collaborative style attempt to work with others

(continued)

to find a solution that satisfies the concerns of all parties. In conflict situations, individuals who have high collaborate scores tend to:

- Seek to identify underlying issues and concerns
- Offer creative and innovative alternatives
- Work for win-win solutions
- View conflict situations as an opportunity for team growth rather than a problem
- Encourage others to work together
- Help others verbalize their issues and concerns.
- Push for win-win solutions even when they are impractical or not feasible.

Accommodate Style—High scores indicate a desire to maintain harmonious relationships even if it means sacrificing what the individual really wants. These individuals cooperate readily, tend to be selfless, and quickly yield to another's point of view. In conflict situations, individuals who have high accommodate scores tend to:

- Be conciliatory
- Readily listen to and try to understand others' points of view, needs, and concerns
- Want to help others get what they want
- Neglect their own concerns in favor of satisfying the concerns of others
- Work toward maintaining a harmonious environment
- Respect all points of view
- Defer too much to the concerns of others and minimize their ability to influence the outcome

Direct Style

- Defends own position

- Wants to win

- Seeks immediate resolution

- Takes charge in conflict situations

- Makes quick decisions about what needs to be done

- Argues own position forcefully

- Quick to assume authority for resolving differences

(continued)

Avoidance Style

- Wants to avoid creating unpleasant situations

- Lets others take responsibility for resolving conflict

- Encourages others to delay direct confrontation

- Accepts the situation

- Suppresses own feelings and needs

- Denies there is a problem to be solved

- Looks for ways to avoid taking a stand that might lead to disagreement

Collaborative Style

- Seeks to identify underlying issues and concerns

- Offers creative and innovative alternatives

- Works for win-win solutions

- Views conflict as an opportunity for team growth

- Helps others verbalize their issues and concerns

- May push for win-win solutions even when impractical and not feasible

- Encourages others to work together.

(continued)

Accommodate Style

- Conciliatory approach
- Ready to listen and understand others' points of view
- Wants to help others get what they want
- Neglects own concerns in favor of others
- Works toward maintaining a harmonious work environment
- Respects all points of view
- Tends to defer too much to others and minimize their ability to influence the outcome

Team Profile Grid

Team members use different
approaches for resolving conflict.

	Direct	Collaborate
Assertive		
	Avoidance	Accommodate

Nonassertive

Conflict Management Styles

Style	Appropriate Situations
Direct	
Avoidance	
Collabortive	
Accommodate	

Next, point to Team Profile Grid and graph each person's primary conflict management style. Discuss the team's profile by asking the following questions:

- Does the team have a predominant conflict management style?
- Does the team's predominant style match how the organization as a whole tends to deal with conflict?

Display the Conflict Management Styles overhead (Figure 10.9). Go through each of the four styles and, for each one, ask:

- When is it appropriate to use this style?
- What are the limitations of this style?

Use an overhead-marking pen and record a few of the group's responses on the overhead. Put up overheads on conflict management styles: Direct Style, Avoidance Style, Collaborative Style, and Accommodate Style (Figure 10.10).

Summarize this discussion by reviewing strengths and cautions for each style.

Team-Building Activity (forty-five to sixty minutes)

Select a team-building activity from Chapter 14.

Healthy Conflict Resolution in Team (sixty to ninety minutes)

Put up overheads Healthy Conflict Resolution in Teams and Steps in Conflict Resolution (Figures 10.11 and 10.12)

Explain that effective teams use agreed upon mechanisms for handling conflict. Next, describe the ways healthy teams manage conflict. Review the Steps in Conflict Resolution overhead with the team, explaining each step. Ask the team to identify a few situations over the past six months that have caused team conflict. Select two or three situations and break the team into two or three groups.

Assign one of the conflict situations to each team. Ask each team to work through the situation using the Steps in Conflict Resolution overhead as a guide. Give each team twenty-five minutes to complete the exercise.

To debrief the exercise, ask one person from each small group to present his or her group's responses. Focus on the agreements proposed to resolve the conflict. After each group presents its responses, ask the entire team:

- Did you identify the triggering event and real issue?
- Did individuals communicate their feelings and points of view?
- Were you able to take others' perspective and understand their point of view?
- What do you think about the proposed agreements? Are they effective ways of resolving the conflict? Is there anything you would recommend adding or changing?

Direct Style

Strengths

- Useful when quick, decisive action is important

- Helps team tackle unpopular or controversial issues

- Important when ethical issues are at stake

Cautions

- Little new information is generated

- If overused, damages relationships

- Can force premature resolution before all options are explored adequately

Avoidance Style

Strengths

- Best approach when issues are trivial or unimportant

- Delays action when emotions are too strong

- Accepts the situation when you don't have the power to change it

Cautions

- Issues fester and do not get resolved

- Doesn't help the team tackle important issues

- May withhold input or information the team needs

(continued)

Collaborative Style

Strengths

- Gains true commitment to solutions and agreements

- Merges a diversity of views to get the best decision

- Helps team address the deeper issues

Cautions

- Can create paralysis and frustration trying to build a consensus solution

- Team must have time to work the issue

- Learning and insight can become more important than resolving the conflict

Accommodate Style

Strengths

- It is important to maintain good relationships

- The other person's ideas or concerns are more important than your own

- Demonstrates the importance of listening to others and valuing their points of view.

Cautions

- Can appear weak or not committed to own point of view

- Desire for harmony can outweigh getting the best decision

- Can be too quick to give up and agree

Healthy Conflict Resolution in Teams

- A desire for resolution, not a desire to win

- Expression and acceptance of feelings

- A climate of mutual trust or a desire to establish trust

- Acceptance of conflict as natural rather than good or bad

- Willingness to take time to resolve issues

Steps in Conflict Resolution

1. Identify triggering event(s)

2. Name the problem or issue— jointly defined

3. Communicate positions and feelings

4. Communicate cooperative intentions

5. Take opponent's perspective

6. Reach agreements (specific)

Team Ground Rules (thirty to forty-five minutes)

Summarize the agreements each team proposed to resolve the conflict situations in the Health Conflict Resolution exercise. Ask the team to take a look at these assessments and identify any common themes. List the common themes on a chart. Tell them that ground rules can help manage conflict. In fact, ground rules often prevent conflicts from developing.

Put up the overhead Conflict Resolution Ground Rules (Figure 10.13).

Show the team the Conflict Resolution Ground Rules (Figure 10.13). Say to the team, "Take a look at the list of common themes we've identified. How can we turn these into ground rules that will help prevent conflict?" Chart the team's ideas. Go through each idea and make sure it is clearly understood by everyone on the team. When the team has a workable set of ground rules, ask them, "If everyone follows these, will the team be able to prevent conflict or improve the way it deals with conflict? Encourage the team to keep modifying the ground rules or adding new ones until they can confidently answer yes to these two questions.

Summarize and Close Day 1 (twenty to thirty minutes)
Introduction and Review Day 1 (fifteen to twenty minutes)
Assertive Messages Techniques (forty-five to sixty minutes)

Put up the overhead Benefits of Assertive Messages (Figure 10.14).

Explain to the group that they are going to learn a communication technique that can help them deal with conflict. Define an assertive message as "a statement which clearly expresses your thoughts and feelings about a situation." Review the Assertive Messages overheads (Figure 10.14). These figures define assertive messages and explain why they are important. They also explain the guidelines for delivering an assertive message and provide an example of an assertive message. Distribute the three examples of assertive messages (Figure 10.15).

Check to see if the group has any questions. Distribute the Assertive Message Worksheets and example (Figure 10.16). Review the worksheet. Ask participants to choose a situation outside the immediate team in which they need to deliver an assertive message. Ideally, it should be a work situation. If a participant doesn't have an appropriate work situation, a personal one will do. Also, tell them to select a situation they do not mind talking about with another person. Give participants ten to fifteen minutes to complete the worksheet. Once everyone has finished the worksheet and has a message, pair up participants. Instruct them to describe the situation and the message to their partner. Ask each person to provide his/her partner with feedback and suggestions to help improve the message.

Debrief the exercise by asking the following questions:

- How do you believe this technique might benefit the team?
- What did you learn from the practice session about delivering these messages effectively?

Answer any remaining questions about the assertive-message technique.

Conflict Resolution Ground Rules — Example

- Deal with realistic issues we can solve

- No labeling or insulting

- Everyone takes responsibility for creating, promoting, or allowing the conflict

- Keep humor appropriate

- Express feelings openly

- Use "I" statements

- Use specific examples

Benefits of Assertive Messages

Assertive messages help team members deal with conflict by:

- Openly stating expectations

- Honoring different points of view

- Taking responsibility for resolving conflict

Guidelines for Assertive Messages

The following guidelines help to deliver assertive messages:

Step 1—<u>Describe the Incident or Behavior</u>

Write down the facts of the situation or describe the behavior in objective terms.

Example

Last week you agreed to review my draft of the new vendor selection policy. I told you I needed your comments by Friday and you said, "That's no problem." I am still waiting for your comments a week later.

(continued)

Assertive Messages

Step 2—<u>Tell the Other Person How You Feel</u>

Describe how you feel about the person's behavior or action.

Example

I am annoyed because I still don't have your input. It's irritating that I have called to remind you three times.

Assertive Messages

Step 3—<u>Tell the Other Person What You Think</u>

Describe your thoughts about the incident or behavior.

Example

I think it's going to be difficult for me to keep working with you on this project. I do need your help, but I want us to be clear about how we're going to work together. Reviewing the draft procedure is only the first phase of the project. I think we need to agree on how we go forward.

(continued)

Assertive Messages

Step 4—<u>Ask the Other Person to Comment</u>

Give the other person an opportunity to comment.

Example

Is this how you remember the sequence of events? Is my description of your behavior accurate?

Discuss the other person's view of the situation, including how his or her perception differs from yours.

Assertive Messages

Step 5—<u>Propose a Resolution and Seek the Other Person's Agreement</u>

- Propose a resolution.

- Offer a proposal that helps move the relationship from conflictive to collegial.

Example

Can we set a new date to get the procedure finalized with your comments? We're two weeks behind schedule. Can you get your comments to me by the end of this week? Let's agree on a date that's feasible.

EXAMPLE OF AN ASSERTIVE MESSAGE

Step 1—<u>Describe the Incident or Behavior</u>

Everyone agreed with my proposal to start the staff meeting a half hour earlier on Tuesday. But since we made that agreement, Ann has been late every week. We delay the meeting which means we usually start at least 20 minutes late. When she came in late last week, she apologized but said, "This earlier starting time doesn't work for me. I didn't agree with it from the beginning."

Step 2—<u>Tell the Other Person How You Feel</u>

I was upset when you said you didn't agree with the half hour change in our staff meeting start time. We discussed it thoroughly and you were one of the first ones to agree with my proposal.

Step 3—<u>Tell the Other Person What You Think</u>

I thought the changes would help all of us. I wasn't sure about your reaction but was pleased you agreed so quickly. I think the new time isn't working well and that's why you've been late every week.

Step 4—<u>Ask the Other Person to Respond</u>

Am I right in my assumption that you're finding it difficult to get to the meeting on time? Did you really agree with the change in time when I proposed it?

Step 5—<u>Propose a Resolution and Seek the Other Person's Agreement</u>

Everybody's time is valuable and we don't want to spend more time in meetings than we need to. Are you willing to see if the new time can work for you? If not, I'll suggest we go back to our original meeting time.

EXAMPLE OF AN ASSERTIVE MESSAGE

Step 1—<u>Describe the Incident or Behavior</u>

I submitted a budget for my department to my supervisor. She reviewed it and said it looked fine. When I got back the final budget, several items were eliminated. I checked with accounting to see if there was a mistake. They informed me that my supervisor told them to revise the budget and eliminate several items.

Step 2—<u>Tell the Other Person How You Feel</u>

I received my final budget from accounting and was surprised to see several items deleted. I was concerned when I learned that you had asked accounting to make these changes. I thought you agreed with the budget I submitted.

Step 3—<u>Tell the Other Person What You Think</u>

My department really needs to purchase the new equipment I put in the original budget. From a technology standpoint, we're going to be severely hampered if we can't upgrade our equipment.

Step 4—<u>Ask the Other Person to Respond</u>

Is the information I got from accounting correct? Can we discuss why you eliminated the new equipment?

Step 5—<u>Propose a Resolution and Seek the Other Person's Agreement</u>

If you believe purchasing all the equipment I put in the original budget is too much, can we agree on adding a few items back into the budget? I would be happy to prioritize these requests and give you a budget that is somewhere between my original proposal and the cuts you made.

(continued)

EXAMPLE OF AN ASSERTIVE MESSAGE

Step 1—<u>Describe the Incident or Behavior</u>

During team meetings Jim cuts me off when I begin to talk about our project. Jim is the project leader and he has made it clear in one-on-one discussions that he wants to handle updates on the project's status. But it's a problem when the team leader asks me a question and Jim insists on answering.

Step 2—<u>Tell the Other Person How You Feel</u>

It upsets me when I am asked a question about our project and you answer for me. This happened again in yesterday's meeting. I feel devalued and that my contribution is not important.

Step 3—<u>Tell the Other Person What You Think</u>

I think you want to deliver a consistent message about how the project is going. I appreciate that and think, if you would let me give my input, you would agree with what I have to say.

Step 4—<u>Ask the Other Person to Respond</u>

Do you see why I am so troubled by this?

Step 5—<u>Propose a Resolution and Seek the Other Person's Agreement</u>

Can we agree that if Todd [team leader] asks me a question about the project I can answer it directly? If it's something I'm not sure about I will defer to you.

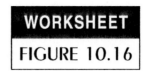

ASSERTIVE MESSAGES WORKSHEET

An assertive message is a statement that clearly expresses your thoughts and feelings about a situation. Assertive messages help you deal constructively with a conflict situation.

Assertive messages help team members deal with conflict by:

- Openly stating expectations
- Honoring different points of view
- Taking responsibility for resolving conflicts

The guidelines for delivering an assertive message are:

Step 1—Describe the Incident or Behavior

From your point of view, describe the incident or behavior you want to discuss with a team member. Write down the facts of the situation or describe the facts of the situation or describe the behavior in objective terms. For example:

> Last week you agreed to review my draft of the new vendor selection policy. I told you I needed your comments by Friday and you said, "That's no problem." I am still waiting for your comments a week later.

Step 2—Tell the Other Person How You Feel

Next, describe how you feel about what the individual's behavior or actions. For example:

> I am annoyed because I still don't have your input. It's irritating that I have called you to remind you three times.

Step 3—Tell the Other Person What You Think

Describe or explain your thoughts about the incident or behavior. For example:

> I think it's going to be difficult for me to keep working with you on this project. I do need your help but I want us to be clear about how we're going to work together. Reviewing the draft procedure is only the first phase of the project. I think we need to agree on how we go forward.

(continued)

Step 4—Ask the Other Person to Respond

Once you have described the incident, your feelings and opinions give the other person a chance to respond. For example:

> Is this how you remember the sequence of events? Is my description of your behavior accurate?

Discuss the other person's view of the situation, including how his or her perception of the incident or behavior differs from yours.

Step 5—Propose a Resolution and Seek the Other Person's Agreement

It is important to propose a resolution to the incident or an agreement that deals with the behavior. This helps ensure the relationship moves from a conflictual one to a collegial one. For example:

> Can we set a new date to get the procedure finalized with your comments? We're two weeks behind schedule. Can you get your comments to me by the end of this week? Let's agree on a date that's feasible.

When delivering assertive messages it is important to:

- Use "I" statements
- Give the message directly, face-to-face
- Give it at the earliest opportunity while the incident or behavior is fresh in your memory and the other person's

DELIVERING ASSERTIVE MESSAGES WORKSHEET

Describe a situation in which you need to deliver an assertive message.

Write out the message using the guidelines.

When will you deliver the message?

What new agreement will you seek?

The remaining team-building activities Team-Building Exercise, Accountability Agreements, Evaluate the Team-Building Session, and Close the Session can be conducted as in Chapter 6.

STEP 5—DOCUMENT THE RESULTS AND IMPLEMENTATION PLAN

This can be conducted in the same manner as described in Chapter 7.

STEP 6—EVALUATE THE EFFECTIVENESS OF THE TEAM-BUILDING SESSION

In conducting Step 6, you can also follow the procedures described in Chapter 8.

Aligning Teams with Strategy

INTRODUCTION

Organizations use teams as a way of achieving strategic goals and objectives. In fact, to gain the maximum advantage, the team's mission and goals need to be aligned with the organization's strategy and goals.

This alignment has several benefits for the team. First, it makes it easier for team members to understand how their work contributes directly to the organization's success. Alignment also helps the team leader sort out priorities when there are multiple demands facing the team. Finally, organization and team alignment focus everyone on the most important work that needs to be done.

THE TEAM-BUILDING PROCESS

The one-day team-building process can be modified to help the team improve its mission and goal alignment.

Step 1—Identify the Need

You and team leader need to discuss how the team supports the broader organization. A decision can be made on whether the leader believes there is a need to strengthen alignment.

Step 2—Gain the Commitment

This step is conducted as described in Chapter 3.

Step 3—Collect Information and Identify Issues

The Team Inventory in Chapter 4 includes questions that assess alignment of team mission and goals. Similarly, interview questions can be used to probe for strategic alignment. For example, asking questions such as, "How does this team's work contribute to the success of the organization?" or "How do your team's goals support the organization's goals?" will help you determine the extent to which the team's work is aligned with the organization's mission and goals.

Step 4—Design and Lead the One-Day Team-Building

Figure 11.1 presents the Objectives and Agenda for the team-building session. The following Leader's Guide will help you conduct the team building:

LEADER'S GUIDE TO ALIGNING TEAMS WITH STRATEGIC DIRECTION

Introduction (ten to fifteen minutes)

Welcome participants and review the Objectives and Agenda (Figure 11.1). Explain the importance of aligning the team's mission and goals with the organization's mission and strategic objectives.

Importance of Alignment (fifteen to twenty minutes)

Put up overhead The Importance of Alignment (Figure 11.2).

Figure 11.2 presents the benefits of alignment between the team and the strategies and goals of the organizations.

Review the Feedback (twenty to thirty minutes)

Review the Mission of the Organization (thirty to forty-five minutes)

Lead a discussion of the mission and allow participants to describe, generally, how the team supports it. Generate a list of ways in which the team believes it aligns with the organization's mission.

Create the Team Mission (forty-five to sixty minutes)

Conduct the mission creation process as described in Chapter 6. In some instances, the team may already have its mission in place.

Objectives

- Understand the importance of aligning the team's mission with the organization's mission.

- Agree on the team's mission and how it supports the work of the organization.

- Understand the organization's key strategic goals.

- Agree on the team's goals and how they support the organization's goals.

(continued)

Agenda

Topic	Time
• Welcome and introduction	Ten to fifteen minutes
• Importance of alignment	Fifteen to twenty minutes
• Review of feedback	Twenty to thirty minutes
• Corporate mission and purpose	Thirty to forty-five minutes
• Team mission	Forty-five to sixty minutes
• Evaluate alignment	Thirty-five to forty-five minutes

Lunch

• Corporate and business unit goals	Forty-five to sixty minutes
• Team goals	Sixty to ninety minutes
• Evaluate alignment	Forty-five to sixty minutes
• Next steps	Fifteen to twenty minutes
• Close session	Five to ten minutes

The Importance of Alignment

Team missions and goals need to support the broader organization's mission and strategic objectives:

This is important because:

- Team members can see how their work directly impacts the organization's results.

- It is easier to set priorities and sort out multiple priorities.

- Everyone is focusing on the work that is most important to the entire organization.

Evaluate Alignment (thirty-five to forty-five minutes)

Ask the team to evaluate its alignment by asking the following questions:

- If the team fulfills its mission, how will that help the organization achieve its corporate mission?
- What does the fulfillment of the team's mission mean to:
  - Customers?
  - Shareholders?
  - Other employees?
- If the team does not fulfill its mission, how will it impact the organization?

The team needs to discuss each question and modify its mission as necessary. The trainer should stress that good alignment ensures the team will help the organization fulfill its broader purpose. This means, for example, that the organization will be harmed if the team does not achieve its mission. Similarly, fulfilling the team's mission should benefit customers, shareholders, and other employees. The trainer continues modifying the mission statement until it is well aligned with the organization's mission.

Corporate and Business Unit Goals (forty-five to sixty minutes)

Review the organization's strategic goals and objectives. If the team is part of a larger business unit, these goals should also be discussed.

Establish or Review Team Goals (forty-five to eighty minutes)

The trainer guides the team through the goal-setting process described in Chapter 6, instructing the team that at least seventy-five percent of its goals need to link directly to corporate and business unit goals. Figure 11.3 provides a format for leading this discussion.

Evaluate Alignment (forty-five to sixty minutes)

The team lists its goals in the Proposed Team Goals column and the team evaluates alignment of its proposed goals with organization and business-unit objectives, using the following rating system:

1. **Perfect alignment**—the goal clearly supports the corporate goal or business unit goal.
2. **Some alignment**—the goal somewhat supports the corporate goal or business unit goal.
3. **No alignment**—the goal does not support either the corporate goal or business unit goal.

The team discusses the reason for its ratings. The trainer helps the team determine if seventy-five percent of its goals or more meet criteria (1) or (2). If not, the goals, particularly those rated (3), are modified until they do so. Help the team modify its goals by asking, "How might we change this goal so that it supports either a corporate or business unit goal?" Brainstorm ideas with the team. If the team continues to have trouble aligning a goal ask, "Why is it important to the corporation or your business unit that you meet this goal?" Discuss this with the group and modify the goal so that its alignment with corporate or business goals is clear.

The other team-building activities can be conducted as described in Chapter 6.

Steps 5 and 6

These can be conducted as described in Chapters 7 and 8.

ALIGNING TEAM GOALS WITH STRATEGIC OBJECTS

Corporate Goals

· · · · ·

Business Unit Goals

· · · · ·

Proposed Team Goal(s)	Corporate Goal Supported	Support Corporate/Business Unit Goals	Revised Goal
	Rating: *Reason:*	*Rating:* *Reason:*	
	Rating: *Reason:*	*Rating:* *Reason:*	
	Rating: *Reason:*	*Rating:* *Reason:*	
	Rating: *Reason:*	*Rating:* *Reason:*	
	Rating: *Reason:*	*Rating:* *Reason:*	
	Rating: *Reason:*	*Rating:* *Reason:*	

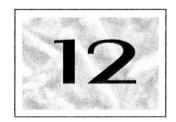

Rebuilding Trust

INTRODUCTION

Trust is essential to team effectiveness. Several things create trust between team members, including:

- Keeping commitments to one another
- Acting consistently
- Displaying integrity
- Sharing information willingly
- Listening with understanding
- Respecting different points of view
- Communicating with honesty and candor
- Taking an active role in the team
- Believing others have the team's best interest in mind
- Willingness to ask for and accept help

Team building can help establish mutual trust. Conducting team building with newly formed teams creates agreements about how to work together. This helps teams get off to a "trustful" start.

In other situations, teams must deal with breakdowns in trust. There are several reasons that trust erodes.

- Differences of opinion become exaggerated.
- The team experiences problems meeting goals and deadlines and team members start to blame one another.

- Team members become competitive instead of collaborative.
- Cliques or factions develop.
- Team members feel there are inequities in work assignments, recognition, etc.
- The team is working under intense pressure and this reduces tolerance for mistakes and/or sensitivity to individual needs.
- Team members don't keep commitments to one another.
- There is a perception some individuals are doing more than their share of work, others less than their share.
- Team members misrepresent the team to others or talk negatively about the team. For example, they tell people outside the team that the team is taking the wrong approach to an important project.
- Individuals gossip about one another rather than confront problems or issues directly.
- Conflicts are unresolved and as a result differences deepen.
- Mistakes are covered up by the team leader.
- Other teams challenge or attack the team's competence or performance.
- Some team members will not admit to mistakes.
- Personality or style differences make it difficult for one person to tolerate another.

An example of a trust breakdown is what happened to a management team while building a new plant. Initially, they were excited about this expansion opportunity and worked long hours to get the job done.

Team relationships remained supportive throughout the first two years of the new plant's operation. However, the plant's projected revenue earnings decreased dramatically at the beginning of its third year. Relationships began to erode when the revenue targets were missed for two consecutive quarters. Team members blamed one another. Some individuals became secretive and stopped sharing information with their peers. This caused several unpleasant surprises. The trust that was once so characteristic of this team became virtually nonexistent.

The problems experienced by such teams are not unique. They and others suffering from similar trust-related breakdowns can benefit from an effective team-building session.

USING THE SIX-STEP TEAM-BUILDING PROCESS

Step 1—Identify the Need—and Step 2—Gain the Commitment—can be conducted as described in Chapters 2 and 3.

STEP 3—ASSESS THE NEED

Trust has different meanings to different people. Unlike goals, roles, or processes, understanding the attitudes, behaviors, or actions that create or undermine trust can be elusive. Thus, trainers need first to diagnose the following:

- How does each person on the team define "trust"?
- What are the behaviors, attitudes, and actions that are indicators of trust?
- What are the behaviors, attitudes, and actions that undermine trust?
- Is team building the appropriate remedy?

Diagnosing Breakdowns in Trust (Figure 12.1) presents an interview format that can help you diagnose the situation.

STEP 4—DESIGN AND LEAD THE TEAM BUILDING

The Agenda and Objectives for conducting the team-building session focused on trust are provided in Figure 12.2. This session can be done in one day rather than two.

Unlike other team-building workshops, the trainer needs to devote more time to discussing feedback-gathering techniques as well as the feedback itself. The team must thoroughly understand how each person defines trust conceptually and operationally. In addition, there must be a collaborative effort to target the key issues.

Review the Data-Gathering Process (fifteen to thirty minutes)

Explain to the team how the data were collected, analyzed, and summarized. A team experiencing trust issues needs to feel confident that the process has been inclusive and objectively executed. It also needs reassurance that anonymity will be preserved. Remind participants they will see the major trends in the responses to the interviews and/or questionnaires. The data are a compilation of everyone's viewpoints and they therefore may not agree with everything presented. Also, let the team know that after the data are presented, they will have an opportunity to discuss and select the most important issues.

Present the Data (thirty to forty-five minutes)

The trainer should distribute copies of the data. Allow the participants a few minutes to read through the information. Then, go through the material and answer questions to clarify the information. It is critical that, before working with the data, all participants understand one another's views. In some instances, the trainer may choose to explain the information point by point rather than letting participants read through it individually. This can be done

DIAGNOSING BREAKDOWNS IN TRUST

The following questions will help identify the issues that need to be resolved in the team-building session:

1. How do you define "trust"? What words come to mind when you think about trust?

2. Think about your interaction with other team members. What are the behaviors, attitudes, and actions that demonstrate trust?

3. What behaviors, attitudes, and actions cause you to mistrust others?

4. How could team building help the team improve trust between team members?

5. What can you do to help the team improve or rebuild trust?

Agenda

Topic	Time
• Welcome and Introduction	Five to ten minutes
• Review the Data Gathering Process	Fifteen to thirty minutes
• Present the Data	Thirty to forty-five minutes
• Defining Trust and Its Attributes	Forty-five to sixty minutes
• Feedback Techniques	Thirty-five to forty minutes
• Feedback Exercise	Forty-five to sixty minutes

Lunch

• Individual Feedback Activity	Sixty to ninety minutes
• Team Agreements	Sixty to ninety minutes
• Next Steps	Thirty to forty minutes
• Close Session	Five to ten minutes

(continued)

Objectives

- Gain a common understanding of how the team defines trust.

- Understand the attitudes, behaviors, and actions that strengthen trust or undermine trust.

- Gain agreement on the major issues that must be addressed to rebuild trust.

- Learn a structured feedback technique to work through issues related to trust.

- Agree on what individuals and the team as a whole will do to begin rebuilding trust.

by using an overhead projector or flip chart. This is helpful if the feedback is likely to incite disagreement or controversy.

Define Trust and Its Attributes (forty-five to sixty minutes)

After the team has absorbed the feedback, lead a discussion of the data using the following questions:

- How does the team define "trust"? What common themes do you see?
- What attitudes, behaviors, and actions do most team members feel create trust?
- What attitudes, behaviors, and actions do most team members feel undermine trust?

Chart the team's collective definition of "trust" derived from the key themes. Likewise, chart the attitudes, behaviors, and actions that create trust and those that undermine it. The goal of this discussion is to identify the issues that need to be addressed. Similarly, the team needs to identify the behaviors that are critical to reestablishing trust. The trainer can ask the following questions to determine if these goals have been achieved.

- Is the definition of "trust" we've developed a good description of what's important to everyone?
- If everyone on the team exhibited these trust-creating attitudes, behaviors, and actions, could the team rebuild trust?
- Conversely, if no one on the team exhibited the attitudes, behaviors, and actions that undermine trust, can the team begin to reestablish trust?

The trainer works with the team until there is a consensus that the desirable and undesirable qualities have been adequately diagnosed and understood.

There are times when it is not possible to address all the trust-related issues during the team building. For example, there may be issues that pertain to the team's relationship with other teams or are driven by organizational factors. In these instances, you need to help the team categorize the issues into (1) issues that the team can control or that can be resolved during the team building; (2) issues which others must address; and (3) organizational issues which are beyond the team's control and not likely to change. The trainer will work with the team to focus on the issues that it can control and resolve during team building.

Feedback Techniques (thirty to forty minutes)

Put up the overheads Benefits of Giving Feedback and Feedback Guidelines (Figure 12.3).

Participants need to understand how to give and receive feedback before engaging in the Individual Feedback Activity (Figure 12.6). The guidelines in Figure 12.3 present the key points of delivering and receiving feedback. Review these guidelines and answer any questions.

Feedback Exercise (forty-five to sixty minutes)

Pass out the handout Experiential Exercise (Figure 12.4).

Conduct an experiential exercise that allows participants to practice giving and receiving feedback. Figure 12.4 offers guidelines and details to aid you.

Individual Feedback Activity (sixty to ninety minutes)

Put up the overhead Goals for the Feedback Activity (Figure 12.5).

Explain that this activity has several goals:

- To teach participants how to give and receive feedback in a trust-building manner.
- To resolve the key issues identified in pre-team-building feedback.
- To better understand the wants and needs of other team members.

It also provides an opportunity for each team member to understand how he or she helps create or undermine trust. Finally, each person will better understand how he or she is perceived by others, and have an opportunity to adopt or enhance trust-building behaviors.

Distribute the Individual Feedback Activity and the Ground Rules for Delivering Feedback (Figure 12.8).

Figure 12.6 provides a format for writing a feedback message. Distribute enough copies to each participant so that they can address one to each member of the team. Also distribute the example of a feedback message (Figure 12.7). After participants have completed the message sheets, put the team in groups of three. Team members give each other the feedback and then the groups are re-formed. This continues until each person has had an opportunity to give and receive feedback.

The guidelines for receiving feedback should be reviewed before participants present their feedback. This helps individuals remember how important it is to be nondefensive, open, and receptive to what others suggest. It is also helpful to create ground rules for delivering the feedback—whether this is done in trios or with the entire group. This helps create a safe environment and encourages team members to engage fully in the process. Figure 12.8 provides an example of ground rules. Ask each person to look at the feedback he or she received from the group and identify the major issues or themes.

Benefits of Giving Feedback

Teams can rebuild trust by using feedback to open up communication.

Effective feedback has several advantages for individual team members and the team as a whole:

- It provides insight into behavior about which an individual may not be aware.

- It helps individuals describe patterns of behavior that are hindering/enhancing trust.

- It helps team members understand the impact of their behavior on others.

- It provides an opportunity for learning and growth.

- It helps teams get relationships back on track.

(continued)

Feedback Guidelines

- Offer positives first, suggested changes second.

- Be specific versus general.

- Be descriptive versus evaluative.

- Take into account the needs of the receiver and your own needs.

- State the feedback clearly and check for comprehension.

- Do not overload others with too much feedback.

- Make sure the feedback is something the individual can change.

EXPERIENTIAL EXERCISE: DEVELOPING TRUST IN RELATIONSHIPS

GOALS

1. To explore how individuals can build or rebuild trust.

2. To help participants understand what is important to others.

3. To open up communication between team members.

GROUP SIZE

Any number of pairs of participants.

TIME REQUIRED

Forty-five to sixty minutes

MATERIALS

Copies of the Developing Trust in Relationships worksheet for each participant.

PHYSICAL SETTING

A room large enough for the participants to talk privately.

PROCESS

1. The trainer tells participants they are going to have an opportunity to explore the dynamics of trusting relationships.
2. Participants are paired up and given a copy of the Developing Trust in Relationships worksheet.
3. Each pair sits together away from other pairs. The group is advised they have thirty minutes of this activity.

(continued)

4. Following the activity the group reassembles. The trainer asks participants the following questions:
   - What did you learn about what's important to your partner?
   - What was it like to give feedback to another person?
   - What would have made it easier to give the feedback?
   - What would have made it more difficult to give the feedback?

Developing Trust in Relationships

Instructions: Both individuals are to complete each statement. One person should respond initially to the statement. Then the other person should respond. Discuss your answers and work together to understand what's important to each of you.

1. I would describe our relationship as _____.

2. One way in which we are alike is _____.

3. One way in which we are different is _____.

4. If our relationship were a film, it would be called _____.

5. I am most trustful of you when _____.

6. If I could change one thing about our past relationship it would be _____

_____.

Goals for the Feedback Activity

- To teach participants how to give and receive feedback in a trust-building way.

- To resolve the issues identified in the feedback.

- To better understand the wants and needs of other team members.

- To help individuals understand how their behaviors enhance or undermine trust.

- To help team members understand how they are perceived by others.

INDIVIDUAL FEEDBACK ACTIVITY

1. Select an area in which you want to give an individual team member feedback. Pick something that you believe is undermining trust.

Issue:

2. Write out your feedback message for the individual selected. Think about what you would like the individual to:

- Stop doing
- Do less of
- Do more of
- Start doing

3. Use the feedback guidelines to write out your message. It is particularly important that you state behaviors or actions as specific rather than general. This will help the individual better understand your requests.

Feedback Message:

---

4. Once you have written your message, decide what you will say to check for the comprehension and accuracy of your message. Typically, this is done by asking a question. For example:

- Is this how you see it?
- Can you see why I am so concerned about this?
- Is this something you were aware of?
- What's your reaction to this?
- Can we work together toward resolving this issue?

INDIVIDUAL FEEDBACK ACTIVITY EXAMPLE

1. Select an area in which you want to give an individual team member feedback. Pick something that you believe is undermining trust.

Issue:

On numerous occasions, Carl has complained to me about other team members. Rather than talking to them directly, he comes to me and criticizes their work, attitude, etc. I am uncomfortable hearing this, knowing he has not talked to the people involved.

Lately, in team meetings, he will look at me and make facial expressions when Spencer or Karen talk. I think it's his way of letting me know he doesn't respect their contribution. These are the two people on the team about whom he complains the most. Because I have not told him how I feel about his criticisms, he thinks I agree with him.

---

2. Write out your feedback message for the individual selected. Think about what you would like the individual to:

- Stop doing
- Do less of
- Do more of
- Start doing

3. Use the feedback guidelines to write out your message. It is particularly important that you state behaviors or actions as specific rather than general. This will help the individual better understand your requests.

Feedback Message:

Carl, I would like you to express your concerns about Spencer's and Karen's work directly to them—not to me. Over the past two weeks you have said to me, "They don't meet deadlines," "I don't get accurate information from them" and, "They're in over their heads in their new jobs."

It will help everyone on the team if you talk with them about your concerns. Telling me won't solve the problem you have with them and I don't want to be drawn into the issue. I don't have any problems with their work and they seem to be doing a good job. You obviously feel different and you need to talk with them about it, not me.

---

4. Once you have written your message, decide what you will say to check for the comprehension and accuracy of your message. Typically, this is done by asking a question. For example:

- Is this how you see it?
- Can you see why I am so concerned about this?
- Is this something you were aware of?
- What's your reaction to this?
- Can we work together toward resolving this issue?

GROUND RULES FOR
DELIVERING FEEDBACK

- Make sure the feedback describes exactly what you want to happen to improve trust and can provide impetus for action.
- State the feedback in terms of observed behavior and data.
- Listen to everything the person says before you respond.
- Ask questions to clarify the feedback so that you understand what's being requested of you.
- Avoid accusatory and judgmental statements both when you are giving and receiving feedback.

Instruct them to write one or two things they plan to do to address those issues. Then put the team back into small groups. Each person discusses his or her list and corrective actions. Reconvene the entire group and ask team members to take turns sharing the results of their discussion and the commitments made.

As an alternative, participants can distribute the feedback sheets to one another. This is done as a whole group, and participants deliver the feedback sheets to each other. Once everyone has had an opportunity to read their sheets, participants are instructed to write down the two or three key messages they have received. Ask them to identify the common themes first and to record other comments under the key themes. Finally, ask them to list one or two actions they will take to address the issues. This alternative works best if individuals record feedback themes and actions planned on a sheet of flip chart paper.

Overall, during this activity, it is important for the trainer to be sensitive to the group's dynamics as well as to each participant's comfort levels. Some of the things the trainer needs to take note of are:

- Comments that become personal attacks (e.g., name calling, accusations, belittling)
- Arguing about the feedback
- Silence or nonresponsiveness to feedback
- Reluctance by a participant to engage in this activity
- Defending behavior or actions or rebutting the feedback

Ground rules can help prevent some of these problems. However, the trainer must guide this activity carefully and work to minimize these difficulties.

Let the group decide if they prefer to work in small groups or use the whole team approach. Small groups are usually preferred if trust is low and each person has several things to address.

Team Agreements (sixty to ninety minutes)

The team should be encouraged to establish a few accountability agreements that support rebuilding a trusting team environment. This encourages the team to confirm and document the trust-building behaviors that are most important to them.

Conclude this activity by thanking participants for their willingness to work together to rebuild trust. Remind the team this is an important first step and how much the team benefits if everyone keeps the commitments they have just made. Finally, encourage the team to support one another as they implement new behaviors.

Next Steps (thirty to forty minutes)

The team's action plan needs to include a process for reviewing individual and team agreements regularly. Ideally, the team should meet again in thirty days and evaluate its progress. This provides an opportunity to engage in another round of individual feedback. When the team has made progress, this can be very energizing. The trainer needs to work closely with the team during this initial thirty-day period. Coaching and counseling can help the leader or individual team members implement agreements effectively.

Close Session (five to ten minutes)

Thank the group for their participation and hard work.

Quick Team Interventions

INTRODUCTION

This chapter provides examples of five quick team interventions. These can be used when it is not feasible to conduct the two-day session or when the team has specific issues that it needs to address.

The quick interventions provide team-building approaches for the following issues:

- Team purpose and mission
- Role clarification
- Team meetings
- Team decision making
- Interpersonal relations

QUICK INTERVENTION: TEAM PURPOSE AND MISSION

This is a one-and-a-half- to two-and-a-half-hour session. It is designed to:

- Create a statement of the team's mission and shared purpose
- Clarify agreement about the team's role in the organization and its contribution to the organization
- Resolve confusion about the team's purpose and build agreement about its mission

This session is useful for teams who are confused about their overall purpose or unclear about where they fit into the total organizational picture. It is also helpful when turnover or growth has significantly changed team membership. Finally, if a team is anticipating a change, this session helps it determine its future role.

LEADER'S GUIDE FOR QUICK INTERVENTIONS

Prework for the Session

The trainer gives a copy of the Mission and Shared Purpose worksheet to each participant (Figure 13.1). Participants are asked to complete the worksheet and bring it to the meeting.

Welcome and Introduction (fifteen to twenty minutes)

Put up the overhead Agenda and Objectives (Figure 13.2) and the overhead Importance of Mission Statements (Figure 13.3).

Welcome participants and review the Agenda and Objectives. Explain the purpose and importance of a well-defined and agreed upon team mission.

Team Mission and Shared Purpose (one to one and a half hours)

1. Put participants in groups of three. Provide a flip chart for each group. Ask one person in the group to lead the discussion and chart the group's ideas. Instruct participants to give everyone an opportunity to share their responses to the Mission and Shared Purpose Worksheet. Each group should chart the common themes and ideas. Instruct the groups also to chart, on a separate sheet of paper, questions or concerns about the team's mission.

2. Bring the team back together and ask one person in each group to present their list of common themes.

3. Facilitate the team in combining the common themes into one- or two-draft statements. Continue to combine ideas, delete items, and capture key thoughts until the team has a draft mission statement. Ask participants to review the lists of questions and issues generated

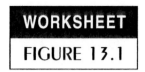

MISSION AND SHARED PURPOSE WORKSHEET

1. How would you describe the purpose of this team?

2. Is your statement of purpose in Question 1 *the team's purpose* as opposed to the broader organizational purpose? If not, how would you differentiate the team's purpose?

3. Do you believe others on the team would define the team's purpose the same way?

4. As you have defined the team's purpose, is it meaningful and important? If not, what would you change to make it more meaningful to you?

Agenda

- Welcome and introduction
- Draft mission statements
- Finalize mission statement
- Document next steps
- Evaluate the team-building session

Objectives

- Create a statement of the team's mission and shared purpose.

- Agree on the team's role and contribution of the organization.

- Resolve confusion about the team's purpose.

- Help everyone on the team gain a common understanding of what the team is expected to contribute to the organization.

Importance of Mission Statements

A shared, meaningful purpose is important for several reasons:

- It builds a common sense of direction and momentum.

- Team commitment is enhanced by working toward a commonly understood purpose.

- Individuals have an opportunity to shape a purpose that reflects what's important to them.

- Teams understand their scope of authority and boundaries.

- It is a joint creation of the team's collaborative efforts.

- Molding its purpose together helps team members respond to challenges confident of the support and help of their teammates.

during the small group discussion. Check to see if all of these have been resolved. Continue modifying the statement, answering questions and clarifying issues until the team reaches agreement on its mission.

4. Record the agreed upon statement on a flip chart and ask participants to do a final review.

5. Get agreement on the mission statement. To close the session thank participants for their hard work and efforts. Remind them that mission statements are dynamic and will need to be changed if their role in the organization changes.

As an alternative, you can:

1. Ask the team to take a few days to review the statement they have created. Get a volunteer from the team to type up the statement and distribute copies.

2. Reconvene the team within five to seven days of the first meeting. Post the mission statement and ask team members if they still agree with it.

3. Gather the team's feedback and edit the statement as necessary.

4. Get final agreement on the statement.

Document Next Steps (ten to fifteen minutes)

The trainer concludes the discussion by summarizing any next steps.

Evaluate the Session (five to ten minutes)

Spend a few minutes getting participants' feedback on the meeting. The trainer can ask:

- What worked well about this meeting?
- What improvements could you suggest?
- Thank participants for their hard work.

QUICK TEAM INTERVENTION: ROLE CLARIFICATION

This is a four- to six-hour session. It is designed to:

- Clarify the purpose of each team member's role
- Describe how each role on the team supports other roles
- Clarify mutual expectations
- Eliminate conflicts and/or misunderstandings due to role ambiguity or overlap

LEADER'S GUIDE FOR ROLE CLARIFICATION
Prework for Session

The trainer provides participants with a copy of the Role Clarification Worksheet (Figure 13.4). Each person needs to complete it and bring it to the meeting. It is essential that everyone completes the assignment. The prework allows the team to conduct the role clarification meeting in the four to six hours.

Welcome and Introduction (ten to fifteen minutes)

Put up the overheads Agenda and Objectives (Figure 13.5) and Benefits of Role Clarification (Figure 13.6).

Welcome the participants and review the Agenda and Objectives. Explain the benefits of role clarification and why it is important for teams to be clear about what each person contributes.

Clarifying Each Role (three to four hours)

The trainer leads the team through the following activity:

1. Give each person a sheet of flip chart paper or newsprint. You will also need to give them a marker. Ask each person to transfer the information on his or her Role Clarification Worksheet to the chart.

2. Solicit a volunteer to start the clarification discussion. This works best if the individual posts his or her chart so that all team members can see it.

3. The trainer leads a discussion designed to clarify the individual's roles by:

   a. Asking team members if they have questions about the individual's role.

   b. Soliciting agreement with how the individual has defined his or her role or identifying proposed changes.

   c. Discussing the individual's role until agreement is reached between the person and the team.

The trainer records on a separate sheet agreed on changes. However, if issues arise that cannot be resolved, these need to be recorded separately as next steps.

1. Steps 2 and 3 are repeated until everyone on the team has clarified his or her role.

ROLE CLARIFICATION WORKSHEET

Please answer each question and bring this worksheet with you to the team-building session. You may use additional sheets if needed.

1. What is your role on the team? Think about the contribution that you are expected to make to ensure the team fulfills its mission and goals.

2. List what you believe are your four to six major responsibilities. Focus on the major deliverables or outputs you provide. These responsibilities, in aggregate, should represent how you spend at least eighty percent of your time.

3. What do you need from others in order to do your job?

4. Do you have any questions about how your role supports or overlaps with others?

Agenda

- Welcome and introduction
- Role clarification exercise
- Mutual support agreements
- Document next steps and actions
- Evaluate the team-building session

Objectives

- Clarify each team member's role and contribution to the team.

- Ensure team members' roles are aligned with and support the team's mission and goals.

- Identify how team members support one another in the execution of their roles.

Benefits of Role Clarification

Role clarification helps teams and team members:

- Describe each person's contribution.

- Understand how each person's role supports other roles.

- Agree on mutual expectations.

- Eliminate conflicts or misunderstandings.

- Ensure everyone's work is aligned with and supports the team's mission and goals.

Document Next Steps and Actions (thirty to forty minutes)

The trainer concludes the session by summarizing the role agreements made during the meeting. An action plan documenting next steps needs to be created that:

1. Lists any issues that require further clarification or agreement. For example, you may want to review role changes with customers or other teams to ensure their agreement and support.

2. Documents issues that require additional discussion. For example, a large project team assigned quality assurance responsibilities to two team members. During the role clarification discussion, agreement was reached on how the two individuals would share this role. However, responsibility for taking corrective action was still unclear. As a next step, the two individuals agreed to meet separately with the team leader and work out an agreement.

Evaluate the Session (fifteen to twenty minutes)

Spend a few minutes getting the participants' feedback on the meeting. To do this you can refer back to the Objectives and ask team members how effective the session has been in meeting each goal.

VARIATIONS IN THE ROLE CLARIFICATION PROCESS

Another role clarification technique encourages team members to consider how much time they allocate to each major responsibility. This approach is useful if there is confusion about priorities or which tasks are most important. Figure 13.7 provides an example of the prework each person completes and brings to the session. Pass out Handout 13.4. The trainer takes the team through the following steps:

1. Beginning with the team leader, each individual describes his or her role and four to six major responsibilities. Each person also explains the percentage of time allocated to each responsibility area.

2. The team evaluates each person's list of major responsibilities and time allocation. Lead this discussion by asking each person how their activities support the team's goals. This helps the individual and team members evaluate whether or not the list of responsibilities and time allocated to each is appropriate.

3. Agreed on changes in major responsibilities or time allocation are documented.

To conclude this activity you can post each person's responsibility list.

Ask the team, "If each person uses their time as agreed on, will the team be able to fulfill its goals?" This final check may result in additional changes.

EXAMPLE OF ROLE CLARIFICATION PREWORK ALLOCATING PERCENTAGE OF TIME TO MAJOR RESPONSIBILITIES

Role: Creating marketing communication material

Major Responsibilities	Time Allocation
Design marketing brochures	30%
Help select advertising agencies	5%
Create public relations CD's	10%
Coordinate marketing campaigns for new products	30%
Monitor master project list and resolve priority conflicts	25%

QUICK INTERVENTION—TEAM MEETINGS

This is a two- to three-hour session designed to:

- Help the team diagnose its problems with meetings
- Create a plan to improve team meetings
- Identify how team members can share responsibility for effective meetings

Effective meetings are often the best way to share information, make decisions, plan the future, and solve problems. Team meetings can be a productive way of getting the group's collective work accomplished. When meetings achieve results, teams are energized and have a real sense of accomplishment.

This session enables everyone on the team to participate in creating a system and environment for effective meetings. The team has the opportunity to assess the quality of its meetings and develop techniques to improve its effectiveness. This intervention aims largely at finding ways to get more done in less time. It also also helps the team agree on how each individual can share responsibility for effective meetings. It guides teams in examining their team participation and interaction and identifies ways to strengthen their contribution to meeting success.

LEADER'S GUIDE ON TEAM MEETINGS

Welcome and Introduction (five to ten minutes)

Put up the overheads Objectives and Agenda (Figure 13.8).

Welcome participants and review the Objectives and Agenda (Figure 13.8).

Define Meetings (five to ten minutes)

Put up the overheads What Is a Meeting? (Figure 13.9) and Meeting Task and Process (Figure 13.10).

Present the definition of a meeting (Figure 13.9) and engage the team in a discussion of the type and frequency of their meetings. Share with the team the distinction between meeting "task" and "process" (Figure 13.10). Let the team know this team-building session will help it improve its meeting processes and as a result enable them to do a better job executing its tasks.

Evaluate Team's Meetings (forty-five to sixty minutes)

Pass out the handout Evaluation of Team Meetings (Figure 13.11).

Distribute the Evaluation of Team Meetings (Figure 13.11) and ask each participant to evaluate the team's meetings. Then go through the checklist and chart the results of the team's assessment. On one sheet, list the areas the team "does well" and on a separate sheet list the areas in which the team "does not do" or "does sometimes." Looking at the Do Not Do/Do Sometimes list, ask the team to brainstorm ways to make meetings more effective. Next, instruct

Objectives

- Diagnose the team's problems with meetings.

- Identify the ways in which team members can share responsibility for effective meetings.

- Create a plan to improve team meetings.

Agenda

- Welcome and introduction
- Define meetings
- Evaluate team's meetings
- Sharing responsibility
- Evaluate team-meetings technique
- Evaluate the team-building session

What Is a Meeting?

A meeting occurs any time two or more people get together face-to-face, electronically, or in a conference call in order to:

- Share information

- Make decisions, plan or take some other action

Meetings can be categorized as information sharing, action taking, or sometimes both.

Meeting Task and Process

Every meeting is comprised of *task* and *process.*

Tasks—refers to what the team is trying to accomplish in the meeting. The tasks are the reasons the group has come together and are the outputs the team wants to achieve.

Process—refers to how the team works together to accomplish its tasks. Meeting processes are the techniques a team uses to help achieve its task outputs.

Research shows that at least ninety percent of problems with meetings can be solved by improving processes.

EVALUATION OF TEAM MEETINGS

Instructions: Please read the statements below and evaluate the team's meetings.

Meeting Preparation

	1 Do Not Do	2 Do Sometimes	3 Do Well
Plan an agenda.	☐	☐	☐
Distribute an agenda.	☐	☐	☐
Determine meeting purpose and objectives.	☐	☐	☐
Talk to key stakeholders and identify their interests.	☐	☐	☐
Arrange for a meeting room, materials, and other logistics.	☐	☐	☐
Determine the decision-making method.	☐	☐	☐
Assign meeting roles such as facilitator, recorder, or timekeeper.	☐	☐	☐
Review the meeting purpose, objectives, and agenda at the beginning of the meeting.	☐	☐	☐
Set up or review ground rules.	☐	☐	☐
Agree on time limits for the meeting.	☐	☐	☐
Follow the agenda and stay on track.	☐	☐	☐
Encourage everyone to participate.	☐	☐	☐
Discourage self-oriented behaviors, such as dominating discussions, criticizing others, complaining, etc.	☐	☐	☐
Document meeting decisions, agreements, and next steps using an action plan or other format.	☐	☐	☐
Assign responsibility for preparing a meeting record, summary, or minutes.	☐	☐	☐
Evaluate the meeting and identify what worked well and what needs to be improved.	☐	☐	☐
Plan the agenda for the next meeting.	☐	☐	☐
Assign responsibility for setting up the next meeting.	☐	☐	☐

the group to look at the Do Well list and the list of improvements just brainstormed. Ask them, "If you continue to do the things on the Do Well list and implement the improvements we just brainstormed, will team meetings be productive and get results?" Continue to generate ideas until the team believes it has a good plan for effective meetings.

Sharing Responsibility (forty-five to sixty minutes)

Put up the overhead Sharing Responsibility for Effective Meetings (Figure 13.12) and pass out the handouts Sharing Responsibility Assessment (Figure 13.13) and Sharing Responsibility Action Plan (Figure 13.14).

Describe the various ways team members can share responsibility for effective meetings. Ask each person to evaluate the group's meeting behaviors using the Sharing Responsibility Assessment. Divide the team into groups of three to four and ask them to discuss their evaluations with each other. Instruct the groups to complete the Sharing Responsibility Action Plan. To do this they must (1) decide if the team demonstrates "too little," "just the right amount," or "too much" of each task and process behavior; (2) identify the task or process behaviors that are most lacking; (3) identify the task or process behaviors the team needs more of; and (4) list one to three recommendations. Reconvene the team and ask each group to present their list of actions. Instruct the team to look at the actions and determine if any important task or process functions still need to be addressed. Continue to discuss the various responsibilities and make agreements until everyone has a role in helping create an effective meeting environment.

Evaluate Team-Meetings Technique (fifteen to twenty minutes)

Put up the overhead Evaluating Team Meetings (Figure 13.15).

Review the decisions and agreements the team has made during the session. Teach the team a technique for evaluating and continuously improving team meetings. Advise the group that it is important to periodically evaluate their meetings and identify what's going well and what needs to be improved. Remind them that when improvements are identified, it is important to act on them immediately. This is another opportunity for sharing responsibility.

Evaluating the Team-Building Session (five to ten minutes)

Use the technique just demonstrated to evaluate the team-building session. Thank the team for their participation.

Sharing Responsibility for Effective Meetings

Every member of the team has responsibility for ensuring meetings are effectively set up, conducted, and the results implemented.

Task-Oriented Behaviors

Recording—listing ideas and data so the entire team can see it

Timekeeping—monitoring time contracts

Setting Priorities—focusing on key issues first

Summarizing—pulling ideas together

Explaining—clearing up confusion or confirming information

Data Seeking—focusing on facts, data and information

Decision Making—determining if the team is ready to make a decision

Sharing Responsibility for Effective Meetings

Every member of the team has responsibility for ensuring meetings are effectively set up, conducted, and the results implemented.

Process-Oriented Behaviors

Facilitating—helping the group move through the agenda and stay on track

Focusing—reminding the group of the outcomes they need to achieve and what the next step should be

Regulating—helping balance communication and making sure everyone has an opportunity to participate

Building Consensus—looking for common ground and areas of agreement

Consensus Testing—checking to see if everyone is in true agreement with the decision

Complimenting—acknowledging the contribution of others

SHARING RESPONSIBILITY ASSESSMENT

Task-Oriented Behaviors	Individuals on the Team Who Routinely Perform Each Role
Recording—listing ideas and data	
Summarizing—pulling ideas together	
Timekeeping—monitoring time contracts	
Setting Priorities—focusing on key issues first	
Explaining—clearing up confusion	
Data Seeking—focusing on facts and data	
Decision Making—determining if the team isready to make a decision	

SHARING RESPONSIBILITY ASSESSMENT

Process-Oriented Behaviors	Individuals on the Team Who Routinely Perform Each Role
Facilitating—helping the group move through the agenda and stay on track	
Focusing—reminding the group of the outcomes they need to achieve	
Regulating—balancing communication and involvement	
Building Consensus—looking for common ground and agreements	
Consensus Testing—checking to see if everyone is in true agreement with the decision	
Complimenting—acknowledging the contribution of others	
Other Behaviors: _____ _____ _____	

SHARING RESPONSIBILITY ACTION PLAN

Task-Oriented Behaviors

Too Little   Just the Right Amount   Too Much

Which task-oriented behaviors are
most lacking?

Which task-oriented behaviors do we need
more of?

Process-Oriented Behaviors

Too Little   Just the Right Amount   Too Much

Which process-oriented behaviors are
most lacking?

Which process-oriented behaviors do we
need more of?

Recommended Actions:

1. _____

2. _____

3. _____

Evaluating Team Meetings

Teams can continually improve their meetings.

Evaluating team meetings provides an opportunity to identify what went well and what needs to be improved. It is important to act immediately on the improvement areas.

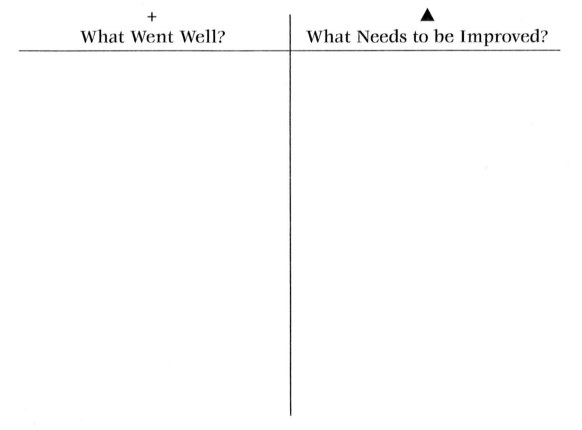

+ What Went Well?	▲ What Needs to be Improved?

Allow a few minutes at the end of each meeting and evaluate it.

QUICK INTERVENTION—DECISION MAKING

This is a four- to six-hour session. It is designed to:

- Clarify team decision-making authority.

- Agree on how each team member is to be involved in key decisions.

- Build a sense of shared responsibility for effective decision making.

This module helps ensure all team members understand the range of decision-making alternatives and when each is most appropriate. It builds agreement about how key decisions will incorporate the skill, knowledge, and viewpoints of those who need to be involved. Finally, it teaches teams when and how to use consensus decision-making. This module is useful when teams are experiencing the following problems:

- Some team members feel excluded from participation in key decisions.

- A team is not using consensus decision-making appropriately or effectively.

- The team leader doesn't believe he or she is getting appropriate involvement in decisions.

- The team is not clear about its decision-making authority or boundaries.

- It is unclear who on the team is supposed to make certain decisions.

The module includes a tutorial on decision making and a decision-charting activity. You can lead the team through both the tutorial and decision charting in one session, or you can break these up into two sessions.

LEADER'S GUIDE—UNDERSTANDING DECISION MAKING

Welcome and Introduction (fifteen to twenty minutes)

Put up the overheads Objectives and Agenda (Figure 13.16).

The trainer welcomes the participants and reviews the Objectives and Agenda.

Importance of Effective Team Decision Making (twenty to thirty minutes)

To begin the discussion ask the team to brainstorm a list of reasons why it is important for a team to make good decisions. The following questions can help stimulate discussion:

- How does effective decision making help the team achieve its mission and goals?

- What impact does decision making have on the team's ability to meet its customer's needs?

Objectives

- Clarify the team's decision making authority.

- Understand the various options for team decision making.

- Agree on how each individual will be involved in key team decisions.

- Build a sense of shared responsibility for effective decision-making.

- Understand how to build consensus.

(continued)

Agenda

- Welcome and introduction
- Importance of effective decision making
- Team decision-making options
- Application exercise
- Building consensus
- Decision charting
- Evaluate the team-building session

- How does effective decision making create an environment in which everyone can contribute their best?

- What types of problems can the team prevent by using an effective decision-making process?

The Team Decision-Making Options (forty-five to sixty minutes)

Put up the overheads Importance of Effective Decision Making (Figure 13.17), Team Decision-Making Options (Figure 13.18), and Factors to Consider When Choosing a Decision-Making Option (Figure 13.19).

Review the importance of effective team decision making (Figure 13.17) and the team decision-making options (Figure 13.18). Check to see if there are questions about any of the four options described or about the definition of consensus. Present the Factors to Consider list (Figure 13.19). Let the team know that these factors help the leader and team members decide which option is appropriate in any given situation.

Application Exercise (twenty to thirty minutes)

Put up the overheads Decision Scenarios (Figure 13.20) and Decision-Making Situations (Figure 13.21).

Divide the team into groups of two or three. Distribute the Decision Scenarios. Instruct the small groups to read each scenario and select the appropriate decision-making option. Ask them to list the factors that influenced their choice of decision-making method. As an alternative, to save time, assign a different scenario to each group. After fifteen to twenty minutes, lead a discussion of each scenario and the recommended decision-making option. Figure 13.21 lists the preferred choice for each scenario. Check with the group to see if there are any remaining questions about the decision-making options, when to use each, or the factors for selecting an option.

Building Consensus (thirty to forty minutes)

Pass out the handouts Values Clarification Activity (Figure 13.22) and Consensus Guidelines (Figure 13.23) and put up the overhead Consensus-Building Ground Rules (Figure 13.24).

Tell the team that you want to give them an opportunity to practice building consensus. Divide the team into two groups and distribute the Values Clarification worksheets. Read the instructions and give the group twenty-five minutes to complete the activity. Let the group know you do not expect them to reach a consensus in twenty-five minutes. Advise them the point of the exercise is to practice consensus-building skills and to better understand what it takes to gain consensus. Debrief the exercise with the Consensus Guidelines. Instruct the small groups to identify which guidelines the group demonstrated during their values discussion. Lead a discussion of each group's consensus-building experience. Advise the group the checklist can be useful in develop-

Importance of Effective Decision Making

There are several reasons why effective decision making is important for teams:

- It ensures the right people are involved in the right decisions in the right way.

- Individuals are clear about decision-making authority and limits.

- It helps teams select the decision-making option most appropriate to the situation.

- Team growth is enhanced by its ability to work together and reach a true consensus.

Team Decision-Making Options

The most typical forms of decision making include:

Authority or Expert

This is the traditional way decisions are made in many work settings.

The decision-making power resides in the "boss" or in someone considered to be an expert.

While this is a quick way to make decisions, it does little to develop the team members' skills or to build a joint sense of responsibility for decisions.

The quality of the decision made depends solely on the decision-maker's breadth and depth of knowledge.

(continued)

Team Decision-Making Options

The most typical forms of decision making include:

Consultative

In the consultative decision-making style one person (usually the team leader) still makes the decision but gathers input and/or buy-in before deciding on the course of action.

Consultative decision making requires more time but usually results in a better decision than the authoritative style.

The acceptance of this approach depends on the perception that those asked for input actually had influence on the decision.

It is important to have clear ground rules on exactly how the consultation will work.

Team Decision-Making Options

The most typical forms of decision making include:

Majority Vote

In this voting style of decision making the majority rules.

It is a quick way to make decisions but can result in "win/lose" situations with the "losers" not supporting the final decision.

It is important to encourage discussion of opposing positions when using this style.

In general, this method should be a fallback if a team cannot reach a true consensus.

(continued)

Team Decision-Making Options

The most typical forms of decision making include:

Consensus

Consensus decision making takes time but maximizes commitment to the decision.

Consensus is not unanimous agreement but means that everyone can live with and fully support the decision.

Team members must openly express their views to reach a true consensus. A consensus decision is usually forged out of different perceptions, opinions, and diverse viewpoints.

This style of decision making should be used for important team decisions and when buy-in is critical.

Factors to Consider When Choosing a Decision-Making Option

- Time—How much time is available?

- Importance—How important versus how trivial is the issue?

- Expertise—How much expertise and information do group members have?

- Capability—How experienced is the group in making decisions together?

- Buy-In—How much buy-in is needed to ensure implementation?

Decision Scenarios

Select the decision-making option that is appropriate for each of the following situations. Identify which factors were most important in making your selection.

Situation

1. A supervisor and her team of technicians work across three shifts. They have just received a large grant to purchase new equipment. The grant has no restrictions and the group may purchase whatever equipment they feel is most needed. The grant must be spent before the end of the fiscal year, in three months. How should the decision be made?

   Option Selected _____

Factors

_____

_____

_____

_____

_____

_____

_____

_____

Decision Scenarios

Select the decision-making option that is appropriate for each of the following situations. Identify which factors were most important in making your selection.

Situation   **Factors**

2. The plant safety coordinator has informed the facilities manager that on the latest safety test lead has been found in the water. This poses an immediate health risk. The safety coordinator has done testing at different water supply sources and cannot locate a pattern of contamination. What should the manager do?

Option Selected _____

3. An organization just completed a customer satisfaction survey. The results show that the team needs to improve several aspects of its performance. The team is expected to come up with solutions to the issues identified in the survey. What is the appropriate option to use in deciding how to respond?

Option Selected _____

(continued)

Decision Scenarios

Select the decision-making option that is appropriate for each of the following situations. Identify which factors were most important in making your selection.

Situation	**Factors**
4. An information technology team is interested in contracting with a major consulting firm for a range of services. A representative of the consulting firm has met with the team leader and offered a cost-effective way to pilot some of their information management systems. The team leader is under pressure to lower costs and provide more efficient systems. Some team members are concerned about engaging an outside consultant. They feel they can do most of the things the consultant can do and want the opportunity to develop the new information systems themselves. What's the appropriate decision-making option?	_____ _____ _____ _____ _____ _____ _____ _____

Option Selected _____

Decision-Making Situations — Example

Select the decision-making option that is appropriate for each of the following situations. Identify which factors were most important in making your selection.

Situation	**Factors**

1. A supervisor and her team of technicians work across three shifts. They have just received a large grant to purchase new equipment. The grant has no restrictions and the group may purchase whatever equipment they feel is most needed. The grant must be spent before the end of the fiscal year, in three months. How should the decision be made?

Time
_____

Importance
_____

Expertise
_____

Buy-in
_____

_____

_____

_____

_____

Recommended Option(s) *Consultative or Consensus*

(continued)

Decision-Making Situations—Example

Select the decision-making option that is appropriate for each of the following situations. Identify which factors were most important in making your selection.

Situation

Factors

2. The plant safety coordinator has informed the facilities manager that, on the latest safety test, lead has been found in the water. This poses an immediate health risk. The safety coordinator has done testing at different water supply sources and cannot locate a pattern of contamination. What should the manager do?

Time

Importance

Expertise

_____

_____

_____

_____

_____

Recommended Option(s) *Authoritative/Expert*

3. An organization just completed a customer satisfaction survey. The results show that your team needs to improve several aspects of its performance. The team is expected to come up with solutions to the issues identified in the survey. What is the appropriate option to use in deciding how to respond?

Buy-in

Importance

_____

_____

_____

_____

_____

_____

Recommended Option(s) *Consensus; Fallback - Majority Vote*

Decision-Making Situations—Example

Select the decision-making option that is appropriate for each of the following situations. Identify which factors were most important in making your selection.

Situation

4. An information technology team is interested in contracting with a major consulting firm for a range of services. A representative of the consulting firm has met with the team leader and offered a cost-effective way to pilot some of their information management systems. The team leader is under pressure to lower costs and provide more efficient systems. Some team members are concerned about engaging an outside consultant. They feel they can do most of the things the consultant can do and want the opportunity to develop the new information systems themselves. What's the appropriate decision-making option?

Recommended Option(s) _____*Consensus*_____

Factors

Importance
_____

Buy-in
_____

_____

_____

_____

_____

_____

VALUES CLARIFICATION ACTIVITY

Instructions: You and your group members have been asked to select the values that are most important to the team. In a prior meeting, the team brainstormed the following list of values:

- Flexibility
- Honesty
- Cooperation
- Dependability
- Empathy
- Sharing
- Trust
- Respect
- Efficiency
- Risk Taking
- Equity
- Openness

Each individual selects their top five values and indicates the reason for each selection on the next sheet. Next, the group works together and makes a consensus decision on their top five values. You will have ten minutes to make your individual selections and fifteen minutes to reach consensus. Please select a leader to facilitate the consensus building. *Record on the flip chart only the values on which you reach consensus.*

VALUE CLARIFICATION WORKSHEET

List of Values	Reason It Is Important

CONSENSUS GUIDELINES

Instructions: Please read through the checklist and discuss the guidelines for building a true consensus. Identify those the team demonstrated during its values discussion and those it did not demonstrate. These guidelines are useful ground rules when working toward consensus.

- ❏ Asked questions of others and didn't just try to sell ideas.
- ❏ Small agreements were acknowledged and built on to try and get a major agreement.
- ❏ Everyone participated in the discussion and it was not dominated by a few individuals.
- ❏ The group did not try to talk someone out of his or her point of view but sought ways to try to address the person's concerns.
- ❏ People were willing to stand for their point of view.
- ❏ Different views were clearly stated before each viewpoint was discussed.
- ❏ The views of all members were given equal consideration.
- ❏ Group members criticized ideas and positions, not each other.
- ❏ Ideas and suggestions were viewed from all perspectives and different perspectives were encouraged.
- ❏ All members behaved responsibly to each other.
- ❏ Real issues and differences were surfaced and clarified.

Consensus-Building Ground Rules

- Stand for your point of view; don't worry that others may prove you wrong.

- Ask questions; don't just sell your idea.

- Listen hard, especially to people with opposing positions. View differences of opinion as a help rather than a hindrance in reaching the best decision.

- Avoid trying to talk someone out of his or her viewpoint. Instead, seek ways to modify the decision to address the person's concerns.

- Don't let a few members dominate the discussion. Ask quieter, less aggressive group members for their ideas, and listen to them carefully.

- Hold out if you don't agree. Try to modify the decision so that it is more acceptable to you.

- Seek small agreements and build on these to get closer to consensus.

ing ground rules for working toward consensus. Brainstorm a list of ground rules that will help the team reach consensus. Figure 13.24 offers an example of what these ground rules might look like.

Decision Charting (forty-five to sixty minutes)

Pass out the handout Decision Charting Matrix (Figure 13.25) and put up the overhead Decision Charting Options (Figure 13.26).

Advise the team that as a final activity you want them to create a decision matrix. Tell them this will clarify how team members will be involved in key decisions. Distribute a copy of the decision charting matrix (Figure 13.25) and post a copy of the matrix on a flip chart. Begin by asking the team to brainstorm a list of key decisions. List these in the Decisions column of the posted matrix. Next, ask the team to identify if these are team or individual decisions. Ask them to take a few minutes to identify which team decisions they want to be involved in and what level of involvement they want. Explain the involvement options listed on the overhead and give participants five to ten minutes to make their choices. Then, ask each person how he or she wants to be involved in team decisions and chart each request on the matrix. When the matrix is finished, ask participants to examine it and determine if everyone is satisfied with their level of involvement. Continue making changes to the matrix until there is agreement by all team members.

Evaluate the Team-Building Session (five to ten minutes)

Close the session by reviewing the decision-making options, factors for selecting the appropriate option, consensus-building guidelines, and the decision charting matrix. Get feedback on the meeting and thank everyone for their participation.

IMPROVING INTERPERSONAL RELATIONS

Effective interpersonal relations are essential to a team's ability to work together productively and collegially. Several things contribute to effective relationships, including:

- A willingness to communicate openly and honestly about a range of issues
- The ability to tackle controversial or sensitive issues and work cooperatively toward resolution
- Respect for the feelings, ideas, and values of one another
- Acknowledging the worth and contribution of others
- A willingness to help one another
- Openness to new ideas and perspectives that may be very different from one's own
- Inclusive team processes and procedures

DECISION CHARTING MATRIX

Key Team Decisions	Team or Individual Decision	Your Role		
		Informed	Consulted	Involved
1.				
2.				
3.				
4.				
5.				
6.				
7.				
8.				
9.				
10.				

Decision Charting Options

Please indicate how you want to participate in the team's key decisions by using the following choices:

"Involved"—You want to be involved in making the final decision.

"Consulted"—You want to give input to the decision before it is made, but you don't want to be involved in making the final decision.

"Informed"—You want to be informed about the decision after it is made by others.

- A belief that others are trustworthy and have the team's best interest in mind

INDICATORS OF INTERPERSONAL RELATIONS PROBLEMS

Often teams say they have good interpersonal relations when problems exist. The team may be slow to recognize that certain behaviors indicate interpersonal difficulties. The following signs reveal that a team may be having interpersonal problems:

- Differences in personality style, work style, or similar disparities make it difficult for team members to tolerate others.
- Some individuals withdraw from group discussions and interaction.
- Team discussions degenerate into arguments and sharp remarks.
- Ideas offered by some team members are routinely dismissed.
- The team quickly polarizes rather than trying to work through issues.
- Individuals try to make others look bad, expose mistakes, etc.
- Team members do not keep commitments to one another.
- Individuals don't listen to one another.
- There is competition rather than collaboration between team members.
- Body language indicates anger, lack of patience, frustration, etc.
- Agreements and decisions made in meetings are not upheld.
- The team's humor is derisive and demeaning.

STRENGTHENING INTERPERSONAL RELATIONS

There are several things a team can do to improve its interpersonal relations. One- to two-hour team-building exercises can be used to help teams address interpersonal problems. Chapter 14 provides examples of experiential exercises that help groups deal with interpersonal issues.

Experiential Exercises

BIRTHDAY LINE-UP
Goals

1. To help participants gain insight into their communication skills
2. To help participants understand how to build agreement and consensus
3. To gain insight into how group communication breaks down

Time Required

Approximately thirty-five to forty-five minutes

Physical Setting

A room large enough so that participants can form a straight line and reconfigure themselves

Process

1. Instruct the participants to form a straight line.
2. Give the following instructions:

   Your task is to line up in order of your birth date, starting with January 1 on the far left through December 31 on the far right. Your birth date is the month and day, not the year. You cannot talk or use written communication that shows your birth date, like a driver's license. All other forms of communication—for example, sounds or gestures—are allowed. When everyone believes the group is in the right order, raise your hands. This will let me know the team has reached consensus. Any questions?

3. Give the group twenty to twenty-five minutes to do the exercise. Make notes and observe how the group:

   • Communicates nonverbally.
   • Uses gestures and other means to resolve confusion and disagreement.
   • Works together to reach consensus.

4. When all participants raise their hands (or after twenty-five minutes), go down the line and ask each person his/her birthday. If the group is in the right order, congratulate them. Ask the following questions:

   • How did you communicate with each other?
   • What made communication so difficult?
   • How did you know whether someone was in agreement or disagreement?
   • Did anyone feel pressured to come to consensus?
   • What did you learn about effective communication, especially when there is confusion?
   • What did you learn about communicating with others when there are differences of opinion?
   • What does it take to reach consensus?

5. If the team did not get the line-up correct, that is, everyone on the team is not in sequential order by birth date, also ask:

   • How did communication breakdown(s) occur?
   • What could have been done to prevent these mistakes or misunderstandings?
   • How do communications breakdowns or misunderstandings occur on the team?
   • Are there any parallels with what happened in this exercise?

VARIATION

1. Participants can be asked to select any significant date rather than their birth date.

2. You can make the exercise more challenging by:

   • Telling the participants that, in addition to no words or written communication, they cannot use hand gestures to indicate numbers, for example, holding up five fingers on one hand and three fingers on the other to indicate May 3.

TEAM COLLAGE
Goals

1. To offer the participants an opportunity to share their perceptions about the team

2. To help participants build deeper relationships with one another

3. To allow the participants to use a creative process to explore feelings about the team

Time Required

Approximately one hour

Materials

1. At least as many magazines as there are participants

2. A pair of scissors for each participant

3. One or two pages of flip chart paper and at least one felt-tipped marker for each participant

4. A roll of masking tape or transparent tape for each participant

Physical Setting

A room large enough so participants can spread out and have plenty of space in which to create their collage

Process

1. You give the following instructions:

   The members of this team have worked together and developed perceptions about the team. Today you're going to have the opportunity to share your perceptions. I've brought a number of magazines, pairs of scissors, flip chart paper, and tape. When I tell you to start, begin looking through the piles of magazines and take one that appeals to you. In addition, you are to take one pair of scissors, one or two sheets of flip chart paper, as many felt-tipped pens as you would like, and a roll of tape. Then, find a spot in the room and tape your flip chart paper to the wall. Go through the magazine and cut out pictures that describe the team's interpersonal relationships and dynamics. Think about how the team communicates, collaborates, shares power, gives feedback, handles mistakes, resolves conflict, listens to each other, respects differences of opinion, and so on. Your collage should reflect both the team's strengths and weaknesses. It should also illustrate what the team needs to do to improve its interpersonal relations.

2. After answering questions, tell the participants that they have twenty-five minutes.

3. After twenty-five minutes, ask the participants to stop their work. Each person describes his or her collage to others in the group. After everyone has finished, you ask:

- What do you see as the team's interpersonal strengths?
- What do you believe are the team's interpersonal weaknesses?
- What are one or two things the team can do to improve interpersonal relations?

Encourage the team to identify recurring themes and build consensus around the most commonly mentioned areas of strength, weakness, and improvement. Chart these responses.

4. To conclude the activity the trainer summarizes team strengths, weaknesses, and improvement areas.

VARIATION

Rather than asking each individual to do a collage, form pairs or trios. Ask these small groups to create the collage. This allows team members to discuss similarities and differences of perception while creating their collage.

TEAM PICTURE

Goals

1. To offer participants an opportunity to graphically depict how the team is working now and how it can improve its effectiveness

2. To allow participants to create a vision for the team

3. To allow participants to use a creative process to describe the team

Time Required

Approximately one hour

Materials

1. One or two sheets of flip chart paper

2. At least two or three felt-tip markers for each participant

3. A five-inch strip of masking tape for each participant

Physical Setting

A room large enough so participants can spread out and have plenty of room to draw their pictures

Process

1. Give the following instructions:

   You will now have an opportunity to draw a team picture. Please take one or two sheets of flip chart paper, at least two felt-tip markers, and a strip of tape. Your task is to draw two pictures of this team. The first picture depicts the team as it is now. It should reveal how you feel about the team and capture one or two themes that best describe the team as you see it. The second picture should depict your vision of what you would like the team to be in the future. You can divide one sheet of paper in half and draw both pictures on one sheet, or draw each picture on a separate sheet of chart paper.

2. After answering questions, tell participants that they have twenty minutes.

3. After twenty minutes, ask the participants to stop their work. Each participant describes his or her pictures to the entire group. Ask the entire team, "What common themes are expressed in the team visions?" Chart the participants' responses under the heading, Team Vision. Ask the team, "What else would you like to add to complete the vision? Think about the ideal situation. What other suggestions do you have?" Continue to chart participants' ideas until they are satisfied with the vision.

4. You can conclude the exercise with the team vision. As an alternative, ask:

- What would each team member need to do in order to achieve the vision?
- What are barriers to our vision? What do we need to do to overcome them?
- What opportunities will we have in the next three to six months to move toward accomplishing our vision?

Record participant responses to some or all of these questions. Identify which responses can be turned into team actions, and list on the Action Plan.

WHAT DID YOU HEAR?

Goals

1. To illustrate how mistakes and disruptions in communication occur
2. To gain an awareness of how team members communicate with one another
3. To gain an understanding of what works and does not work in information sharing

Time Required

Forty to sixty minutes

Materials

The Information Sheet (Figure 14.1)

Physical Setting

A room large enough so that participants can move around in small groups

Process

1. Ask for six to eight volunteers (or approximately half of the team).
2. Ask the volunteers to go outside the meeting room.
3. Distribute the Information Sheet (Figure 14.1) to the team members who remained in the meeting room. Ask each person to read the Information Sheet. After checking to see if there are any questions, collect the sheets.
4. Bring the volunteers back into the room. Each volunteer is paired up with an individual who read the Information Sheet. Give the following instructions:

   Please explain to your partner the most important information on the Information Sheet. Each person can transmit the information in his or her own way, without help. The volunteer is allowed to ask questions to clarify what the communicator said.

5. Allow the pairs three to five minutes to transmit and receive the information.
6. Then display the Information Sheet on the overhead or flip chart and ask the volunteers the following questions:
   - How much of this information was communicated to you?
   - Did you receive all the information you considered to be pertinent?
   - What information was omitted that you consider important?
     Volunteers then discuss their experience.
7. Lead a discussion about how what happened in this exercise is similar to what happens in the workplace.

INFORMATION SHEET

There is a rumor that everyone on this team will get a big promotion. It's important that each person do a few things to qualify for promotion.

First, come to work thirty minutes early for the next two weeks.

Second, make sure you wear blue every Friday.

Third, smile whenever you enter the building.

Although it's not required, bringing strawberries or chocolate to the boss will help ensure your promotion.

It's a good idea not to tell too many people about this, otherwise they might get suspicious. Make sure you only tell these rules to people born in May and August.

GETTING CONSENSUS

Goals

1. To allow participants to investigate the dynamics involved in decision-making

2. To help participants experience the way in which they resolve conflict

Time Required

Sixty to ninety minutes

Materials

The Getting Consensus sheet (Figure 14.2)

Physical Setting

A room large enough so that participants can form small groups

Process

1. Assemble the participants into subgroups of five to six members each.

2. Distribute copies of the Getting Consensus worksheet (Figure 14.2) and ask participants to read it. After checking for questions about the task, give each subgroup these instructions:

   Appoint a leader of your subgroup. This person will facilitate the discussion and encourage everyone to work toward consensus. You will have thirty minutes to reach consensus.

3. After thirty minutes stop the activity and ask the following questions:

   - How many groups reached consensus?
   - Was it true consensus or did some people feel pressured to agree?
   - How did the group handle conflicting views?
   - What attitudes and behaviors helped you reach agreement?
   - What attitudes and behaviors made it difficult to reach agreement?
   - What values surfaced?
   - How did these values make it more difficult or less difficult?
   - What did you learn about consensus decision-making that you can apply to day-to-day work?

GETTING CONSENSUS

Situation

You are a member of a task force that has been asked to oversee the downsizing of a department. There are ten individuals in the department and jobs for only six people. These six people will be reassigned to other groups and the remaining four will be out of work. Everyone must agree on the six who will be offered new jobs. Voting is not allowed. You will have thirty minutes to reach agreement.

The ten people in the department are as follows:

1. A fifty-year-old divorced woman who reentered the workforce three years ago after raising five children.

2. A thirty-five-year-old engineer who is known to be a confirmed racist.

3. A former priest who left the Catholic Church under questionable circumstances but who is performing well on the job.

4. A thirty-year-old woman who is putting herself through school.

5. A forty-year-old white male whose wife is dying of cancer.

6. An opinionated woman who has a strong track record and has been lobbying for promotion.

7. A twenty-six-year-old man who is a strident Republican.

8. A woman who works two jobs to support her invalid parents.

9. A man who was formerly a member of the Democratic National Committee.

10. A talented man with several years of service who is a homosexual.

TEAM MEMBER CHARACTERISTICS
Goals

1. To help participants obtain more realistic perceptions of their attitudes and behaviors

2. To improve relationships among team members

3. To gain awareness of how each team member can improve his or her effectiveness

Time Required

Approximately sixty to ninety minutes

Materials

The Team Member Characteristics list (Figure 14.3)

Physical Setting

A room large enough so that participants can form small groups

Process

1. The participants are instructed to form triads and are given copies of the Team Member Characteristics list (Figure 14.3).

2. Each participant is instructed to circle the five positive characteristics and the five negative characteristics that best describe him or her. Allow ten minutes for individuals to make their selection.

3. After everyone has completed the list, ask one person in each group to begin the discussion by sharing the positive and negative characteristics chosen. The person provides a brief explanation about why these characteristics were selected. Then the other members of the group provide feedback to the individual. The feedback should describe areas of agreement or disagreement with the person's perception. Stress that it is important to give feedback on both positive and negative perceptions. Feedback such as, "You don't have any negative traits" is not acceptable. The trainer states that the goal of this exercise is to help each person understand how others perceive their strengths and weaknesses as a team member.

4. Allow ten to twelve minutes for individuals to share their perceptions and get feedback from others.

5. After the groups have finished the exercise, ask:
   • What are some of the things you learned about yourself?
   • Were your perceptions accurate?
   • Was the feedback useful?

6. Ask everyone to think about the feedback they received and to write down one to two things they will do in response to it. Instruct individuals to share these commitments with their small groups.

TEAM MEMBER CHARACTERISTICS

Positive Adjectives That Describe You	Negative Adjectives That Describe You
1. Frank	1. Unmotivated
2. Assertive	2. Competitive
3. Honest	3. Unrealistic
4. Decisive	4. Rigid
5. Open	5. Stubborn
6. Analytical	6. Aloof
7. Adaptable	7. Unwilling
8. Reliable	8. Flighty
9. Cooperative	9. Unreliable
10. Hardworking	10. Passive
11. Motivated	11. Self-centered
12. Helpful	12. Complaining
13. Trustworthy	13. Selfish
14. Enthusiastic	14. Complacent
15. Talented	15. Argumentative
16. Creative	16. Demeaning
17. Wise	17. Disorganized
18. Skilled	18. Apathetic
19. Problem solving	19. Defensive
20. Intelligent	20. Uncommitted

MY CONTRIBUTION TO THE TEAM

Goals

1. To offer participants an opportunity to give and receive feedback

2. To allow participants to compare their self-perceptions with others' perceptions of them

3. To encourage individuals to learn how they can be more effective as team members

Time Required

Approximately sixty to ninety minutes

Physical Setting

A room large enough so that participants can form small groups

Process

1. Explain that this is an opportunity for each person to share what he or she contributes to the team and get feedback from others about their self-perception.

2. Ask each person to take a few minutes and write down their responses to the following questions:

   • "I see myself as a valuable member of the team because _____."

   • "I believe I could be more valuable to the team if I _____."

3. Ask for a volunteer to begin the discussion and give the person two to three minutes to answer both questions.

4. After the volunteer has finished, ask the other group members to spend five to ten minutes providing the individual with feedback on their perceptions of him or her. Stipulate that those giving feedback should introduce their comments with the phrase, "I see you . . . ."

5. Steps 3 and 4 are repeated until everyone has had a chance to share their self-perception and get feedback from others.

6. Lead a summarizing discussion by asking these questions:

   • How close were your self-perceptions to others' perception of you?
   • What traits, attitudes, and behaviors were described as most valuable to the team?
   • What kinds of traits, behaviors, and attitudes did individuals offer in order to be a more valuable team member? Were there any common themes?

GROUP PROJECT
Goals

1. To participate in an exercise that helps participants experience group dynamics

2. To help participants examine how they work together to accomplish a task

Time Required

Approximately thirty-five to forty-five minutes

Materials

Flip chart paper, tape rolls, felt-tip markers, scissors, Styrofoam cups, and multicolored construction paper

Physical Setting

A room large enough so that participants can spread out and do a building project

Process

1. Divide the group into three to four teams.

2. Give participants the following instructions:

   You are going to do a project together. I am going to distribute the following materials to each team:

   - one sheet of paper.
   - one roll of tape
   - two felt-tip markers
   - one pair of scissors
   - five Styrofoam cups
   - three sheets of construction paper

   Each team is going to use these materials to construct an art object. You need to create a sculpture or statue that is at least five feet high. It must be a free-standing art object—that is, it can't be taped to the floor—and will be evaluated based on its height (that is, at least five feet) and creative design. You will have ten minutes to plan your object and twenty minutes to build it. I will start timing once all the materials are distributed. Any questions?

3. Distribute the materials and instruct the group to begin planning their artwork. After ten minutes, let them know that the planning period is over and that they should begin building.

4. Give the group a time warning after fifteen minutes. After twenty minutes, instruct the group to stop work.

5. Ask each group to describe their art object. Measure each to determine if it meets the five-foot requirement. You can use someone in the class who is close to five feet as your "yardstick." Check to make sure each one is also freestanding, that is, not taped to the floor or a table.

6. Congratulate the team on their artwork's creativity and their ingenuity in meeting the criteria.

7. Debrief the exercise by asking the following questions:

   - How many individuals were actively involved in the planning process and the building process?
   - Did one person emerge as the leader or did the leadership rotate?
   - Who influenced the discussion most? Who influenced the least? How?
   - Who in the team was most motivated to carry the task through to completion?
   - How well did team members cooperate with one another?
   - Was there competition between group members?
   - What process was used to agree on the design of the artwork?
   - Did the artwork gradually evolve or did it completely change scope and direction? Who initiated changes?
   - What did you learn about your own behavior?
   - How was this experience similar to experiences on the team?

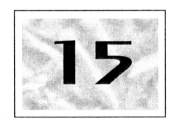

Supporting Teams

INTRODUCTION

The Team-Building Workshop presents various ways to use team building to strengthen team performance and thereby to enhance organizational success. It is a mistake to assume teams are the only way to meet today's competitive challenges. The decision to use teams must be evaluated in consideration of the organization's broader strategy, structure, and systems. But when the decision is made to commit to a team-based organization, teams must be supported.

This is a critical issue because teams, and consequently team building, will succeed only if they receive support. What does it mean to "support teams"?

When an organization is committed to teams, the top management makes it known that team execution represents the future of the organization. Policies, practices, structures, values, and systems that don't support teams change. Rewards and recognition, including advancement, are closely tied to team performance. The highest priority projects are assigned to teams. Barriers to team execution are eliminated and resources are provided, whether this is training, personnel, technology, or other things. Finally, teamwork is encouraged at all levels of the organization. Informal teamwork is as prevalent as formal teams.

LEADING TEAMS

The team leader plays a major role in supporting teams. Throughout this book we have described the leader's role in ensuring the success of team building. Team leaders who are responsive to team needs, interested in team growth, and willing to change help teams deliver their best. Here are other things managers can do to support their teams.

Every year, the team changes in some way. As the team grows and matures, leaders must examine whether they are leading in a way that meets the team's needs. For example, as team members develop new skills, the leader needs to do likewise. One opportunity to do this is to look at the feedback gathered prior to the team-building session. The leader should ask, Is my leadership contributing to any of the problems expressed? or Is my leadership contributing to, or inhibiting, the team's growth and development? An honest examination usually reveals ways in which the manager can develop stronger leadership skills. This is essential for continued team development. When managers demonstrate their commitment to personal growth, team members are more willing to work to improve their performance. When managers exhibit a willingness to stretch and acquire new skills, team members gain the confidence to do likewise.

Second, managers must use different strategies to help teams deliver their best. Teams have different needs as they move from inception to maturity. The challenge is to lead a team through its stages of development so that its output makes an increasingly greater contribution to organizational success. What does this look like for each stage of development?

When teams first come together, individuals are getting to know one another. Generally everyone is on his or her best behavior. This is when team members feel the least safe. Leaders should expect teams to be hesitant to share ideas or participate openly in team processes. This is a testing phase and team members want to know their boundaries. They are appraising how much involvement the leader desires versus how much control the leader will exercise. Also, there isn't a great deal of creativity yet. The leader needs to provide clear structure, share his or her expectations, and encourage involvement. The leader's vision of what the team can accomplish working together is a powerful way to communicate the team's potential and encourage full enrollment.

As the team gets to know one another, conflicts between members, challenges to the leader, and other unsettling behaviors are manifested. This can be a creative and productive time. Team members are getting comfortable with one another, exploring new relationships, and sharing different viewpoints. It is critical for the leader to encourage this behavior. Managing the group's energy, channeling conflict into creative ideas, and keeping the team focused on its mission and goals are important. This is the leader's opportunity to begin planning high-involvement meetings that require active participation and shared leadership. The team learns that constructive conflict can lead to innovation and the opportunity to deliver breakthrough results.

Gradually, team members develop a strong sense of team identity, and settle into their roles. The team has a sense of success and achievement. However, the leader may find individuals are so determined to prevent conflict that they don't share controversial ideas and avoid dealing with team problems. Similarly, there can be such an emphasis on agreement that the best ideas aren't surfaced or discussed. The leader needs to discourage groupthink and encourage the expression of diverse views. It is important to help team members develop respect for new ideas, different approaches, and uncommon perspectives. Leaders who help teams stretch their thinking facilitate both individual and team growth. This is the time to use team building to bring out issues and challenge the team to take a major step in improving results, processes, and relationships.

Finally, team members figure out how to engage differences and get the job done at the same time. The leader's challenge is to prevent complacency. This is difficult because the team may resist change. Leaders help maintain or renew team momentum by introducing new challenges and setting higher standards. Feedback from customers and other key stakeholders identifies opportunities for continued growth. Similarly, the leader challenges the team to play a stronger role in meeting strategic challenges.

COACHING TEAMS

Successful team leaders think of themselves as coaches. They recognize their role is to help the team accomplish its mission, goals, and deliver the best products or services to customers. Consequently, they are actively engaged in coaching individuals and the team. These leaders are quick to spot coaching opportunities and use everything, both success and failure, as opportunities to coach. This accelerates team growth and facilitates strong individual performance.

VALUING DIFFERENCES

Teams don't work well unless each member feels valued. This feeling begins with the leader. Each person brings a unique set of skills and abilities to the team. The collective application of these enables the team to perform and excel. Effective leaders value not just the contribution made but also each person. When team members feel the results they produce are more important than who they are, morale suffers. Consequently, it is important to recognize each person's special contribution to the team.

Some individuals' work will bear more directly on goal achievement than others. But each person delivers results that help the team succeed. The leader's recognition of this builds each person's sense of worth and yields strong commitment to the team.

BUILD INVOLVEMENT AND SHARED LEADERSHIP

Leaders encourage shared leadership by the way they communicate. Figure 15.1 illustrates how team leaders can do this. Team members interpret information sharing as access to power and a sign of trust. The leader has an opportunity to use communication techniques as a way to facilitate growth. Similarly, Figure 15.2 describes what managers can do to increase shared leadership by empowering teams to take on increasing responsibility for the work performed.

FIGURE 15.1

BUILDING INVOLVEMENT THROUGH COMMUNICATION

Level of Shared Leadership

Hierarchical Transition to Team	Participative	High Involvement	Shared Leadership
• Routine information • New developments • Special announcements • Employees kept up-to-date • Employee views sought periodically on selected issues	• Deeper/more thorough information provided to help improve work performance • Broader range of information shared • Use information to consciously build expertise • Employees encouraged to seek information	• Employees have access to most of information managers have • Important to understand strategic issues and priorities • Information outside the organization is as important as internal • Strong two-way information flow; managers learn as much from employees as employees learn from managers	• Employees responsible for ensuring ... ... information • Employee to employee or team to team, information flow without managers in the communication chain

Communication and Information Sharing

FIGURE 15.2

CREATING SHARED LEADERSHIP

Managers use several methods to create shared leadership. Typical activities characterize each level of employee involvement, from low to high. The following descriptions will help you identify the current level of participation in your group and provide ideas for how to increase shared ownership.

Hierarchical Transition to Team	Participative Involvement	High Involvement	Shared Leadership
• Managers regularly schedule meetings in which they brief employees on routine operations. • Special meetings are called to announce new developments. • Periodic roundtable discussions seek employees' views on problems or issues before making a decision. • Some managers may involve employees by using suggestion systems. • "Press conference" meetings allow employees to voice concerns and/or request information about events.	• Task forces are used to address a particular issue. Selected employees (often from more than one department) are asked to solve specific problems rather than offer a broad range of ideas. • Managers regularly ask groups of employees within their department to solve a particular problem relating to the department's effectiveness or find a way to improve something the department is doing (policy, program, or process). • Managers from different departments put together cross-functional teams to improve some aspect of their working relationship.	• Managers ask employees to take on management responsibilities, e.g., budgeting, scheduling, planning, etc. • Managers create long-term project teams and serve as the team coach. • Managers meet with team members for planning, problem solving, and coordinating with other teams. There is an emphasis on the strategic as well as the day-to-day. • Information is communicated to the team about customers and the organization's performance as a whole. Information is shared extensively.	• Members of the team are responsible for setting goals, budgeting, scheduling, and interacting directly with customers. • The manager's time and energy are focused on strategic issues. Managers meet with the team regularly to provide resources, information, and guidance. • Managers rarely get involved in day-to-day operational decisions and activities but are still accountable for team performance. • Representatives from many departments form short-term project teams to deal with issues of strategic importance to the organization, such as new product development.

(continued)

FIGURE 15.2

(CONTINUED)

Hierarchical Transition to Team	Participative Involvement	High Involvement	Shared Leadership
	• Managers use routinely scheduled staff meetings to get input before planning team activities or making critical decisions. • Employees recommend more effective ways for work to be designed.	• Managers meet periodically with employee teams who are addressing team or organizational issues. These meetings report the status of work-in-progress and allow managers the opportunity to provide input, give feedback, and keep the team on track.	• Managers coach teams and continuously expand their boundaries.

CONCLUSION

Team building is an important strategy for team performance, growth, and development. It is a process that begins with identifying a need and renews itself by ongoing examination of ways to strengthen a team's contribution to the organization. The success of team building requires an organizational commitment to teams. It is ensured by the leader's dedication to personal growth as well as team growth and development.

Suggested Reading

Agreements for Excellence. IMPAQ Organizational Improvement Systems, 1991.

Burke, W. Warren. *Organization Development,* 1982.

Doyle, Michael, and David Strauss. *How to Make Meetings Work,* 1976.

Dyer, William G. *Team Building: Current Issues and New Alternatives,* 1995.

Graham, Robert J. *Project Management As If People Mattered,* 1989.

Huse, Edgar R., and Thomas G. Cummings. *Organization Change and Development,* 1988. Pp. 63–76.

Katzenbach, Jon R., and Douglas K. Smith. *The Wisdom of Teams,* 1993.

Moran, Linda, Ed Musselwhite, and John H. Zenger. *Keeping Teams on Track,* 1996.

Phillips, Steven L., and Robin L. Elledge. *The Team-Building Source Book,* 1990.

COMPLETE SET OF OVERHEADS FOR THE TEAM-BUILDING WORKSHOP

FIGURE 5.3

Objectives

The objectives of this data feedback meeting are the following:

- Agree on the team's strengths and weaknesses.

- Identify the major issues that need to be addressed.

- Plan the next steps.

FIGURE 5.4

Agenda

- Introduction
- Review the feedback.
- Identify major themes.
- Plan the next steps.
- Close the session.

FIGURE 5.5

Data Gathering Meeting Ground Rules

- Ask questions to clarify data, but don't criticize findings you don't agree with.

- Listen to others' perspective.

- Respect differences of opinion.

- Focus on the issues that are having the greatest impact on team performance.

- Participate actively in discussions.

FIGURE 5.6

Data Discussion Questions

- What major themes or issues do you see?
- What team strengths emerge?
- What are the major weaknesses of the team?
- In what areas do you agree with the data?
- In what areas do you disagree with the data?
- Are there any major issues the team needs to address that are not reflected in the data?
- Where should the team begin in order to improve its effectiveness?
- Which issues are the most important to address in the next three months?
- Can the team address all these issues or are some outside your control?
- What major categories could we group these issues into?

FIGURE 6.1

Objectives

- Review the characteristics of effective teams so that everyone understands what it takes to build a successful team.

- Discuss the team's feedback so that everyone understands how others perceive the team's strengths and weaknesses.

- Agree on the team's mission, that is, a shared, meaningful purpose.

- Agree on four to six specific, measurable team goals.

- Agree on the roles and responsibilities of each team member and the team leader.

- Agree on how the team will work together and create agreements to ensure individual and mutual accountability.

- Assess the team's skills and create a learning plan.

- Create an action plan that documents team agreements, decisions, and next steps.

- Evaluate the team-building session in order to identify ways to improve future team-building sessions.

FIGURE 6.2

Agenda: Building the Essentials of Team Effectiveness

DAY ONE

TOPIC	TIME
• Welcome and introduction	Five to ten minutes
• Review agenda and objectives	Five to ten minutes
• Expectations	Fifteen to twenty minutes
• Characteristics of teams	Fifteen to twenty minutes
• Review of feedback	Forty to sixty minutes
• Shared mission and purpose	Forty-five to sixty minutes
• Break	Ten minutes
• Team goals	Forty-five to seventy minutes

LUNCH

• Team-building activity	Forty-five to sixty minutes
• Roles and responsibilities	Ninety minutes to two hours
• Summarize day one action plan	Twenty to thirty minutes
• Close day one	Five to ten minutes

Agenda: Building the Essentials of Team Effectiveness

DAY TWO

TOPIC	TIME
• Introduction	Five to ten minutes
• Review day one	Twenty to thirty minutes
• Common, collaborative approach	Forty-five to sixty minutes
• Break	Fifteen minutes
• Accountability agreements	Ninety minutes to two hours

LUNCH

• Team-building activity	Forty-five to sixty minutes
• Skill assessment and plan	Sixty to ninety minutes
• Finalize action plans	Twenty to thirty minutes
• Next steps	Twenty to thirty minutes
• Evaluate team-building session	Ten to fifteen minutes
• Close day two	Five to ten minutes

FIGURE 6.5

What Is a Team?

A team is a group of interpendent individuals who have complementary skills and are committed to a shared, meaningful purpose and specific goals.

They have a common, collaborative work approach, clear roles and responsibilities, and hold themselves mutually accountable for the team's performance.

Effective teams display confidence, enthusiasm, and seek continuously to improve their performance.

FIGURE 6.6

Characteristics of Effective Teams

Real teams are characterized by the following:

❏ A shared, meaningful purpose or mission

❏ A set of specific and measurable goals

❏ A common and collaborative work approach

❏ Well-defined roles and responsibilities

❏ Mutual accountability for the team's response

❏ The skills required to do the job and a commitment to continuous learning and improvement

❏ Passion, as demonstrated by confidence and enthusiasm to do their best

FIGURE 6.7

Components of Team Mission

A team's shared and meaningful purpose describes what it is expected to contribute to the organization.

It describes the following:

- The common direction of the team and explanation of why it exists

- The customers the team serves and those who receive its outputs

- The products and/or services it provides

- Its overall contribution to the organization and how it fits into larger picture

- Any other characteristics that are important to the team's success (e.g., quality, service and technology)

FIGURE 6.8

SMART Goals

Team goals need to meet the following "SMART" characteristics:

S–Specific

M–Measurable

A–Attainable

R–Results-oriented

T–Time-based

An example of an effective goal statement is the following:

"Improve customer responsiveness so that all requests are responded to within forty-eight hours."

"Upgrade every department's information technology system by installing the latest version of XPLS-WIN by June 30."

FIGURE 6.9

Sample Roles and Responsibilities

Instructions:

- Describe your role on the team in one or two sentences.
- List your four to six major responsibilities. This list should represent how you spend ninety percent of your time.

Example:
Role:

- Plan, facilitate, and help implement the results of team-building session.

Major Responsibilities:

- Collect feedback before the team-building session to determine how each person views the team's strengths and weaknesses
- Work with the team leader to design the two-day session and plan the agenda
- Coordinate all logistics required to make the team building successful
- Facilitate the team-building session and ensure all objectives are met
- Prepare a follow-up report that documents the results of the team building

FIGURE 6.10

Clarification Questions

- Does anyone have any question about this individual's role on the team?

- Are there any concerns about what this individual has presented?

- Do you feel something important has been omitted and needs to be added?

- Are there any changes you would suggest that would strengthen this individual's contribution to the team?

FIGURE 6.11

Feedback Questions: Evaluating Day One

- What did you find helpful about today's team-building session?

- Are there any issues discussed today that were not adequately addressed?

- Is there anything about the way the session was conducted that you would like to see handled differently tomorrow?

FIGURE 6.12

Common and Collaborative Approach

Effective teams reach agreement on how they will work together. This is their common approach. They also ensure that they work collaboratively, using the skills and talents of each team member.

The major aspects of common and collaborative approach are:

- making decisions
- conducting meetings
- providing opportunities for everyone to participate
- communicating within the team and sharing information
- valuing the contribution of each team member
- demonstrating mutual support, trust, and commitment
- working with other teams
- interacting interpersonally
- responding to changes with flexibility
- handling work agreements and utilizing skills
- encouraging innovation and new approaches
- resolving conflicts

FIGURE 6.13

Definition of Accountability

Accountability is a commitment team members make to themselves and their team members to demonstrate attitudes, behaviors, and actions that promote team effectiveness.

Accountable team members fully accept their membership in the team and feel personally responsible for the team's results.

A second aspect of accountability is mutual accountability. This means team members feel responsible to one another for everything that happens within the team. Commitments made to the team are important and upheld. The team provides feedback and makes agreements in order to deal with problems that arise and continuously improve its performance.

FIGURE 6.14

Mutual Accountability

Team members demonstrate mutual accountability when they:

- Hold themselves accountable for everything that happens within the team, rather than expecting the team leader to hold them accountable.

- Are willing to take personal responsibility for what they have or have not contributed to the team.

- Represent the team accurately to others.

- Accept the team's feedback and modify their behaviors based on that feedback.

- Believe it is important for each member to understand how his or her personal choices affect the team.

- Consider how their actions will impact other members of the team and do what is in the best interest of the team.

FIGURE 6.15

Contracting
for Accountability

Accountability agreements are contracts
team members make with each other. They
are designed to clarify:

(1) What the team wants to do in order to
    improve some aspect of its
    performance.

(2) What each team member will do to
    uphold the agreement.

Accountability agreements are different
from team norms or ground rules. These
agreements are designed to help the team
handle issues that are blocking team
effectiveness or impeding team growth.
They require thorough discussion by all
team members.

FIGURE 6.16

The Four Principles of Accountability Agreements

1. Team members agree to hold themselves accountable for keeping the agreements.

2. Team members agree to hold one another accountable for keeping the agreements.

3. The team agrees to use regular feedback to keep themselves and others accountable.

4. Team members work together to help one another fulfill the accountability agreements.

FIGURE 6.17A

Sample Team Agreement

Issue: Keeping commitments and meeting deadlines.

Agreement

Team members will keep their commitments to one another.

Clarifications

1. Speak up if you can't do something you've been asked to do.
2. If you cannot meet a commitment, give the other person as much advance notice as possible.
3. Put team commitments and priorities first.

FIGURE 6.17b

Sample Team Agreement

Issue: Involving others in special projects.

Agreement

Team members will look for ways to involve others in special projects.

Clarifications

1. Talk to others to see if they have the skills required and don't assume they have nothing to contribute.

2. Explain what you need from others so they can make an informed decison about whether or not they can help.

FIGURE 6.17c

Sample Team Agreement

Issue: Handling conflicts and disagreements.

Agreement

Team members will work with one another to resolve conflicts or disagreements.

Clarifications

1. Talk directly to the person with whom you have the disagreement or conflict before you involve the team leader.

2. State your view of the issue and listen to the other's view.

3. Be willing to compromise and work toward a solution both parties can agree to.

4. Don't get other team members involved in the discussion who are not part of the conflict or disagreement.

FIGURE 6.18

Skills Assessment and Plan

Skill Assessment Questions

- Are there any skills critical to achieving the team's mission and goals missing or underrepresented on the team?

- Are there others outside the team who can provide these skills?

- Does the team need to upgrade its technical or functional expertise in any area?

- Is there a need for training in any of the following skills:
  - problem solving
  - decision making
  - communication, that is, feedback, listening, speaking up, etc.

- Are there any other areas in which the team needs training in order to fulfill its mission and achieve its goals?

FIGURE 9.3

Agenda: Project Teams

Day One

Topic	Time
• Introduction	Five to ten minutes
• Expectations	Five to ten minutes
• Definition of a team	Fifteen to twenty minutes
• Characteristics of effective cross-functional project teams	Fifteen to twenty minutes
• Review charter and team feedback	One and a half to two hours
• Team vision of success	Sixty to ninety minutes

LUNCH

Topic	Time
• Team-building activity	Sixty to ninety minutes
• Team leader and team member roles and responsibilities	Sixty to ninety minutes
• Summarize day one	Twenty to thirty minutes
• Close day one	Ten to fifteen minutes

Agenda: Project Teams

Day Two

Topic	Time
• Introduction	Ten to fifteen minutes
• Review day one	Fifteen to twenty minutes
• Project phases and key milestones	Sixty to ninety minutes
• Common approach and accountability agreements	Sixty to ninety minutes

LUNCH

Topic	Time
• Stakeholder analysis and plan	Sixty to ninety minutes
• Skill resource assessment	Sixty to ninety minutes
• Finalize action plan and agreements	Thirty to forty minutes
• Next steps	Ten to fifteen minutes
• Evaluate team building	Ten to fifteen minutes
• Close two-day session	Five to ten minutes

Objectives: Project Teams

- Understand the characteristics of effective project teams so that everyone has a shared picture of success.

- Review the team's charter so that all team members understand what is expected.

- Agree on the team's vision of success.

- Agree on team member, team leader, and sponsor roles and responsibilities.

- Create accountability agreements in order to clarify mutual expectations about how the team will work together.

- Plan major project phases and identify key milestones.

- Design a stakeholder plan based on a stakeholder analysis.

- Assess skills and resources in order to identify what the team requires in order to be successful.

- Create an action plan that documents actions, agreements, and next steps.

FIGURE 9.4

Definition of a Project Team

Cross-functional project teams come together only for the life of a project. They bring together individuals with complementary skills from various disciplines or functions and are chartered to achieve a specific mission and project goals. To be effective they must agree on a collaborative work approach, roles, and mechanisms to hold one another accountable, and have the skills and resources required.

FIGURE 10.3

Objectives

- Gain a clear understanding of the nature of conflict.

- Review the team's feedback and identify the issues that need to be resolved.

- Understand personal styles of handling conflict.

- Learn techniques for conflict resolution.

- Create accountability agreements that will serve as conflict resolution guidelines.

- Agree on the next steps.

AGENDA
Resolving Team Conflict

Day One

Topic	Time
• Introduction	Five to ten minutes
• Hopes and concerns	Twenty to thirty minutes
• Ground rules	Fifteen to twenty minutes
• Defining conflict	Thirty to forty minutes
• Review of feedback	Thirty to forty minutes
• Conflict management styles	Sixty to ninety minutes

LUNCH

• Team-building activity	Forty-five to sixty minutes
• Healthy conflict resolution in team	Sixty to ninety minutes
• Conflict management ground rules	Thirty to forty-five minutes
• Summarize day one	Twenty to thirty minutes
• Close day one	Ten to fifteen minutes

(continued)

AGENDA
Resolving Team Conflict

Day Two

Topic	Time
• Review day one	Fifteen to twenty minutes
• Assertive messages techniques	Forty-five to sixty minutes
• Team-building activity	Forty to sixty minutes
• Accountability agreements	Sixty to ninety minutes
• Evaluate team-building session	Ten to fifteen minutes
• Close session	Five to ten minutes

FIGURE 10.4

Outcomes
of Destructive Conflict

Conflict is *destructive* when it:

- Diverts energy for a prolonged period of time, making it difficult to get work done.

- Destroys morale.

- Polarizes and divides the team.

- Deepens differences.

- Produces irresponsible interpersonal behavior.

- Does not result in new behaviors.

- Suppresses open and authentic communication.

- Causes team members to avoid addressing issues.

- Discourages creativity or breakthrough thinking.

- Undermines team spirit and cohesion.

- Causes individuals to withhold information or ideas.

(continued)

Potential Outcomes of Constructive Conflict

Conflict is *constructive* when it:

- Opens up and clarifies issues.

- Helps resolve problems and gain closure.

- Releases new information and perspectives.

- Helps individuals share information and ideas.

- Increases involvement of individuals needed to solve the problem.

- Allows authentic communication to occur.

- Builds cohesiveness.

- Affirms direction, priorities, and plans.

- Promotes team and individual growth.

- Facilitates team learning.

- Results in breakthroughs, creativity, or innovative ideas.

FIGURE 10.7

Direct Style

- Defends own position
- Wants to win
- Seeks immediate resolution
- Takes charge in conflict situations
- Makes quick decisions about what needs to be done
- Argues own position forcefully
- Quick to assume authority for resolving differences

Avoidance Style

- Wants to avoid creating unpleasant situations

- Lets others take responsibility for resolving conflict

- Encourages others to delay direct confrontation

- Accepts the situation

- Suppresses own feelings and needs

- Denies there is a problem to be solved

- Looks for ways to avoid taking a stand that might lead to disagreement

Collaborative Style

- Seeks to identify underlying issues and concerns

- Offers creative and innovative alternatives

- Works for win-win solutions

- Views conflict as an opportunity for team growth

- Helps others verbalize their issues and concerns

- May push for win-win solutions even when impractical and not feasible

- Encourages others to work together.

Accommodate Style

- Conciliatory approach
- Ready to listen and understand others' points of view
- Wants to help others get what they want
- Neglects own concerns in favor of others
- Works toward maintaining a harmonious work environment
- Respects all points of view
- Tends to defer too much to others and minimize their ability to influence the outcome

FIGURE 10.8

Team Profile Grid

Team members use different
approaches for resolving conflict.

	Direct	Collaborate
Assertive		
	Avoidance	Accommodate

Nonassertive

FIGURE 10.9

Conflict Management Styles

Style	Appropriate Situations
Direct	
Avoidance	
Collabortive	
Accommodate	

FIGURE 10.10

Direct Style

Strengths

- Useful when quick, decisive action is important
- Helps team tackle unpopular or controversial issues
- Important when ethical issues are at stake

Cautions

- Little new information is generated
- If overused, damages relationships
- Can force premature resolution before all options are explored adequately

Avoidance Style

Strengths

- Best approach when issues are trivial or unimportant

- Delays action when emotions are too strong

- Accepts the situation when you don't have the power to change it

Cautions

- Issues fester and do not get resolved

- Doesn't help the team tackle important issues

- May withhold input or information the team needs

Collaborative Style

Strengths

- Gains true commitment to solutions and agreements

- Merges a diversity of views to get the best decision

- Helps team address the deeper issues

Cautions

- Can create paralysis and frustration trying to build a consensus solution

- Team must have time to work the issue

- Learning and insight can become more important than resolving the conflict

Accommodate Style

Strengths

- It is important to maintain good relationships

- The other person's ideas or concerns are more important than your own

- Demonstrates the importance of listening to others and valuing their points of view.

Cautions

- Can appear weak or not committed to own point of view

- Desire for harmony can outweigh getting the best decision

- Can be too quick to give up and agree

FIGURE 10.11

Healthy Conflict Resolution in Teams

- A desire for resolution, not a desire to win

- Expression and acceptance of feelings

- A climate of mutual trust or a desire to establish trust

- Acceptance of conflict as natural rather than good or bad

- Willingness to take time to resolve issues

FIGURE 10.12

Steps in Conflict Resolution

1. Identify triggering event(s)

2. Name the problem or issue—jointly defined

3. Communicate positions and feelings

4. Communicate cooperative intentions

5. Take opponent's perspective

6. Reach agreements (specific)

FIGURE 10.13

Conflict Resolution Ground Rules

- Deal with realistic issues we can solve

- No labeling or insulting

- Everyone takes responsibility for creating, promoting, or allowing the conflict

- Keep humor appropriate

- Express feelings openly

- Use "I" statements

- Use specific examples

FIGURE 10.14

Benefits of Assertive Messages

Assertive messages help team members deal with conflict by:

- Openly stating expectations

- Honoring different points of view

- Taking responsibility for resolving conflict

Guidelines for Assertive Messages

The following guidelines help to deliver assertive messages:

Step 1—<u>Describe the Incident or Behavior</u>

Write down the facts of the situation or describe the behavior in objective terms.

Example

Last week you agreed to review my draft of the new vendor selection policy. I told you I needed your comments by Friday and you said, "That's no problem." I am still waiting for your comments a week later.

Assertive Messages

Step 2—<u>Tell the Other Person How You Feel</u>

Describe how you feel about the person's behavior or action.

Example

I am annoyed because I still don't have your input. It's irritating that I have called to remind you three times.

Assertive Messages

Step 3—<u>Tell the Other Person What You Think</u>

Describe your thoughts about the incident or behavior.

Example

I think it's going to be difficult for me to keep working with you on this project. I do need your help, but I want us to be clear about how we're going to work together. Reviewing the draft procedure is only the first phase of the project. I think we need to agree on how we go forward.

Assertive Messages

The following guidelines help to deliver assertive messages:

Step 4—<u>Ask the Other Person to Comment</u>

Give the other person an opportunity to comment.

Example

Is this how you remember the sequence of events? Is my description of your behavior accurate?

Discuss the other person's view of the situation, including how his or her perception differs from yours.

Assertive Messages

Step 5—<u>Propose a Resolution and Seek the Other Person's Agreement</u>

- Propose a resolution.

- Offer a proposal that helps move the relationship from conflictive to collegial.

Example

Can we set a new date to get the procedure finalized with your comments? We're two weeks behind schedule. Can you get your comments to me by the end of this week? Let's agree on a date that's feasible.

FIGURE 11.1

Objectives

- Understand the importance of aligning the team's mission with the organization's mission.

- Agree on the team's mission and how it supports the work of the organization.

- Understand the organization's key strategic goals.

- Agree on the team's goals and how they support the organization's goals.

Agenda

Topic	Time
• Welcome and introduction	Ten to fifteen minutes
• Importance of alignment	Fifteen to twenty minutes
• Review of feedback	Twenty to thirty minutes
• Corporate mission and purpose	Thirty to forty-five minutes
• Team mission	Forty-five to sixty minutes
• Evaluate alignment	Thirty-five to forty-five minutes

Lunch

• Corporate and business unit goals	Forty-five to sixty minutes
• Team goals	Sixty to ninety minutes
• Evaluate alignment	Forty-five to sixty minutes
• Next steps	Fifteen to twenty minutes
• Close session	Five to ten minutes

FIGURE 11.2

The Importance of Alignment

Team missions and goals need to support the broader organization's mission and strategic objectives:

This is important because:

- Team members can see how their work directly impacts the organization's results.

- It is easier to set priorities and sort out multiple priorities.

- Everyone is focusing on the work that is most important to the entire organization.

FIGURE 12.2

Agenda

Topic	Time
• Welcome and Introduction	Five to ten minutes
• Review the Data Gathering Process	Fifteen to thirty minutes
• Present the Data	Thirty to forty-five minutes
• Defining Trust and Its Attributes	Forty-five to sixty minutes
• Feedback Techniques	Thirty-five to forty minutes
• Feedback Exercise	Forty-five to sixty minutes

Lunch

• Individual Feedback Activity	Sixty to ninety minutes
• Team Agreements	Sixty to ninety minutes
• Next Steps	Thirty to forty minutes
• Close Session	Five to ten minutes

Objectives

- Gain a common understanding of how the team defines trust.

- Understand the attitudes, behaviors, and actions that strengthen trust or undermine trust.

- Gain agreement on the major issues that must be addressed to rebuild trust.

- Learn a structured feedback technique to work through issues related to trust.

- Agree on what individuals and the team as a whole will do to begin rebuilding trust.

FIGURE 12.3

Benefits of Giving Feedback

Teams can rebuild trust by using feedback to open up communication.

Effective feedback has several advantages for individual team members and the team as a whole:

- It provides insight into behavior about which an individual may not be aware.

- It helps individuals describe patterns of behavior that are hindering/enhancing trust.

- It helps team members understand the impact of their behavior on others.

- It provides an opportunity for learning and growth.

- It helps teams get relationships back on track.

Feedback Guidelines

- Offer positives first, suggested changes second.

- Be specific versus general.

- Be descriptive versus evaluative.

- Take into account the needs of the receiver and your own needs.

- State the feedback clearly and check for comprehension.

- Do not overload others with too much feedback.

- Make sure the feedback is something the individual can change.

FIGURE 12.8

Goals for the Feedback Activity

- To teach participants how to give and receive feedback in a trust-building way.

- To resolve the issues identified in the feedback.

- To better understand the wants and needs of other team members.

- To help individuals understand how their behaviors enhance or undermine trust.

- To help team members understand how they are perceived by others.

FIGURE 12.8

Ground Rules for Delivering Feedback

- Make sure the feedback describes exactly what you want to happen to improve trust and can provide impetus for action.

- State the feedback in terms of observed behavior and data.

- Listen to everything the person says before you respond.

- Ask questions to clarify the feedback so that you understand what's being requested of you.

- Avoid accusatory and judgmental statements both when you are giving and receiving feedback.

FIGURE 13.2

Agenda

- Welcome and introduction
- Draft mission statements
- Finalize mission statement
- Document next steps
- Evaluate the team-building session

Objectives

- Create a statement of the team's mission and shared purpose.

- Agree on the team's role and contribution of the organization.

- Resolve confusion about the team's purpose.

- Help everyone on the team gain a common understanding of what the team is expected to contribute to the organization.

FIGURE 13.3

Importance
of Mission Statements

A shared, meaningful purpose is important for several reasons:

- It builds a common sense of direction and momentum.

- Team commitment is enhanced by working toward a commonly understood purpose.

- Individuals have an opportunity to shape a purpose that reflects what's important to them.

- Teams understand their scope of authority and boundaries.

- It is a joint creation of the team's collaborative efforts.

- Molding its purpose together helps team members respond to challenges confident of the support and help of their teammates.

FIGURE 13.35

Agenda

- Welcome and introduction
- Role clarification exercise
- Mutual support agreements
- Document next steps and actions
- Evaluate the team-building session

Objectives

- Clarify each team member's role and contribution to the team.

- Ensure team members' roles are aligned with and support the team's mission and goals.

- Identify how team members support one another in the execution of their roles.

FIGURE 13.6

Benefits of Role Clarification

Role clarification helps teams and team members:

- Describe each person's contribution.

- Understand how each person's role supports other roles.

- Agree on mutual expectations.

- Eliminate conflicts or misunderstandings.

- Ensure everyone's work is aligned with and supports the team's mission and goals.

FIGURE 13.8

Objectives

- Diagnose the team's problems with meetings.

- Identify the ways in which team members can share responsibility for effective meetings.

- Create a plan to improve team meetings.

Agenda

- Welcome and introduction
- Define meetings
- Evaluate team's meetings
- Sharing responsibility
- Evaluate team-meetings technique
- Evaluate the team-building session

FIGURE 13.9

What Is a Meeting?

A meeting occurs any time two or more people get together face-to-face, electronically, or in a conference call in order to:

- Share information
- Make decisions, plan or take some other action

Meetings can be categorized as information sharing, action taking, or sometimes both.

FIGURE 13.10

Meeting Task and Process

Every meeting is comprised of *task* and *process.*

Tasks—refers to what the team is trying to accomplish in the meeting. The tasks are the reasons the group has come together and are the outputs the team wants to achieve.

Process—refers to how the team works together to accomplish its tasks. Meeting processes are the techniques a team uses to help achieve its task outputs.

Research shows that at least ninety percent of problems with meetings can be solved by improving processes.

FIGURE 13.12

Sharing Responsibility for Effective Meetings

Every member of the team has responsibility for ensuring meetings are effectively set up, conducted, and the results implemented.

Task-Oriented Behaviors

Recording—listing ideas and data so the entire team can see it

Timekeeping—monitoring time contracts

Setting Priorities—focusing on key issues first

Summarizing—pulling ideas together

Explaining—clearing up confusion or confirming information

Data Seeking—focusing on facts, data and information

Decision Making—determining if the team is ready to make a decision

Sharing Responsibility for Effective Meetings

Every member of the team has responsibility for ensuring meetings are effectively set up, conducted, and the results implemented.

Process-Oriented Behaviors

Facilitating—helping the group move through the agenda and stay on track

Focusing—reminding the group of the outcomes they need to achieve and what the next step should be

Regulating—helping balance communication and making sure everyone has an opportunity to participate

Building Consensus—looking for common ground and areas of agreement

Consensus Testing—checking to see if everyone is in true agreement with the decision

Complimenting—acknowledging the contribution of others

FIGURE 13.15

Evaluating Team Meetings

Teams can continually improve their meetings.

Evaluating team meetings provides an opportunity to identify what went well and what needs to be improved. It is important to act immediately on the improvement areas.

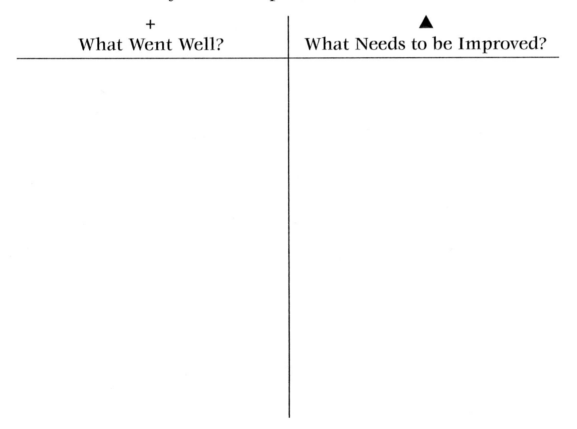

+ What Went Well?	▲ What Needs to be Improved?

Allow a few minutes at the end of each meeting and evaluate it.

FIGURE 13.16

Objectives

- Clarify the team's decision making authority.

- Understand the various options for team decision making.

- Agree on how each individual will be involved in key team decisions.

- Build a sense of shared responsibility for effective decision-making.

- Understand how to build consensus.

Agenda

- Welcome and introduction
- Importance of effective decision making
- Team decision-making options
- Application exercise
- Building consensus
- Decision charting
- Evaluate the team-building session

FIGURE 13.17

Importance of Effective Decision Making

There are several reasons why effective decision making is important for teams:

- It ensures the right people are involved in the right decisions in the right way.

- Individuals are clear about decision making authority and limits.

- It helps teams select the decision-making option most appropriate to the situation.

- Team growth is enhanced by its ability to work together and reach a true consensus.

FIGURE 13.18

Team Decision-Making Options

The most typical forms of decision-making include:

Authority or Expert

This is the traditional way decisions are made in many work settings.

The decision-making power resides in the "boss" or in someone considered to be an expert.

While this is a quick way to make decisions, it does little to develop the team members' skills or to build a joint sense of responsibility for decisions.

The quality of the decision made depends solely on the decision-maker's breadth and depth of knowledge.

Team Decision-Making Options

The most typical forms of decision making include:

Consultative

In the consultative decision-making style one person (usually the team leader) still makes the decision but gathers input and/or buy-in before deciding on the course of action.

Consultative decision making requires more time but usually results in a better decision than the authoritative style.

The acceptance of this approach depends on the perception that those asked for input actually had influence on the decision.

It is important to have clear ground rules on exactly how the consultation will work.

Team Decision-Making Options

The most typical forms of decision making include:

Majority Vote

In this voting style of decision making the majority rules.

It is a quick way to make decisions but can result in "win/lose" situations with the "losers" not supporting the final decision.

It is important to encourage discussion of opposing positions when using this style.

In general, this method should be a fallback if a team cannot reach a true consensus.

Team Decision-Making Options

The most typical forms of decision making include:

Consensus

Consensus decision making takes time but maximizes commitment to the decision.

Consensus is not unanimous agreement but means that everyone can live with and fully support the decision.

Team members must openly express their views to reach a true consensus. A consensus decision is usually forged out of different perceptions, opinions, and diverse viewpoints.

This style of decision making should be used for important team decisions and when buy-in is critical.

FIGURE 13.19

Factors to Consider When Choosing a Decision-Making Option

- Time—How much time is available?

- Importance—How important versus how trivial is the issue?

- Expertise—How much expertise and information do group members have?

- Capability—How experienced is the group in making decisions together?

- Buy-In—How much buy-in is needed to ensure implementation?

Decision Scenarios

Select the decision-making option that is appropriate for each of the following situations. Identify which factors were most important in making your selection.

Situation

1. A supervisor and her team of technicians work across three shifts. They have just received a large grant to purchase new equipment. The grant has no restrictions and the group may purchase whatever equipment they feel is most needed. The grant must be spent before the end of the fiscal year, in three months. How should the decision be made?

Option Selected _____

Factors

_____

_____

_____

_____

_____

_____

_____

_____

Decision Scenarios

Select the decision-making option that is appropriate for each of the following situations. Identify which factors were most important in making your selection.

Situation	**Factors**

2. The plant safety coordinator has informed the facilities manager that on the latest safety test lead has been found in the water. This poses an immediate health risk. The safety coordinator has done testing at different water supply sources and cannot locate a pattern of contamination. What should the manager do?

Option Selected _____

3. An organization just completed a customer satisfaction survey. The results show that the team needs to improve several aspects of its performance. The team is expected to come up with solutions to the issues identified in the survey. What is the appropriate option to use in deciding how to respond?

Option Selected _____

Decision Scenarios

Select the decision-making option that is appropriate for each of the following situations. Identify which factors were most important in making your selection.

Situation

Factors

4. An information technology team is interested in contracting with a major consulting firm for a range of services. A representative of the consulting firm has met with the team leader and offered a cost-effective way to pilot some of their information management systems. The team leader is under pressure to lower costs and provide more efficient systems. Some team members are concerned about engaging an outside consultant. They feel they can do most of the things the consultant can do and want the opportunity to develop the new information systems themselves. What's the appropriate decision-making option?

_____

_____

_____

_____

_____

_____

_____

_____

Option Selected _____

FIGURE 13.21

Decision-Making Situations

Select the decision-making option that is appropriate for each of the following situations. Identify which factors were most important in making your selection.

Situation

1. A supervisor and her team of technicians work across three shifts. They have just received a large grant to purchase new equipment. The grant has no restrictions and the group may purchase whatever equipment they feel is most needed. The grant must be spent before the end of the fiscal year, in three months. How should the decision be made?

Factors

Time

Importance

Expertise

Buy-in

_____

_____

_____

_____

Recommended Option(s) *Consultative or Consensus*

Decision-Making Situations—Example

Select the decision-making option that is appropriate for each of the following situations. Identify which factors were most important in making your selection.

Situation

2. The plant safety coordinator has informed the facilities manager that on the latest safety test lead has been found in the water. This poses an immediate health risk. The safety coordinator has done testing at different water supply sources and cannot locate a pattern of contamination. What should the manager do?

Recommended Option(s) *Authoritative/Expert*

3. An organization just completed a customer satisfaction survey. The results show that your team needs to improve several aspects of its performance. The team is expected to come up with solutions to the issues identified in the survey. What is the appropriate option to use in deciding how to respond?

Recommended Option(s) *Consensus: Fallback - Majority Vote*

Factors

Time

Importance

Expertise

_____

_____

_____

_____

_____

Buy-in

Importance

_____

_____

_____

_____

_____

_____

Decision-Making Situations

Select the decision-making option that is appropriate for each of the following situations. Identify which factors were most important in making your selection.

Situation	**Factors**

4. An information technology team is interested in contracting with a major consulting firm for a range of services. A representative of the consulting firm has met with the team leader and offered a cost-effective way to pilot some of their information management systems. The team leader is under pressure to lower costs and provide more efficient systems. Some team members are concerned about engaging an outside consultant. They feel they can do most of the things the consultant can do and want the opportunity to develop the new information systems themselves. What's the appropriate decision-making option?

Importance

Buy-in

_____

_____

_____

_____

_____

Recommended Option(s) _____ *Consensus* _____

FIGURE 13.24

Consensus-Building Ground Rules

- Stand for your point of view; don't worry that others may prove you wrong.

- Ask questions; don't just sell your idea.

- Listen hard, especially to people with opposing positions. View differences of opinion as a help rather than a hindrance in reaching the best decision.

- Avoid trying to talk someone out of his or her viewpoint. Instead, seek ways to modify the decision to address the person's concerns.

- Don't let a few members dominate the discussion. Ask quieter, less aggressive group members for their ideas, and listen to them carefully.

- Hold out if you don't agree. Try to modify the decision so that it is more acceptable to you.

- Seek small agreements and build on these to get closer to consensus.

FIGURE 13.25

Decision Charting Matrix

Key Team Decisions	Team or Individual Decision	Your Role		
		Informed	Consulted	Involved
1.				
2.				
3.				
4.				
5.				
6.				
7.				
8.				
9.				
10.				

FIGURE 13.26

Decision Charting Options

Please indicate how you want to participate in the team's key decisions by using the following choices:

"Involved"—You want to be involved in making the final decision.

"Consulted"—You want to give input to the decision before it is made, but you don't want to be involved in making the final decision.

"Informed"—You want to be informed about the decision after it is made by others.

INDEX

ABOUT THE AUTHOR

Vivette Payne is a consultant and writer who specializes in organization, team, and personal development. Her particular interest is working with fast-growing organizations to guide the implementation of growth-facilitating human resource systems and processes.

Ms. Payne is president of the Avery Payne Group, a network of consultants that brings clients a depth and range of skills in organizational, team, and personal development. She works with clients in both the private and the public sector.

Ms. Payne holds a bachelor's degree in psychology and a master's degree in organizational development.

She is the author of *First-Level Leadership: Supervising in the New Organization* (AMA, 1998).